A CULTURAL HISTORY OF
CHILDHOOD AND FAMILY

VOLUME 3

A Cultural History of Childhood and Family

General Editors: Elizabeth Foyster and James Marten

Volume 1
A Cultural History of Childhood and Family in Antiquity
Edited by Mary Harlow and Ray Laurence

Volume 2
A Cultural History of Childhood and Family in the Middle Ages
Edited by Louise J. Wilkinson

Volume 3
A Cultural History of Childhood and Family in the Early Modern Age
Edited by Sandra Cavallo and Silvia Evangelisti

Volume 4
A Cultural History of Childhood and Family in the Age of Enlightenment
Edited by Elizabeth Foyster and James Marten

Volume 5
A Cultural History of Childhood and Family in the Age of Empire
Edited by Colin Heywood

Volume 6
A Cultural History of Childhood and Family in the Modern Age
Edited by Joseph M. Hawes and N. Ray Hiner

A CULTURAL HISTORY

OF CHILDHOOD AND FAMILY

IN THE EARLY MODERN AGE

Edited by Sandra Cavallo and Silvia Evangelisti

BLOOMSBURY

LONDON · NEW DELHI · NEW YORK · SYDNEY

Bloomsbury Academic
An imprint of Bloomsbury Publishing Plc

50 Bedford Square
London
WC1B 3DP
UK

1385 Broadway
New York
NY 10018
USA

www.bloomsbury.com

Hardback edition first published in 2010 by Berg Publishers, an imprint of
Bloomsbury Academic
Paperback edition first published by Bloomsbury Academic 2014

British Library Cataloguing-in-Publication Data
A catalogue record for this book is available from the British Library.

ISBN: HB: 978-1-84788-796-2
PB: 978-1-4725-5469-7
HB Set: 978-1-84520-826-4
PB Set: 978-1-4725-5474-1

Library of Congress Cataloging-in-Publication Data
A catalog record for this book is available from the Library of Congress.

Typeset by Apex CoVantage, LLC, Madison, WI, USA
Printed and bound in Great Britain

CONTENTS

ILLUSTRATIONS

CHAPTER 8

GENERAL EDITORS' PREFACE

The literature on the histories of children and the family has reached a critical mass. The proliferation of encyclopedia, conferences, and professional associations reflects the vitality of these closely related but independent fields. The two subjects are naturally linked; Western conceptions of the family have virtually always included children, and children and youth are irrevocably shaped by their time growing up in families.

A Cultural History of Childhood and Family aims to bring order to these sometimes disparate histories and historiographical traditions with original material written especially for these volumes. More than six dozen editors and authors from five continents and thirteen countries were commissioned to take a comprehensive look at the subject from a Western perspective with more than casual glances at the world beyond. Based on deep readings of the secondary literature and on representative primary sources, each of the chapters is an original work of synthesis and interpretation.

It is our hope that imposing a standard table of contents on a project covering literally thousands of years and hundreds of ethnicities, religious faiths, and communities will help us find otherwise hidden patterns and rich contrasts in the experiences of children and families and in humankind's attitudes about them. There is inevitably a bit of overlap; issues related to children and the family do not form and develop according to convenient beginning and ending dates. But there is also a variety of viewpoints, even on similar topics. Indeed, as general editors we embrace the divergence of interpretations, emphases, and even writing and organizational styles that emerge from these five dozen chapters. Some of the diversity follows naturally from the vastly different conditions facing children and their families in different eras, while in other cases it is inspired by the authors' expertise and personal approaches to the field.

There have always been many childhoods and many families in the West. The purpose of these volumes is not only to look at the constructions of childhood and the family, particularly as they reflect evolving ethnic, gender, religious, national, and class assumptions, but also the lived experiences of children and of the families in which they spend so much of their lives. The symbiotic relationship between child and parent, between brother and sister, and between the individual and the family to which he or she belongs is reflected in the intertwined historical literature on children and families. By studying both, we can learn more about each.

Elizabeth Foyster
Clare College, University of Cambridge

James Marten
Marquette University

Introduction

SANDRA CAVALLO AND SILVIA EVANGELISTI

In recent years, scholars have underlined the tremendous impact that the religious changes taking place in sixteenth-century Europe had on the family and childhood and the importance that Protestants as well as Catholics attributed to children and parents for building a disciplined society and a confessional state. These changes developed within an ideological context where state-sponsored laws placed increasing emphasis on the political and economic role of the household and sought to regulate marriage and sexuality, as well as the transmission of private wealth. At the same time, a long tradition of studies has celebrated the Renaissance as a key period for the development of new ideas about civility, civilization, and knowledge and the role of education in forging the individual. According to this view, these values provided the ideal cultural context for the emergence of new discourses about family and childhood; these ideas were then widely disseminated through the aid of print and pictorial images, reaching a vast audience made of privileged circles, as well as of a less exclusive public. Indeed, chapters in this volume indicate that too much emphasis has perhaps been placed on the role of the Protestant Reformation in defining the profile of the early modern family and that far more attention needs to be given to the legacy of the Renaissance in establishing the parameters along which definitions of the ideal family developed in this period. Thus, the Renaissance, the Protestant and Catholic reformations, and the state can be seen as three propelling forces that sought to civilize, educate, and discipline adults and children of both sexes while asserting class, gender, and age hierarchies.

In exploring the cultural contexts in which early modern family and childhood were inscribed, this volume, however, looks beyond the idealized image often emerging from the written and visual representations of the family and considers the extent to which theories and normative discourses affected social practice. Some of the chapters, in particular, indicate that our understanding of the early modern family and childhood would benefit from a greater attention to material culture and to visual sources in order to counterbalance the use of written, prescriptive sources. Moreover, building on recent scholarship, the chapters question some of the traditional metanarratives in family history, challenging generalizations based, for example, on geographical or confessional divides, or notions of the emergence of the affective family. In so doing, the book highlights the diversity of family arrangements in a variety of cultural and religious contexts in Europe and the early colonies.

As well as providing some general background information that will form the context for the volume, the following pages offer an overview of the interpretative frameworks adopted in the chapters and an introduction to the themes in recent scholarly discussion on the family that are most relevant to the contributions in this collections.

IDEAS ON CHILDHOOD AND FAMILY LIFE:
1400–1650

The period between the fifteenth and the mid-seventeenth centuries saw unprecedented discussion about childhood and the family and a proliferation of visual representations of domestic and family life touching on both its public and its most intimate aspects. In the fifteenth century, ideas about family and childhood were discussed in a variety of genres from the literature on good household government and pedagogical texts to handbooks for domestic medicine and children's health. The theories that developed around the family described an ideal system according to which the household was a metaphor for authority and social order, and its good management was the first step toward the proper governance of the city and state. All members of the family group, including children and servants, were expected to take an active part in the making of the household and the preservation of its wealth and status.

The advent of print allowed for new ideas and prescriptive discourses to circulate in Europe and the newly acquired colonial territories in Asia and America. Printing of course popularized theories about childhood, family, and gender roles. Books of advice, and prescriptive literature, were translated in vernacular languages and reached larger circles of the learned public, which included women. So did religious and devotional texts. In sixteenth-century Catholic Europe, for example, a number of books published after the reform program launched by the Council of Trent in the middle of the sixteenth century specifically addressed the three different states of female life: the virginal and marital states and widowhood. In Protestant Europe, moralists, pedagogues, and physicians took a particular interest in children and contributed to a wide production of books devoted to their care and upbringing. The Protestants' emphasis on Bible-reading as a practice that should be found in every household, associated with the availability of books in portable format, has been seen by some scholars as an element of distinction that made the culture of books particularly important for Protestants—maybe more than for Catholics. This contributed to the rise of a cultural context in which ideas about childhood and child rearing were thoroughly discussed.[1] Research on visual and material culture attests that these ideas also reached people through visual means of communication, like paintings and prints hanging on the walls of the house, or school books or catechisms, which offered persuasive messages about domestic life.[2]

As some of the chapters included in this volume show, written and visual discourses propagated the ideal model of the nuclear, patriarchal family. They underlined the centrality of the married couple and their children, while downplaying the role of other components of the extended family. This version of the family was rigorously organized along gender lines that stressed the authority of the father over his wife, children, and servants, though it encouraged at the same time partnership and intimacy within the marriage. Various artistic interpretations of the Holy Family focused on the Holy Couple and pointed more than before to the intimate relationship and affective bonds between husband, wife, and children. Interestingly, however, while contemporary visual arts reinforced the idea and importance of the nuclear family, they also contributed to challenging it, thus offering a nuanced version of the ideal family model. A number of paintings refiguring the birth of the Virgin, for example, displayed busy domestic interiors where the event takes place attended by mainly female figures who bring food to the mother and wash the newborn baby. These scenes that linked servants to crucial and symbolic life cycle moments of family life, conveyed a clear message: servants too were an integral part of the family, and they also worked for its physical and spiritual reproduction.

The religious redefinitions of the sixteenth century made an important contribution to theorization about the family. The historiography on the Reformation and the Counter-Reformation has provided a rather complex understanding of these two major religious changes of the sixteenth century.

We are now aware of the different lines of thinking that developed within each of the two confessions, explored with particular reference to Protestant culture. Moreover, we can no longer avoid acknowledging the transconfessional similarities existing between the two reform programs, notwithstanding the radical theological differences that of course remain firmly in place. Protestant and Catholic states gave great importance to the family and considered its hierarchical organization a fundamental step in order to guarantee the formation of obedient subjects. Reformers from both sides saw the family as a spiritualized unit and the primary place for the moral and religious formation of good Christians, and they made wives and children increasingly subordinate to the husband and father. Family and marriage were at the center of a process that aimed at imposing norms and behaviors for moralizing society as a whole.[3] More precisely, this disciplinary program sought to increase the state's and the church's control over the family by emphasizing the importance of marriage and the married couple for guaranteeing an ordered society. Although Protestants and Catholics held notably different views on marriage, they both saw it as the only legitimate space for experiencing sexual relations, thus confining sexuality to the conjugal context. All forms of premarital and extramarital sexuality were condemned, and adultery was denounced as a violation of the conjugal bond. In practice, a double standard existed, and adultery was considered a crime above all when committed by a woman. This moralizing impetus was reflected in the increasing development of charitable institutions that aimed at disciplining, containing, and to a certain extent punishing illicit sexual behavior and its consequences. In sixteenth- and seventeenth-century Europe, civic and ecclesiastical authorities promoted the creation of asylums for ex-prostitutes and for poor and unmarried women and of foundling hospitals for orphans and abandoned children.

Doubtless the moralizing input directed toward the family also affected parent-child relations.[4] In Protestant culture the paternal figure acquired particular new importance. Martin Luther envisaged that there should be no difference between the secular and spiritual state. Since Protestants rejected religious celibacy, the minister of God was also a father. He held spiritual as well as secular authority over his children and wife. Catholic reformers, on the contrary, confirmed the existence of a clear distinction between the religious and lay states. In line with the precepts of the Council of Trent, they stressed the primacy of key spiritual foundations of religious and monastic life, above all chastity, which anyone willing to enter the secular or regular clergy should observe. The priest and the father could not be united in the same person. The Catholic father therefore watched over his family's Christian piety in cooperation with the priest and sometimes in competition with him. The priest was a symbolic father and the only one between the two of them to be officially invested with spiritual authority. This distinction represents a radical difference between the two confessions whose implications on the family, childhood, and models of masculinity still need to be fully explored by scholars.

In emphasizing the importance of paternal authority, scholars have at the same time underlined the duties and responsibilities of parents toward their children. As a number of chapters in this volume discuss, one of the main aims of parenting was to raise children by means of affection as well as authority. Affection and persuasion, together with authority, defined the family nucleus and were presented as an important element for reinforcing its cohesion. Power relationships within the family were not in contradiction with the considerable attention paid to affection and emotional ties that developed between husband and wife, and between parents and children. Letters, diaries, and autobiographies offer plenty of support to the idea that parents were able to express their loving thoughts toward their children while being prepared to accept the righteous practice of physical punishment when they misbehaved.[5] Visual evidence from the sixteenth century reinforces this point. Bonds of blood and affection were reflected, for instance, in some family portraits in which the emotional links among members and generations of the family—men, women, and children—are underlined by the gestures of the sitters and the physical contacts that they established among themselves by touching their shoulders or arms with their hands.[6] These interpretations of family life emphasize the collective participation of adults and children in affective relations, through which the continuity of the family was also established.

To a certain extent, theories about the family circulated not only through written means but also through that kind of material language spoken by objects and spaces. Indeed, if normative discourses fostered models of domestic behavior, the objects and spaces found in the house did it too. Material items contributed to shaping adults' and children's existence almost as much as written discourses did. This can be clearly seen by looking, for instance, at the transformations in the household environment. Starting toward the late fifteenth and the sixteenth centuries, a reorganization of the household space, and the circulation of new material objects and types of furniture, diversified the functions of the domestic interior and gave greater relevance to important and symbolic moments of family life. Compared with medieval dwellings, the early modern house acquired a more solid, hygienic, and articulate spatial structure. Bricks replaced wood, straw, and clay, and the open space often shared by humans and animals, in particular in the countryside, was now abandoned in favor of a more definite separation of spaces. Different areas were destined for socializing, sleeping, and eating, and dining areas for family were separated from the servants' areas. Specific objects and pieces of furniture allowed young children and babies to be included in the collective activities of the household. These changes in the domestic setting expressed people's search for an increased separation between intimacy and sociability, their desire to assert hierarchies and distinctions within the group, and the adoption of a more mannered social existence, as conformed to the contemporary literature on the household.[7]

Renaissance culture, and in particular the humanistic tradition, placed a great emphasis on children and their education and learning. Cultural as well as economic factors contributed to this new interest on childhood. Indeed, the growth of urban centers, urbane cultural life, and the emergence of commercial capitalism in some areas of Europe, which took place from the last centuries of the Middle Ages onward, created the conditions for an increased social and "psychological investment" in children.[8] More thought was given to child rearing and teaching methods, and more resources were spent in the education of children and youth. Children were conceived as different from adults, and childhood was a phase that would prepare and mould the future full adult person. Parents from the elites, like patricians, merchants, and rich artisans, found in education a system that ensured that their male offspring would be able to properly manage and care for patrimonial interests, or maintain success in commerce or professional life, and that their female children would acquire the skills that allowed for convenient marriage. Dutifully instructed children guaranteed the continuity of the family, its values and ideology, and therefore the social order.

In the wake of the reformations, education increasingly became a major concern for both Protestants and Catholics. Building a confessional state started with the education of adults and above all children. Domestic religious training, and school instruction, both grew more important after the reformations, and the church stressed—even more than before—the obligation of parents to provide education. As the chapter on education points out, the transmission of religious teachings in Europe was guaranteed by the development of schools and institutional training.[9] Protestants and Catholics notably held two different sets of beliefs about children's essential nature, with Protestants maintaining a much more pessimistic view than did their Catholic counterparts. Like Augustine, they regarded children as sinful and depraved. This view became a dominant theme in their pedagogical literature. The ideas elaborated by the Puritan movement are particularly revealing of this trend. Puritans formed a radical religious group that gave systematic and new attention to children, child rearing, and education. They believed that human depravity needed to be treated through discipline and training from a very early age, in order to submit young individuals to God's will. Although it is not clear to what extent these ideas were actually put into practice, Puritans became massively influential in Western pedagogical thought, especially in England and in America, where they had settled almost from the beginning in the first colonies of New England.[10]

Education offers an interesting angle for looking at early modern children and their political role, with particular reference to state building. Recent studies on the colonial family have offered new insights on yet another aspect of the political meaning of childhood in association with processes of cultural reproduction. The attempt to translate European cultural and social models in non-Christian contexts became a primary step for the implantation of new colonial societies. In the American and Asian colonies, children were the object of state-sponsored policies concerning their welfare and education. When children from European backgrounds traveled from Europe to the colonies, they mostly traveled with their parents or their masters, as in the case of young servants, but the orphans moved on their own. In the sixteenth and seventeenth centuries, for example, orphan girls in their teens were shipped from Portugal to Goa and from France to Quebec, with the prospect of marriage. In the colonies, a number of public initiatives, often organized with the support of missionaries, were intended for the education and welfare of children, from the opening of schools and charitable institutions for the children of families with European backgrounds to the schools for native children. Instructed and acculturated to European and Christian values, these children would have contributed to the consolidation and growth of the colonies, almost acting as colonizers in their own right.[11]

The circulation of ideas about childhood and family on a global scale poses questions about the impact of norms and models of family life conceived in Europe, and the ways in which they were applied both across the continent and outside it. Early modern Europe and its colonial territories included different contexts that were ethnically and culturally heterogeneous. Europe of course was not uniquely Christian. Established Jewish communities had been a long-lasting presence, and so were families of converted Muslims who were still deeply embedded in their culture and beliefs, although they were primarily concentrated in certain areas of the continent. Moreover, colonial expansion brought contacts with the non-Christian religious imagination and its practices in Asia and America. Normative discourses might be understood, received, and experienced in different ways according to the cultural contexts to which they applied. Within this framework, ideas, images, and symbols traveled from Europe and bounced back to it sometimes with newly acquired meanings. It is precisely in this framework that the gap between theory and practice offers thought-provoking insights for broadening our understanding of childhood and family life.

FAMILY LIVES: 1400–1650

While the family envisioned in the prescriptive discourse was a stable and relatively uncomplicated body, often simply composed of parents and their children and thus characterized by clearly defined parental roles, the reality of family life was often much more complex and the experience of childhood rife with uncertainties. A number of factors, triggered by economic conditions and demographic patterns, challenged the stability of the conventional biological family. The continuity of domestic life was threatened by the high mortality rate that resulted from poor diet and hygiene, by the repeated outbreaks of plague and famine, and by the effects of intense military activity during the sixteenth and seventeenth centuries. At the same time the endemic infectious diseases that raged across the increasingly densely populated urban environment took a heavy toll, especially on children and migrants. The high death rate meant that marital and filial bonds were often short lived. Certainly, many family units were soon reconstituted though remarriage, while at other times the widowed or the orphan children found a new home in the household of kin, neighbors, or acquaintances. These broken and re-formed households, however, were quite distant, in size and composition, from the idealized family unit celebrated in conduct literature and in the visual celebrations of the Holy Family.

The incidence of migration and the demand for labor, within an economic system in which both agricultural and manufacturing production were firmly based on the coresidential household unit, further added to the fluidity of the household. From the fifteenth century onward, recourse to temporary or seasonal migration in search of employment as a laborer or servant became the norm among the laboring classes of Europe, as did the departure of adolescent males to be apprenticed or to serve in various capacities in another household. The variety of forms taken by domestic employment and the fact that training and the education of unrelated children were largely imparted within the home also produced further diverse types of cohabitations. People bound by ties of filiation, fraternity, or more distant kinship shared a home with high-rank employees, servants, slaves, wet nurses, surrogate children and apprentices.

These considerations fundamentally undermine the thesis that regarded the frequent experience of death and separation as conducive to scant bonds of affection between members of the family. Already discredited on several grounds, this argument appears particularly weak in view of the narrow and anachronistic definition of the family it reflects, one that reduces it to the nucleus of parents and their children. Recent studies on emotions tend instead to adopt a much broader understanding of family and familial relationships. Considerable work, for example, has recently been conducted on the fraternal bond, a tie internally stratified by gender, age, and the custom of primogeniture and by distinctions between siblings and half siblings, between the legitimate and the illegitimate.[12] But the interest of scholars is also being extended to other kinship relationships and, as many chapters in this volume illustrate, to the emotional and spiritual ties of parenthood often forged in childhood with adoptive parents, milk parents, and godparents. Allowing for the wide circulation of children from all classes between different households, for the purposes of training, education, and service, these studies consider the whole range of ties that constituted the emotional landscape of an early modern child or adult both within and outside the family of origin.[13]

The complexity of domestic arrangements makes the family household of this period difficult to encapsulate within the standard classification of family forms formulated by historical demographers. For example, the two models seen as dominant family types, the nuclear and the extended or multiple, refer to conventional households constituted respectively by two parents and their children or by the parents and their children along with one or two grandparents. These neat family forms may indeed have been prevalent in the eighteenth and nineteenth centuries, the periods on which, given the availability of complete series of data, the great majority of studies on family structures have concentrated. However, these were in the minority during the period covered by this volume, when the high level of mortality made lone-parent or widowed householders numerous, while domestic units resulting from multiple remarriages, and hence populated by children from different parents, were very common.

The demographic models that for some decades since the 1960s have dominated scholarly thinking about the family thus appear inadequate if we are to appreciate the reality of domestic arrangements in this period. Moreover, the conceptual vocabulary coined by historical demographers appears increasingly obsolete and is progressively disappearing from current scholarship on the early modern family. Notions such as family structure, family life cycle, and life cycle servant are too rigid, and they fail to capture the variety of household forms we encounter, along with their changeability over time and the varied profiles of service providers.

The unconventional forms assumed by the early modern household have received more attention from the colonial historians of early modern empires than from scholars of Europe. Certainly, Latin America displays unprecedentedly high percentages of domestic groups featuring no adult male and of children raised in the homes of people who were not their parents.[14] Yet households that diverge from the paradigmatic nuclear family and the orderly three-generational extended family were not the exclusive prerogative of Spanish America. Since the 1990s, scholars of the old continent have drawn attention to the significant presence of widows and female-headed households in various regions of early modern Europe, and to the imaginative types of cohabitations often resulting from the death of a spouse or father.[15] What is more, the informal adoption of poor or orphaned children was an extremely common phenomenon across Europe.[16] The impetus to raise a foundling, an orphan, or simply a needy child in their homes, and the tendency to forge emotional ties of a familiar kind with the children of others by acting as guardians or godparents, might have been particularly strong in the case of those couples who had no offspring of their own. In the last few years historians have begun to recognize that childless couples made up a significant proportion of families in early modern society and that the composition of their households and the fictive parenting roles they created for themselves deserve attention.[17] The interest of scholars has recently been focused also on the households headed by bachelor men, including not just celibate ecclesiastics but unmarried laymen. These too might have been much more numerous than scholars have been willing to acknowledge, misled by the enduring assumption that marriage was the norm for secular adult males in the early modern period.[18]

Studies on the colonies may also stimulate research into other irregular family forms. Historians of Latin America have highlighted the historically high rates of concubinage, polygamy, and illegitimacy in the Spanish empire and have stressed their association with the racially mixed and socially unequal unions that characterized colonial settlement in this region, where, from the start of overseas expansion, sexual liaisons were formed by European men with Indian or African women they never married.[19] Though certainly on a minor scale, these practices were far from unknown in the patriarchal and highly stratified environment of the old continent. Although long obscured by the emphasis historians have placed on the moralization of sexual mores and the regulation of marriage carried out by religious reformers, and by the implausibly regular family typology proposed by historical demographers, the practice of concubinage and the consequent illegitimacy of offspring seem to have been far from marginal in some regions of Europe, and not confined to the supposedly disorderly popular classes. In sixteenth- and early seventeenth-century Veneto, for example, elite concubinage, typically involving a young noble and a plebeian woman, seems to have been widespread (despite being increasingly stigmatized by the church) and a structural phenomenon in a society that prescribed strict rules of social endogamy.[20]

To some extent, Europe too was, like Latin America, a multiethnic society. Some chapters in this volume emphasize this often neglected aspect by drawing attention to the presence of Muslim and Jewish communities within Europe's fabric, and likewise to the employment of slaves and black servants in its households. The extent to which the family traditions of ethnic and religious groups living in close propinquity influenced each others, and whether any exchange and appropriation of models took place between them, represents an important new avenue of research, already undertaken in some recent studies. In his exploration of marriage rituals, for example, Roni Weinstein has concluded that a unique Jewish culture developed in the Italian context. The marriage patterns of the Jewish Italian community, from the practice of gift giving to wedding ceremonies, from the role of parental authority to the way in which emotions were expressed, presented specific characteristics that were grounded in wider local practice and that were distinct from both the Ashkenazi and the Sephardic traditions.[21] In a similar vein, historians of material culture have showed that the fascination with Islamic artifacts throughout the Renaissance led to the introduction of objects and textiles of exotic appearance into the western domestic interior. Initially imported from the Islamic world, these luxury commodities soon became the object of local imitation by European craftsmen who appropriated the production techniques and decorative patterns of Middle Eastern artisans. Likewise, the appreciation of Islamic furnishing inspired features such as the Spanish *estrado,* a platform furnished with cushions and carpets devoted to female sociability, in the design of western European houses.[22]

As stressed by contributions to this volume, the borrowing of models in the upbringing of children and patterns of family life was even more striking in colonial societies, especially those characterized by a close, daily interaction between the native, European, and black population. Rather than envisaging a map of family practices defined by clear-cut and predetermined religious and cultural divides, it is therefore important to recover the variety that such practices assumed in similar contexts as well as the similarities that might have existed, or developed, between apparently distant cultural realities.

This new attention to diversity has also led to questions about the enduring view that matched specific family forms with broad geographical areas of Europe, in particular the influential thesis formulated by Laslett and Hajnal according to which eastern and southern (or Mediterranean) Europe displayed types of household and household formation that were radically different from those prevailing in northern and western Europe.[23] Evidence has accumulated in the last few years challenging these time-honored orthodoxies. Detailed local and comparative studies by both specialists of the Mediterranean area and experts in eastern Europe have extensively demonstrated that a great variety of family forms could be found within these artificially drawn territorial boundaries.[24]

Recent scholars have also unmasked the ethnocentric assumptions contained within historical demography models influenced by modernization theory, which associate parts of Europe described as backward, "familist," or "collectivist" with the extended family and with high levels of patriarchal power. According to this paradigm, the domestic systems of southern and eastern Europe were characterized by the dominance of the old over the younger generations, whose dependence on the family of origin persisted well into mature age, and by the subordination of much younger wives to their husbands. A much less authoritarian and gender-biased family system, one which promoted individualism and entrepreneurial abilities, prevailed instead in the more advanced northwest of Europe. Here, the dominance of the neolocal family, independent from the elderly, would mean that a more egalitarian marital relationship could develop between spouses who were close in age, while the systematic recourse to the practice of life cycle service (that is, the custom of placing young people in service with other families until they married) granted children early independence from their parents. As the evidence in this volume suggests, these cut-and-dried oppositions appear particularly unsatisfactory if one considers the experience and understanding of childhood up to 1650. Fundamental features such as the age of leaving home, the involvement of children in the labor economy, and the forms of education/training/service outside the family are remarkably similar across the whole of Europe as well as among those involved in transatlantic settlement, and they vary more by class, gender, and legitimacy or illegitimacy of birth than by place.

The tendency to attribute distinctive family forms to entire geographical areas has therefore been abandoned in favor of a more localized approach that finds in the ecological, administrative, legal, and economic contexts the reason for the development of specific domestic arrangements. This microregional turn is particularly appropriate to the study of the 1400–1650 period, given that family reconstitution for most of this period can be conducted only at the local level because of the fragmented and discontinuous nature of the sources. Most assumptions about household structures during this time span have in fact been derived from findings rooted in the following centuries and then projected back as if they were self-evidently in place at an earlier date. As noted by Paolo Viazzo, a tendency to assume that most recent household structures dated from time immemorial has indeed "plagued the whole debate."[25]

The idea of geographical homogeneity has also been challenged by those historians who have investigated the influence of cultural values on the family and on gender relations in particular. Recent comparative research such as that conducted by Jutta Sperling brings to light the differences in gender culture between countries that have often been lumped together as sharing the same Mediterranean culture of honor.[26] These recent works show, for example, that Portugal and parts of Spain were characterized by egalitarian inheritance laws and matrilocality and by high levels of female celibacy and of women in a position of dominance. Property regimes and family structures seem to have been much less agnatic in parts of the Iberian Peninsula than in Italy and France.

National and regional variation also complicates the simple opposition between Protestant and Catholic family and child rearing practices that is often proposed in the literature. We have already stressed the composite nature of Protestant culture both in Europe and in the colonies. But Catholic culture too presents a variety of forms. It is notable, for example, that a new representation of paternity emerges in Spain in the depictions of Saint Joseph as early as the sixteenth century, well in advance of other European countries.[27] This specific chronology seems to stem from the success that Josephine devotion experienced in early colonized South America, thanks to its association with precolonial gods and rulers. Here the figure of the saint was appropriated by the indigenous population and transformed, under the influence of fluid gender codes, into a more ambiguous character, combining male and female traits, and was then exported back to motherland Spain. As this example illustrates, the colonial experience was an important element that set some countries apart from fellow Catholic and European countries, differentiating, for example, the way in which some family roles were perceived and represented.

CONCLUSIONS

The period between the fifteenth and the mid-seventeenth century witnessed a proliferation of discourses about the nature and functions of the family, and the role of parents in the upbringing of children. Renaissance humanist thought redefined the parameters that shaped children's education while promoting a view of the family as mirror of a well-ordered society based on class, gender, and age hierarchies. Then the crucial religious changes generated first by the Protestant and then by the Catholic reformations, together with state-sponsored policies, placed increasing emphasis on the political role of the household and the importance of childhood for building a disciplined and confessional society. The massive production of printed books in vernacular languages and of visual representations of domestic life created the conditions for these ideas to reach a wide audience, which in an age of colonial expansion included Europe and its overseas territories. The period undoubtedly saw a reinforcement of family and in particular of paternal authority. At the same time the value of marriage was enhanced and the bonds of affection between the spouses and between parents and their children were highly regarded in the discourse on the family. The expression of emotions and family bonding were also favored by a rising domestic consumption that improved the level of comfort in the home, making it a much more suitable place for domestic life and rituals. On the other hand, the new status acquired by marriage contributed to the campaign for moralizing sexual customs that made illicit any form of extramarital union.

From the fifteenth century on, therefore, and with increased vigor through the sixteenth century, visual culture and advice literature, religious preaching, and state policy elevated the nucleus of parents and their children to the status of paradigmatic family, reinforcing at an ideological level its social and religious functions and promoting the development of ties of affection between its members. Nevertheless, the most theoretical and ideal conceptualizations of the family were challenged by demographic and economic upheavals, political instability and military activities, and intensified migration. These factors made the family very vulnerable and often short lived. As shown in particular by the recent historiography on the colonial world, the discontinuity of the family household reached its apex in the racially stratified overseas domains; but, as chapters in the volume indicate, in continental Europe, too, unconventional and highly unstable households were a common experience in the family lives of early modern men, women, and children.

CHAPTER ONE

Family Relationships

SANDRA CAVALLO

Many elements suggest that the Western family became more patriarchal during the early modern period, which is to say that the prerogatives of fathers and husbands over wives, children, and subordinates increased substantially. The growth of the state and the impact of the Protestant Reformation have been seen as central forces in these transformations. In their centralizing and disciplining effort, secular and ecclesiastical authorities empowered householders, elevating them to guarantors of public and moral order in their homes. But the process was already underway; since the fifteenth century humanistic writings and town ordinances had established the public authority of the head of household, making him accountable for the conduct of his dependents. Needless to say, in prescriptive literature, sermons, and law codes, heads of households were generally understood to be male. Moreover, the rise of the patrilineage, and therefore of a view of kinship defined solely through the male line, had excluded women from genealogical representation and denied them a legal identity and the direct management of property.

A growing body of research, however, shows considerable variation in the ways in which male authority was exercised in the early modern family. Different environmental conditions and patterns of livelihood considerably diversified domestic arrangements and the nature of the marital and filial bond. Theological belief and ethnic status were additional factors that created diversity. For example, the authoritarian, father-centered model of family life was favored in early America, where it tallied with the settlers' quest for order and hierarchy.

But even in the colonies it was very different for a child to grow up in a Puritan or in a Quaker community, and, in the Spanish empire, to be born of European or mixed-race parents. Sources such as diaries and legal deeds, letters, and judicial records provide precious evidence to highlight these diversities; moreover, they portray the working of family relationships in ways that are often at odds with the normative discourse of the conduct literature. Yet even the prescriptive sources on which scholarship has largely relied, once submitted to comparative analysis, reveal that the patriarchal model of the family is neither static nor monolithic; subtle variations affect the normative representation of familial roles over time, and contradictions are detectable that reveal the weak points in the model promoted. In addition, we should also consider variations in what specific family bonds—for example, those between father and child or between in-laws—represented for different social classes. Frequently, the family life of the higher orders has been taken as a model that can be generalized across the whole social spectrum. In what follows we shall instead pay special attention to the characteristics of family relationships among the lower and middling ranks.

The focus on the working of patriarchy has often led scholars to portray a simplified image of the early modern family, reduced to the relationship between spouses and between parents and their children. In reality, any discussion of family relationships between 1400 and 1650 cannot avoid considering the broad spectrum of ties that made up the family of an individual: with kin, step-kin, and spiritual kin, and with a range of nonkin. The early modern domestic group had a weak biological base, and the high mortality rates and the incidence of widowhood and remarriage made the presence of various degrees of blood relations living under the same roof extremely common; moreover, the home was regularly populated by unrelated persons. Servants constituted a common and often considerable component of the coresidential unit. In the aristocratic household, as at court, servants largely outnumbered family members, but in patrician and mercantile households, too, they were often equivalent in number to the masters of the house. Besides, the presence of adopted or foster children, wet-nursed babies, and youngsters in education or in apprenticeship further complicated the composition of the early modern household, extending emotional ties and the sources of authority, support, and role models well beyond the biological, nuclear family.

THE IDEAL FAMILY

From as early as the 1400s, we see the development in Europe of a literature for the good governance of the family that prescribes in great detail the roles its members should perform in domestic life and that regulates relationships of authority between them.[1] In the following century this genre, originally aimed at the elites, expanded its interlocutors, was printed in the vernacular, and sometimes entrusted to broadsheets and chapbooks, thereby stimulating and reflecting a considerably wider social penetration of the family model it promoted. This appears as a structure based on avowedly hierarchical principles and upon the so-called natural inequality between its members. Inspired by the revived Aristotelian tradition that saw all things in existence as arranged according to a natural order, and hence presenting the social and political order as given and immutable, these texts described family organization as justified by the ascribed attributes of sex, age, and social class. The female gender's scant rationality and the incapacity of minors legitimated the authority and guidance that the father of the household exercised over his wife and children. As for the servants, they belonged to a naturally subordinate class because, being able in body but not so in mind and being prone to vice, they were born to carry out manual tasks and to be guided, also at a moral level, by clever men of virtue who were fit to command. In short, women were naturally inferior to men, children to adults, and servants to masters.

A hierarchical definition of the family was therefore already fully formulated by the 1400s, preceding by over a century both the growth of state legislation that would also legally reinforce the power of husbands and fathers (Chapter 7), and the development of a Christian ethic that would describe the father as "God's vicar" in the governance of the family, thereby adding a divine basis to the natural one of paternal authority (Chapter 8). And yet a sustained reading of advice for household management also reveals a series of innovations, even within the same basic framework, which was to inform the way in which family roles and relationships were conceptualized in the following two centuries. While in the late Middle Ages there was already an emphasis on the civic functions of the father's role, which was supposed to endow children with the necessary virtues for civil coexistence, the importance of the home in forming good subjects was further emphasized in the succeeding centuries by absolutist political discourse: it was in the family that one learned how to submit to the authority of governments.

Obedience to the head of the family was thus the key value informing family organization, and yet he was expected to exercise differing degrees of authority toward family members: constitutional rule over his wife, royal rule over his children, and tyrannical rule over his servants. The husband, in other words, did not have unconditional power over his wife. Moreover, by the late 1400s a more balanced definition of the conjugal relationship emerged that placed an increasing emphasis on the inseparability of the roles of husband and wife, these being frequently compared to the bond between body and soul. Whereas at the start of the century the female role within the family had been portrayed as limited to a purely reproductive function for the continuity of the husband's lineage and the preservation of his property, the wife was now described as the coregent of the household.

At the heart of this change was a general elevation of the civil value of marriage effected by the humanists, even earlier than by religious reformers. Writers such as Erasmus, Agrippa von Nettesheim, and Juan Lluis Vives upheld the importance of the institution of marriage in the education of new generations, and the fact that it fulfils man, giving him a life companion, and must therefore be based on love and on the intimacy of the married couple. At the same time there was continued emphasis on the duty of obedience to the husband, and a regime bordering on seclusion was prescribed for women, whose emotional weakness was constantly reiterated. The woman was seen to exercise a crucial ordering function, bringing beauty and harmony to the small world of the home. And yet in the late sixteenth century these purely domestic tasks were seen to transcend the household setting and acquire a public value: in the treatises of the Protestant theologians, the wife had great responsibility because it was she who by example instilled in the children the virtues of order, industriousness, and thrift that were so indispensable to public life.[2] But contemporary Catholic literature spoke no less highly of wifely duties. In the words of Agostino Valier, writing in 1575, "by raising good fathers, good citizens, good gentlemen and good princes" women "serve as mothers of the people of God."[3]

Even though the role of the mother in the family expanded and was more valued in the treatises of the 1500s, the domestic tasks allotted to the father remained extensive. He had responsibility for choosing good servants, identifying those who were loyal, intelligent, and discreet, and for correcting them where necessary, while his wife saw to feeding and clothing them and nursing the sick, as well as organizing the division of labor between them; moreover, she was supposed to attend to the education of the maidservants, as well as their Christian and moral instruction. In general the household was depicted in these texts as being organized along gender lines, with stronger and more enduring relationships between parents and children of the same sex and between masters and servants of the same sex. The father, moreover, carried great weight in the key decisions regarding the health and upbringing of the children, especially the males; he must select their tutor, and before that the wet nurse, perhaps even the midwife. The mother's role concentrated on the early years, in the phase of learning speech and the basic notions of faith and prayer, but the male children should early on be removed from the overly soft upbringing of the mother. The father, whose role some maintained became crucial as early as after the child's fourth birthday, stood as a model of conduct and manners, even of physical posture: the son should precociously assume an adult demeanor, learning to take up his appropriate place in society, which is to say speaking with people of consequence, giving way to superiors, bowing, and exercising composure.[4]

And yet, despite this idealization of the father figure, the treatise writers of the 1500s often described fathers as unfit for their responsibilities. In reality, bemoaned Giovanni Antonio Flaminio in 1523, they frequently gave an extremely bad example, boasting in front of their children about their mistresses and the violence they had perpetrated, inciting them to rashness and impudence, and mocking any talk of religious matters. "They say that they are males and that they will be men."[5] In other words, the values of masculinity were an obstacle to the formation of good Christians and good subjects. Erasmus, Memmo, and other writers of the period therefore suggested that children should be removed from their parents as early as possible; their upbringing was not the business of the family. Here the father's functions were limited by the traditional trust placed by this society on education outside the home. As we shall see, this remained a common practice for a large part of the period.

But patriarchal authority was limited also in other ways. The very analogy continuously established between the governance of the household and that of the community in the discourse on the early modern family placed the father's actions under constant scrutiny, so that he had to give continuous proof of wisdom in the pursuit of his duties and of genuine, efficient leadership, exercised with consensus, not with terror. The risk of seeming an unfit patriarch was always present, and it gave power to subordinates, to wives and servants in particular, who were better able to manipulate such vulnerability. To avoid open displays of insubordination and scandals that would damage his reputation, the head of household frequently resorted to mediations. He was no absolute patriarch.

FATHERS AND CHILDREN

Recent studies have greatly modified the image of paternal monarchy proposed by historians of the family in the 1970s and 1980s. An attentive reading of the prescriptive literature already shows cracks in this image. Though many humanist texts define fatherhood primarily in terms of authority and discipline, the sermons that prominent friars directed to a larger and socially diverse audience propose a very different image of the father-son relation,

one in which affection and tenderness figure highly.[6] Other sources reinforce the impression that fatherhood in the early modern age was increasingly associated with duty, affection, and care, not just power. For example,
diaries such as that of Constantijn Huygens, the secretary to the Prince of
Orange in the early decades of the seventeenth century, offer a loving representation of paternal domesticity, suggesting the everyday involvement of
fathers in the tiniest aspects of the life of young children.[7] In his journal,
Constantijn meticulously records every instance of progress they make—the
first smile, the first words, the first steps, the emergence of the "no" phase.
He appears to be well acquainted with their wet nurses and the nature of the
bond that children develop with them, and he accurately describes the course
of their illnesses. He then indulges in tender descriptions of family life that recall the atmosphere of Murillo's innovative depiction of the Holy Family (Figure 1.1). Here Saint Joseph, long portrayed as an elderly and marginal figure
whose role in medieval nativity stories was, at best, negligible, is shown as a
young, handsome, and vigorous man actively involved in the upbringing and
care of his son. Indeed, from the late fifteenth century the growth of the cult

FIGURE 1.1: *The Holy Family with a Little Bird*, Bartolomè Esteban Murillo, circa 1650,
oil on canvas, Museo el Prado, Madrid.

of Saint Joseph in the Catholic world promoted new ideals of masculinity that enhanced "mothering fathers."[8] In Spain and the Spanish colonies in particular the imagery of Saint Joseph adopted archetypes employed in depictions of the Virgin and child that stressed the nurturing and physical nature of fatherly love (Figure 1.2). This evidence is in sheer contrast with the image of the father as a severe and authoritarian figure aloof from his children that in the second half of the eighteenth century the new rhetoric of sensibility was to associate with the preceding period.[9] Certainly, however, the extent to which these ideals extended to the Protestant world remains to be explored. Submission to fatherly authority might have been harshly enforced, especially in American colonies, as a reaction to the indulgent modes of child rearing attributed to the natives.[10]

FIGURE 1.2: *Saint Joseph and the Christ Child*, anonymous, sixteenth century, feather mosaic, Museo de las Americas, Madrid.

The emotional bond between fathers and children, male children in particular, appears particularly strong among those classes in which male offspring
were seen to provide continuity for the family name, reputation, social position, and property. This intense love for their children was, in some views,
a feature that, in instances of disagreement, substantially limited the deter-
mination of fathers to enforce their will on children at all costs. This can be
seen in a classic area of generational conflict, that of religious vocation. This
became a frequent occurrence in Catholic countries where first the reformed
orders, then the militant orders of the Counter-Reformation, exerted a
strong attraction on the young, often to the displeasure of their parents.
One is struck by the passionate words and the declarations of love used by
fathers in their attempts to turn their children away from a religious choice;
in his letters to the son who had joined the Jesuits, Guichard Coton "begged"
him to return, employing the language of reason and affection rather than
command. And the children replied in the same terms, acknowledging the
strength of the tie that binds them to their parents and defending their own
choices by invoking a higher obligation rather than any independence from
the father.[11]

The interaction between generations therefore betrayed essential recognition of shared values. This meant that parents on the whole adopted persuasion
rather than coercion in cases of controversial decisions; likewise, children making autonomous choices, of a spouse for example, would crave the agreement
of their parents.[12] Of course there was no lack of cases in which physical and
psychological violence was exerted on children to influence undesirable decisions relating to marriage or vocation, or cases in which there were threats to
disinherit. But it is likely that in many cases parents and children were at one in
their grounds for making these kinds of choices.

However, the picture was not socially uniform, and generational conflicts
appear to have been much more common among the classes that depended
on work for a living—for example, small artisans lacking the material and
symbolic possessions (palaces, estates, chapels) that acted as a glue between
the generations. Here the early economic independence that was demanded of
children often led to them leaving the father's household in their early teens,
and sometimes to migration; the sense of self born of learning to look out for
themselves and be self-sufficient through their own hard work soon led these
young people to demand the freedom to make their own choices independently
of parents' opinions. Paternal authority was therefore frequently questioned.
Gaspare Nadi (1418–1504), a Bolognese mason who for 50 years kept a diary
extensively devoted to family matters, offers continual examples of an attitude

of insubordination that, besides his children and nephew, must have affected youth as a whole, at least among these social strata. He often laments the sudden departures from the home of his numerous children, the decisions to leave their masters or to pursue a religious vocation, things that occurred "without permission" or "against the wishes" of their father. One is struck, however, by the placidity with which he relates meeting these challenges. When his son Antonio, 15 at the time, left Federigo da Santafiore, in whose employment he was, despite the appreciation shown to him by this nobleman, by his fellow workers, and the court, Gaspare was put out but delicately refrained from giving his views: "as his father I was not very pleased, but I did not wish to upset him."[13] Clearly appealing to idealized notions of fatherhood, he fashions himself as a wise father, who patiently endures youthful impetuosity, but his account can also betray resignation and an awareness that, within these social strata, paternal authority had profound limits.

Of course, the frustration of the failed patriarch in seeing his own authority undermined could also lead to reactions of exceptional brutality. In 1630, likewise in Bologna, the Torrone tribunal was examining the case of a mercer who had beaten his eleven-year-old son to death; as testified by the neighbors, the latter "didn't want to do well, he didn't want to learn a trade or go to school, he had gone to the bad ... he had run away from home and he didn't want to work and that was why his father often knocked him about."[14]

HUSBANDS AND WIVES

The image of the marital couple that emerges from the prescriptive literature, depicting a submissive wife and an ever-present husband, overriding head or ultimate supervisor of family affairs, is belied by other sources. Wives of husbands long absent because they were busy at court, or engaged in their religious functions, or in seasonal work or in commerce, effectively took on the management of the household and the family property, an occurrence allowed for by the same texts that laid down the rules for married life. For Tudor gentlewomen like Lady Lestrange, domestic pressures could be so overwhelming as to obliterate the classic limitations on the country lady's mobility that already restricted her within a range of 10 or 20 miles, and to visiting neighbors and local relatives.[15] Paradoxically, it was in fact the most sedentary women, those who fully embodied the model of female domestic segregation endorsed by conduct books, who could be given the greatest responsibilities and some considerable leeway in decisions regarding the family. At the same time, letters offer a more contained image of the freedom that wives would have enjoyed in the running of family affairs than the one we derive from account books: their correspondence with absent husbands is often packed with minute details about household goings-on as if, even from afar, husbands maintained control over the domestic sphere, at least symbolically.

It was, however, in the realm of bodily needs that patriarchal authority was particularly diminished. Women controlled household tasks relating to the management of the body—birth, food, domestic health care, and death—and this tempered significantly the power of men when, in the intimacy of the home, they were confronted with physical vulnerability and depended on women for the fulfillment of basic needs. Care was "disruptive of hierarchies and unimpressed by status."[16]

But there were also enclaves in which responsibility for the household and family business, officially, as well as informally, resided wholly in women's hands. In maritime communities—for example, in the port towns of the Iberian Peninsula, Scandinavia, and Holland—the proportion of the male population at sea for long periods reached some thirty-five percent, or even up to fifty percent. Here we see a total reversal of roles: the traditional limitations on legal female authority were sidestepped by means of proxies granted by the husbands before embarkation, so that wives enjoyed an unusual freedom to make purchases, sales, and other transactions. It is likely that this accustomed them to an independence of opinions and behavior that, at least as far as folklore suggests, was maintained even when the men returned.[17]

Likewise, the unusual property rights enjoyed by women in parts of the Iberian Peninsula carried weight in conferring upon them particular authority within the family. Although the system of handing down family assets prevalent in Europe favored men, or indeed one son only (not necessarily the firstborn), in Portugal, as in the northwest of Spain, daughters inherited on a par with sons, or even more than their male siblings; the dangers of the fishing economy made them the most reliable heirs, and this led to many women owning property shares in ships or trading companies and being prominent among the taxpayers.[18] In other parts of Europe, it was ethnic identity that secured privileges of ownership for women: in the Jewish ghettos of Italy, daughters received greater portions than their brothers, in the form of dowries. Given that the dowry was legally protected, standing as a security for the widow, the transmission of family property through the female line served as a bulwark against the constant threat of pogroms and expulsions, and the risk of seeing the community's assets destroyed or confiscated; the system also counterbalanced the insecurity intrinsic to the mercantile and financial occupations which the Jews were forced to exercise. The inviolability of dowry funds made wives the holders of family property, and this could not but strengthen their position in the family, fuelling the stereotype of the powerful Jewish mother that has thrived to this day. But the influence that these mothers frequently exerted over their married children then made them awkward figures for young Jewish couples who often cohabited with the husband's parents in the early stages of marriage; these cohabitations hampered the young wife's scope of independence and often prompted marital conflict.[19]

In short, female influence in the family varied considerably according to age, as well as with varying patterns of male employment and forms of property transmission. In the same households the figure of the strong mature woman could coexist with that of submissive young wives who were victims of marital violence.

MOTHERS AND CHILDREN

Clearly, in spite of the centrality of the father in the discourse on the family, the mother could remain a crucial point of reference in the life of an adult child; according to some authors it was precisely her constant presence in the home that made her an irreplaceable source of psychological reassurance for her children. Although feelings between mothers and children were discouraged and even reviled in the literature on the family, the bond had already been formed at an early age; this was in spite of the widespread custom of entrusting newborns to the care of a wet nurse. Common among Italian patricians already in the 1400s, the practice spread to the well-off classes based both in the rest of Europe and in the colonies in the following century, but the lower-middle classes also resorted to it, especially in urban settings, albeit less systematically, given the costs involved. The custom has sometimes been seen as a measure that weakened the bond with the mother, who, within the ideology of the lineage, was meant to be a marginal presence in the life of her children. But the logic according to which children were regarded as belonging to the paternal line was considerably weaker among the nonpropertied classes; moreover, the legal rules assigning total responsibility for offspring to the father and his blood kin were frequently sidestepped in practice, even among the privileged. For example, women who, on remarrying, lost guardianship of their children, frequently did not stop being involved in the crucial choices regarding their future. A study of the Roman noblewoman Eugenia Maidalchini shows how she kept in close contact with their guardian, influencing every decision regarding the children of her first marriage, to the point where one can speak of de facto double management of their upbringing.[20]

Nor did the hiring of a wet nurse necessarily entail a cooling of maternal feeling and the privileged relationship with the mother. We learn from the seventeenth-century diary of a poor Amsterdam wine broker how his wife followed the wet nurse to whom, lacking milk, she had entrusted her newborn, all the way to Friesland, despite the distance and the expenses the journey entailed, to avoid being separated from her baby son.[21] In the upper social strata the wet nurse frequently lived in the home, and this favored the persistence of the bond with the mother. In any case, mothers became active figures after the child's weaning, whether in relation to the care of the body, for example in childhood illnesses, or in attention to psychological problems. The noblewoman Eugenia Maidalchini describes in her letters how she had dealt with her two-year-old son's fears of traveling in a coach, or with the regressive behavior of one of the older children, who wanted only to be held in her arms after having been in a life-threatening state of health for two weeks.[22]

The detachment from the mother, if it did happen, usually took place well beyond the age recommended by conduct books. We cannot nevertheless exclude some degree of internalizing of the discourse that represented the maternal figure as a dangerous emasculating influence for male children. In the diary kept between 1552 and 1616, Hans von Schweinichen, a son of the Silesian lesser nobility, actually talked about his mother as an obstacle who had caused him to miss precious opportunities because she was unwilling to let her son go and wished to keep him all to herself.[23]

The mother-daughter bond was a particularly enduring one among the better-off classes, maintained by means of constant correspondence, frequent visits, and stays in the mother's house. Not only was it far from unusual to go home to give birth (or in any case the grandmother's presence at childbirth was common), but as we see once again from the extraordinary correspondence between Eugenia Maidalchini and her mother, which lasted over 30 years, the latter kept an eye on Eugenia from a distance, guiding the daughter's adjustment to formal wifely duties and then those of a widow (which clothes to wear, for example), and imparting advice on how to achieve matrimonial harmony and be a good mother.[24] Indeed this kind of advice became a very popular literary genre in the early modern period.[25]

Later in the female life cycle, relationships with children could also turn nasty. The fact that the father's testament often urged his heirs to look after their mothers and to give them their rightful share of the property betrays a mistrust of the mechanisms that should have protected the widow. After the father's death, conflicts with the mother were indeed extremely frequent, whether on questions of property or residence and care.

EXTENDED FAMILIES

Treatises give us a simplified view of the family, which is depicted as a nuclear unit consisting only of parents and children, even if extended to the servants. In reality, a household was often much more complex; for example, it was fairly common to live at one time or another in extended families. Among the upper social strata the tendency for both spouses, or at least for the wife, to marry when very young meant that the new couple often lived with the husband's family in the early stages of marriage. A woman could give birth to all her children, or a good number of them, before having her own household, enduring in the meantime the intrusions of mothers-in-law who sometimes exerted control even over the sexual intimacy of the couple, checking for example on signs of the daughter-in-law's menstrual cycle.[26] Nor was the situation any easier for the young husband, who continued to be treated as he was before his marriage.[27] These were often difficult cohabitations that could nonetheless have the result of cementing the intimacy of the young spouses, who became allies in a conflict between generations. Yet at other times they had a divisive effect on the couple. Precisely because of the possible interferences in the life of the young people, the conduct book authors of the 1600s discouraged coresidence with parents.[28]

Among the merchant classes, the custom of delaying the division of family assets between siblings, despite the death of the father, frequently also meant that brothers, often married, continued to live under the same roof. Shared habitation in the family palace, albeit in separate apartments, and partaking in at least some of the rituals of domestic life were symbolic incarnations of unity and agreement between the coheirs, who remained in effect a single legal and economic entity until the time when increased prosperity made their splitting possible.[29] Such cohabitation between generations or between adult brothers were therefore frequent not only for economic reasons but also on ideological grounds, or simply because of age. Nonetheless, with the exception of parts of rural eastern Europe, such arrangements were of a temporary nature, and individuals experienced different kinds of family structure—nuclear, extended, and multiple—in different phases of their lives.

Yet the fluidity of the domestic nucleus was a particularly strong feature of the lower and middle classes. Here the composition of the household had very little of a cyclical and structural nature but could change from one moment to the next in response to sudden deaths, wars, and illnesses. The influential argument according to which nuclear and extended families were firmly associated with particular geographical areas finds no correspondence in biographical evidence. For example, the household arrangements experienced by artisans in central Italy were extremely varied and unstable. Moreover, while cohabitations among the higher social classes were usually limited to close relatives (parents, a brother, or at most a paternal uncle) and therefore respect a patrilineal logic (homes were shared with the husband's, not the wife's, parents or relatives), among the laboring classes the whole group of kin, without distinctions of degree of kinship or male or female line, and inclusive of stepkin, represented a resource that could also lead to forms of coresidence.[30] One example comes to us from the experiences of the Florentine coppersmith Masi. As recorded in his diary, Masi married Caterina (who was fatherless) in 1478, and the couple settled in the house of Caterina's uncle, Landino; only eight months later they set up a separate household. A few years after this, the family welcomed Caterina's brother, Francesco, and her mother, Agnola, into their home. Agnola died the following year, while Francesco stayed on in the Masi household for a good 12 years. Upon his sister's death, however, Francesco moved to the house of a deceased paternal uncle, along with a cousin, and the Masi family went back to being nuclear.[31]

Besides the contingencies of fertility, mortality, and illness, the fluidity of the household owed a great deal to conflict, a factor frequently overlooked in the somewhat rigid reconstruction of the family life cycle. Let us take, for example, the turbulent housing situation of mason Gaspare Nadi, characterized by repeated separations from and reunions with his third wife and stepchildren, and by periods of sharing with children from three different marriages and their families. Almost all the ruptures in these different household configurations are presented as motivated by acute domestic conflicts. These events are ambiguous: far from fitting the binary opposition weak or strong adopted by historical demographers to classify family ties in different parts of Europe, they demonstrate the ambivalence of family relationships.[32] These relationships appear highly fragile among social strata that were perhaps particularly prone to quarrelling because of their extreme vulnerability but that were clearly capable in the long run, of setting their disputes and returning to normal.

Even when there was no cohabitation, however, it did not mean that family relationships were unimportant. The definition of family based on coresidence has by now been criticized in various quarters. In both northern and southern Europe, a family member leaving home would keep in touch with parents and other relatives through letter writing and reciprocal visits, by being present at funerals, and by being at the bedside of the sick. For many young people, moreover, the paternal home remained an intermittent shelter to be returned to temporarily in the case of illness or personal difficulties, or at the end of terms of service.[33]

The closeness or distance between where family members settled could, however, have been a significant factor in the endurance of family ties. If we take into consideration relationships between households of relatives who were also neighbors, living in the same village or district of a town, we find an intense circulation of help and resources that had a crucial value in the management of the household and within the family economy.[34] In contrast, in those areas characterized by a strong flow of migration from the country to the city, ties with at least part of the family, the part left behind, were often weakened for those moving away. However, new family relationships became central: those established through marriage in the place of arrival and those with relatives, often siblings, with whom one had shared the experience of migration. In these circumstances the ties between kin belonging to the same generation and facing the same problems of settling and becoming established in a new environment seem to have been particularly strong. Siblings and brothers and sisters-in-law often settled close at hand and mutually participated at weddings and baptisms as witnesses and godparents, but they also acted as guardians of orphans for one another and set up work partnerships or other forms of professional cooperation.[35]

Kin were, moreover, central in providing children with education or training in a particular craft or profession: many studies have noted that in fact boys and girls were often sent as apprentices to a relative rather than a stranger. One might say then that the responsibility for offspring was frequently distributed among the kinship group. This is particularly clear in those not infrequent cases when the child was entrusted to an uncle or an older brother at an early age; the new family took over as the crucial parental structure, thereby informally adopting the young kin. It was mainly families with numerous offspring that had recourse to this kind of expedient, with the avowed purpose of lightening the burden of having to bring up so many children. Indeed, families with many children were far from uncommon among the lower-middle classes. Here the relatively young age at marriage of the spouses and the tendency for widowed men to remarry almost immediately once they lost their wives notably extended their reproductive time span, putting considerable stress on the scant resources of their families. But at the same time the substantial discrepancy in age between siblings created multiple centers of authority within these families, and a consequent sharing of the obligations characterizing the father-son relationship. The older brother was seen as having responsibility for the younger ones, and relationships between siblings were thought of not simply as between equals, and hence in terms of rivalry or solidarity, but also as relations of authority and dependency.[36] Older children already producing income, and likewise a father's or mother's brother, clearly internalized and in part fulfilled these expectations, since they often became the primary providers for some of their siblings, or for nephews and nieces.

SURROGATE PARENTS

Being brought up by a surrogate parent was therefore not uncommon and could even extend beyond the confines of kinship. Godparents and sometimes also better-off neighbors or acquaintances might take on the burden of raising a child from a poor family. In Venice such agreements might well take the form of contracts in which the child was defined as the new parents' *figlio d'anima* (spiritual offspring). The foster parents made a commitment to keep the child in their home as a servant or apprentice until adulthood, and to guarantee his or her future by finding a girl a suitable match and paying her dowry or establishing a boy in a trade.[37] For childless couples and bachelors, these de facto adoptions provided artificial descendants to whom they could hand on their own professional knowledge, sometimes their assets, and even their name; in other cases they were more strictly a form of charity and patronage. Even when the relationship between masters and servants or apprentices was not formalized in terms of adoption, it was still thought of in terms of family relationships, with the master promising to treat the servant as his own son or daughter and looking after his or her physical and spiritual welfare. Bonds of affection frequently did develop between them; not only would masters often leave legacies to their more loyal servants and provision for their old age, but the servants themselves demonstrated trust and attachment, frequently choosing masters as executors of their wills or even making them the beneficiaries of their possessions.[38] Particularly worth noting are the bonds formed with chambermaids and menservants who were privy to their masters' secrets and accompanied them everywhere; likewise, wet nurses, who often breast-fed several babies from the same family and, at court or in aristocratic households, were then made nursemaids to the same children, thereby became the depositaries of a family memory regarding the children's early years and the first manifestations of their physical and psychological temperament.

From the parents, the masters inherited duties to educate and protect but also authority, and they were thus fully within their rights to impose corporal punishments and corrections. But the requirement of total submission to the master often allowed abuse, including sexual violence. At the same time the young people might well not acknowledge the masters as fathers, such is the extreme frequency of apprentices and servants running away or moving from one workshop to another, from one household to the other.[39] There was therefore a significant gap between the ideal and reality.

The removal of children and teenagers from the family of origin was motivated not only by financial reasons. Fostering was a fairly widespread phenomenon across social groups and genders in the early modern period, only declining, in Europe, in the 1600s. In Portugal, for example, the poorest children left for the colonies in the wake of the missionaries or as cabin boys on board ship, while the more privileged entered a seminary or monastery in early adolescence, or left home to serve as pages at court.[40] Others moved to the house of a distinguished tutor; even those who went to university often took up lodgings with one of their teachers there. The daughters of the nobility and the prosperous merchant classes were also frequently entrusted to an elite family so that they could acquire the social skills required of an accomplished gentlewoman—not only manners and style, but the ability, inherent to the female role, to mediate in conflicts, negotiate positions for the family, arrange marriages, and run a grand household.[41] Clearly, there was a pedagogical value attributed to being brought up outside the family; as the conduct literature maintained, children would have "less boldness in the house of others and would learn better manners."[42]

But fostering also carried hopes of acculturation and opportunities for future social advancement. When the host family was socially superior, even mere domestic service often involved the acquisition of reading skills, since masters sometimes took very seriously their obligations to educate ignorant servants.[43] In Peru, indigenous children placed in service with colonial families even acquired a new racial status, that of *ladini*, as well as the master's surname, in recognition of the fact that they were now able to speak Spanish, knew Catholic doctrine, and could dress, style their hair, and behave at table according to Spanish conventions.[44] Children were seen as key vehicles in the acquisition of cultural knowledge, hence fosterage was a common practice in societies stratified by race as well as by class. In early America the often forced fosterage of Indian children had long played a part in English efforts to assimilate native people. Children were abducted to serve in English households, where it was hoped they would grow accustomed to the English "orderly" and "civilized" way of life.[45] Among the higher classes, on the other hand, the circulation of children contributed to the growth of networks of clientage between families, so that the sending of a child was welcomed as a gift and was seen as a mutual honor.[46] The affection it was hoped would take root between the young charges and those entrusted with them would make the latter their patrons in the years to come. All in all, there were complex and variegated reasons behind the custom of entrusting one's children to others.

CONCLUSION

Despite the importance that European and colonial societies attributed to the father's authority, which in many parts of Europe and in the Spanish empire remained legally in force until his death, paternal control over children was limited to just the first years of their lives. Mortality and mobility were important factors, and the high number of fatherless children and of female-headed households in parts of Europe show that in many cases the management of the family and the main parental role were associated with women. Class was another element that could threaten paternal power. Despite their legal prerogatives, poverty often disempowered fathers, delegitimizing their authority to command. Moreover, the upbringing of children was rarely a matter solely for parents; both in terms of affection and authority. Parental roles were distributed among a wide and varied range of people. Horizontal and lateral family connections, such as those between older and younger siblings, in-laws, and between aunts and uncles and their nephews and nieces, frequently played a key role, especially among the less prosperous classes. But many children were raised outside their natal homes by people who were unrelated. Fosterage, be it temporary or protracted, forced or voluntary, declined in Europe only in the 1600s, while remaining a fairly common practice in the colonies, especially in Latin America. Although both maternal and paternal roles expanded considerably over the period, with wives and mothers acquiring more authority over family affairs and fathers amplifying their emotional involvement in their children's lives, familiar relationships continued to bind together individuals remotely connected or unconnected by kinship ties. This blurred considerably the boundaries of what the individual could have regarded as his or her family.

CHAPTER TWO

Community

ILANA KRAUSMAN BEN-AMOS

Early modern families operated within a matrix of social networks and ties that linked them to communities and broader social groupings outside their confines. Throughout the period, families did not operate in isolation as closed domestic units, but rather they were embedded within varied networks and ties that enabled them to perform the immense task of sustaining themselves during the life course and across the generations. Families performed multiple political, economic, and social functions that were invariably designed to preserve the family status, extend economic resources, offer employment to offspring, or allow them access to positions and careers. In an era of high mortality rates and few guarantees for safety against numerous hazards, domestic units relied on the assistance of others in guaranteeing a modicum of viability and in securing the prospects and well-being of their children. No family, wealthy or poor, could sustain itself for long without cultivating ties and commitments within broader communities and networks that were available outside.

It had for some time been the belief that this configuration, which maintained a certain openness between families and the outside world, diminished from late medieval times onward, as families became more privatized and confined to a nuclear unit strictly controlled by male household heads.[1] As much research on families and the social spaces they inhabited now shows, however, while a measure of privatization became apparent—especially in the internal design of elite houses—early modern families remained strongly linked to communities in their immediate locality and sometimes beyond.[2]

Such links were evident in the ties of patronage and sociability that linked elite families to one another, in the varied interactions and systems of rule in localized communities, and in the ties of trade, associations, or neighborhoods that bound large sections of the population in webs of interpersonal relations and obligations. In what follows we take a look at the major networks and institutions that constituted these communities—patrons and friends, rural and urban neighborhoods and ties, associations, and the host of local institutions that increasingly catered to the welfare of families and their children. What will become apparent is that as the period from the fifteenth through the seventeenth century progressed—and the processes of state formation, the Reformation, economic expansion, and the growth of towns became more marked—so the links between families and their communities intensified and became more robust; communities exerted power and penetrated family life, while families themselves vigorously cultivated and pursued their outside networks.

PATRONS, FRIENDS, AND THE
ADVANCEMENT OF CHILDREN

As kings across Europe consolidated their power and increased the size and scope of their governance from 1400 onward, a unique system of rule based on strong personal links between monarchs and the upper classes evolved. Kings were increasingly engaged in relations of interdependence and alliances with nobles, who, in return for their service and loyalty, obtained varied favors, positions, and share of rule. The monarchy—in France, England, Germany, Castile, and in some Italian cities—assimilated into its orbit large sectors of the nobility in patron-client exchanges that benefited them both.[3] These expansive networks of patronage that stretched from a court aristocracy via its brokers and down to the provincial gentry and below impinged on the lives of families and their children in numerous tangible ways. Encompassing kinship ties as well as ties with nonkin, and invariably referred to as both "kinship" or "friendship," patron-client ties were essential for securing the interests of elite families, whose dynastic concerns, accumulation of land, advancement of family members, and aspirations for influence over government all became entwined.

As families across Europe consolidated their holdings by concentrating their property in the hands of one son, they increasingly relied on these patronage ties for establishing alternative employment and careers for noninheriting siblings. By allowing access to positions in varied branches of the government or the church, patron-client alliances enabled families to open up opportunities for younger offspring, while at the same time extending and strengthening their holdings. For example, in fifteenth-century Granada, where previously division of patrimony was the norm, a gradual shift can be observed toward the creation of a *mayorazgo*—an inalienable patrimony that was handed out to the eldest son and remained intact from one generation to the next, with some elite families consequently managing to build up large estates that became the basis of their own power and prestige. Younger siblings, who might also be provided with a small portion or allowance, were at the same time encouraged to go into careers in state service, the church, or the army, where they could hope to amass resources or establish themselves on their own. In England, the process was particularly marked as families among the upper and lower ranks of the gentry or the professions managed to consolidate their estates through the practice of primogeniture, while at the same time sending off younger sons into public office, the church, the armed forces, as well as the mercantile trades or the professions (law and medicine). These alternative careers not only required substantial financial means but also family networks that could prove more decisive in determining the prospects of sons than could sheer familial wealth or social aspirations.[4]

Access to patronage and positions thus became part of an "artful planning of succession," an indispensable mechanism for placing children into careers that could promote their upbringing and fortunes already at an early stage in their lives.[5] To take just one example, when the wife of Arthur Plantagent, Viscount Lisle, followed him in his move away from Hampshire to Calais in 1533 (he was appointed deputy lieutenant), she made extensive arrangements for her three boys from her earlier marriage—who were left behind—relying intensively on family ties to secure their maintenance, education, and subsequently their careers. The youngest boy, age six, was entrusted with the abbot of Reading, then sent to Paris, and later placed in the service of Bishop Gardiner when he was eleven years old. The second son, age eight, was placed with a friend of the family and then entered the service of a leading courtier, Sir Francis Bryan. The eldest son remained in Hampshire under the care of a neighbor until he entered Lincoln's Inn in 1533, and at age twenty he became the servant of Thomas Cromwell, then still at the hub of policy making in Henry VIII's court. Throughout these years the mother who lived in Calais was heavily involved in the affairs of her sons, instructing varied additional friends and relatives to visit and take care of the boys whenever possible.[6] Numerous examples can be found of younger siblings who were sent into houses of patrons and friends during their teens and then moved into careers at court, state service, the church, or the professions. For those families who struggled to maintain a more precarious position in the social hierarchy, the task of sustaining links and investing time and resources in the cultivation of friendship that guaranteed the careers of offspring was particularly precious.[7]

Patronage networks not only provided contacts for potentially lucrative careers but also offered a range of vital support that helped secure and improve the fortunes and position of families throughout the life course and across the generations. As the correspondences of elite families in places like England and France indicate, patronage was critical for arranging suitable marriages, procuring grants of land and wardship (in the case of the early death of the father), and securing pensions and annuities for family members. These patrons offered favors and advice in the settlement of disputes and in extending influence over local officials, in securing service and justice at the law courts, or obtaining release from prison. Friends and patrons offered loans when families fell on hard times—when fortunes were fluctuating, when families became solvent, or when the untimely death of the head of the family disrupted or brought the family to the verge of disintegration. Women were sometimes heavily involved in the art of cultivating these types of networks, playing roles as patrons, clients, or brokers for their husbands and making a broad range of patronage suits for themselves and on behalf of their offspring, dependants, or clients. They acted as patrons or intermediaries who mediated in the advancement of careers or in preferment to secular and religious offices. By the late sixteenth and early seventeenth centuries, the role of friends in the family lives of European gentry and professional classes was paramount, and networks encompassing them intermingled with blood relations that could sometimes stretch over large geographical areas well beyond one's local area or abode.[8]

At the center of these ties was the large house itself, with its inner structure and arrangements designed to perform its key role as the locus for cultivating kin and patronage ties. The Christmas season, holidays, and major life cycle events such as birth, weddings, and funerals were occasions in which gates were opened and hospitality was offered on a large scale. These celebrations sometimes encompassed numerous guests—patrons, clients, friends, and kin, in addition to resident kin, servants, or the local poor—who congregated in an orderly and hierarchical form in the great hall at the center of the house. In England, the late sixteenth century witnessed the so-called great rebuilding of country houses, with halls and rooms sumptuously constructed and the great hall performing its role as a public and ceremonial space. Lavish hospitality to patrons, clients, and their entourage of family and dependents was also evident in France, where it was vigorously acted out with a view toward cultivating and rewarding patrons, pursuing favors, and cementing personal bonding and obligations. Nor was hospitality solely a phenomenon of the countryside; rather, it increasingly formed part of the domestic world of urban elites. In sixteenth-century Spain, the emerging patrician families in the city of Granada built and refashioned big houses that had initially been constructed by the Muslim aristocracy. These large houses, with their granaries, cellars, and stables, and their dozen or more serving men and women, carried coats of arms sculpted above the main entrance, and their gates regularly opened to kin and numerous guests, patrons, and friends.[9]

RURAL COMMUNITIES

Throughout the fifteenth and sixteenth centuries, European society continued to be dominated by rural settlements, where patterns of land ownership and lord-tenant relations penetrated and impinged on familial practices and arrangements. By the fifteenth century, interactions and forms of exchange between tenants and lords varied greatly, but for the most part they encompassed the payment of rents as well as special fees that were extracted from tenants—for milling grain or baking bread on the lord's estate, when buying and selling land, or in the transmission of inheritance to offspring. Lord-tenant exchange also entailed daily interactions and binding commitments, with families coming into contact with, and relying on, their landlords for provision of favors and support, for which they were expected to offer services and deference in return. So, for example, in a sixteenth-century Normandy village, the resident lord seigneur, Gilles de Gouberville, protected his tenants against the royal tax collector, offered them advice and support when they took cases to the court, and was an arbiter in their disputes with their neighbors. He paid for medications for offspring who became ill, distributed clothes and charities to needy families, and offered food gifts or hospitality upon a birth or following the death of tenants, their wives, or children. These acts and provisions were part of an ongoing exchange whereby in return for his offerings, his tenants owed de Gouberville loyalty and gratitude, aptly articulated and expressed in the gifts—apples, chicken, rabbits, or butter—that they sent or brought to him throughout the year. Customs of offering food gifts were evident and potent in many places where lords were resident, signaling the ongoing exchange, dependence, and patterns of rule that penetrated the domestic lives of peasants and their families everywhere.[10]

Rural families were also linked to one another in face-to-face encounters and reciprocal exchanges that encompassed a wide array of favors, services, and material support, alongside hospitality and sociability. These were conveyed in daily affairs and in social gatherings, on streets and public spaces, in festivities or at the church. Families were engaged with one another in interactions involving buying and selling, offering loans and advice, mediating in disputes, visiting the sick, or participating in domestic events and celebrations of birth, marriage, and death. In some places it was the custom to organize help in times of need—when families fell on hard times, when marriages were cemented, and when the younger generation was about to start households of their own. In England celebrations called "help ales" and "bride ales" typically offered communal charity to the newlyweds and those who fell on hard times, merging such acts of reciprocal generosity with merrymaking and festivity. These communal customs remained common well into the late sixteenth century and early decades of the seventeenth century, when they gradually began to erode. In other places, communal customs might threaten familial patterns of transmission of land and marriages. In Germany, the village "spinning bees" (*spinnstube*)—evening gatherings of the unmarried, in which work mingled with drink, gossip, dancing, and amusement—were the locus of the sexual culture of the young, an occasion for the passing of love pledges and playfulness. Given their relative freedom in mate selection, these spinning bees put the entire marriage system, which was tied to landholding and inheritance, under a great deal of pressure.[11]

By the fifteenth century, local communities were also governed by a host of institutions—assemblies and village meetings, varied forms of courts (both ecclesiastical and civil), and local officials increasingly also supported by state officials and central state organs. These local bodies encouraged a more effective form of cooperation between families—in plowing, harvesting, or organizing common grazing—but they also played an increased role in the surveillance and imposition of discipline, invariably affecting patterns of marriage, residential arrangements, leisure and consumption, and relations between families and their neighbors and the community at large. There were many variations across Europe with respect to the strength and effectiveness of these local organs of control, with relatively weak communities more apparent in England and the Low Countries, and stronger ones in central and southern Europe. Yet even in England, the role of community in the surveillance of mobility, patterns of residence, and sometimes marriages became evident, especially from the mid-sixteenth century onward, as suspicions of vagrants and the itinerant poor mounted. Here as well, local authorities increasingly enforced rules and regulations designed to safeguard the interests of parishioners against outsiders and the vagrant poor and applied repressive measures to expel them. Restrictions on female servants, unmarried women, and widows were particularly tight. In Germany, local communities used their power of regulation to discriminate against widows and reinforce the patriarchal family structure by favoring married sons over widows in inheritance or in the selling of property, or by imposing restrictions on widows' transactions of their property. Restrictions on women in access to common resources and varied forms of employment were marked also in the towns, where their entry into guilds, for example, was everywhere practically barred.[12]

The religious changes that were brought about by the Reformation and that vastly transformed religious life over much of Europe tended to reinforce these links between the patriarchal family structure and the community. Protestants vigorously pursued the notion that communities were practically and morally founded on well-ordered households and that these households were places of worship and prayer as well as social institutions. Reformed communities everywhere—both Protestant as well as Catholic—propagated the notion of community by focusing on confessional congregations based on shared belief, as well as on the bonds of mutual obligations between households. Hence one witnesses across Europe the involvement of churches in varied novel schemes for the relief of the poor, as well as an increased use of church courts and consistories in the regulation of behavior and in the maintenance of household morality and order. For example, in Strasburg, the council made laws prohibiting the marriages of servants who in their judgment had inadequate funds to support a viable household. Conversely, they tried to encourage marriages among citizens' families by dowering poor respectable girls, thus helping their proper integration into the civic community. Families sometimes used these courts to help resolve conflicts within their households or among extended families. Across Europe and colonial America, the era of the Reformation and Counter-Reformation witnessed the increased prosecution of offences related to sexual morality, family mores, and domestic authority, all stimulated by the belief that bodies outside the family—church courts as well as secular tribunals and civic authorities—had the right and indeed the obligation to interfere in the domestic lives of members and the conduct of household affairs.[13]

Local governing bodies thus increasingly interfered in the regulation of domestic behavior, marital conduct, and the settlement of disputes within and between families. An increased share of the business of the local courts everywhere (in Europe as well as colonial America) involved interpersonal disputes in which family members—not only husbands and wives, but also children, brothers and sisters, in-laws, friends, and servants—could all become embroiled. Accusations involving slander and allegations of witch-craft were particularly common and had severe repercussions, including harsh punishments at the courts.[14]

Surveillance of familial conduct and resolution of disputes were not achie-ved solely through local governing bodies and the courts but rather via more informal patterns of rule and neighborly exchange. Many disputes were likely to be mediated by third parties—kin and friends, neighbors, clergymen—rather than by the courts, and the power of tight-knit communities to regulate behavior through surveillance, intrusion, and gossip was extensive. In colonial America, neighborly intrusion and gossip served to deter, censure, or punish misbehaving and recalcitrant husbands, wives, and children—by talking and making public their presumed misdeeds. In seventeenth-century Venice, street gossip had an enormous effect on domestic and public conduct. As court cases involving mari-tal litigation in Venice also reveal, gossip was instrumental and accepted as a legitimate part of the testimonies of the kin and friends of the parties involved. Elsewhere, community gossip invariably exacerbated disputes or disrupted the rhythm of daily life, but it could also strongly reinforce gendered norms and codes of behavior. Everywhere the power of gossip to exert pressure—through exposure, harassment, humiliation, and threat to the reputation and good name of individuals and their families—was immense, frequently prompting women and men to conform without the intervention of the authorities or the courts.[15]

MIGRATION NETWORKS
AND THE YOUNG

The period from 1400 onward witnessed a vast increase in trade and markets, with rural areas in both the western and eastern parts of Europe becoming more specialized in what they produced, depending on markets for imports and exports of commodities, and expanding trade networks within Europe as well as in other parts of the world. Concomitantly, there was growth in the proportion of the population residing in larger towns and commercial centers. Between 1500 and 1700, small towns grew moderately, while towns of 10,000 and more (with the possible exception of the Mediterranean area, where urban growth had been achieved in earlier centuries) nearly doubled. Over much of Europe, the increase was particularly intense during the sixteenth century.[16]

The growth of towns was for the most part fueled by the influx of migrants from the countryside. Towns across Europe attracted migrants of all social strata, including younger sons of gentry and wealthy families (who moved to towns with the intention of establishing themselves in public office or the professions or in the mercantile trades) or the middle classes and the poor, who arrived for the purpose of learning a trade and finding a career and employment or a suitable marital match. All types of migrants included many young people, men as well as women in their teens or early twenties, who left their families of origin in the countryside and came to towns to become apprentices and servants in the households of urban dwellers. Despite varied legislation and attempts to limit or prohibit migratory movements, such moves were powerful and evident in many places, and they continued to affect all social strata throughout the period. By the early seventeenth century, for example, one in four men living in the towns of the Dutch republic had come from elsewhere, and massive immigration fueled the vast labor markets of Amsterdam and other towns.[17]

The circumstances created by market expansion and migration to towns impinged on and prompted the links between families, communities, and broader networks, which became an indispensable asset in the pursuit and construction of careers. There was the sheer need for information and contact networks: in helping young migrants in their move to towns, in finding masters or suitable employments, and in taking the initial steps in careers and the conduct of trade, business, or a craft. Among the upper mercantile classes, the assistance of kin and friends was decisive, and other ties became entangled as well.[18] The example of the Behaim family in sixteenth-century Nuremberg offers a glimpse of these types of expanding ties in which kin, occupation, and urban office became enmeshed. The Behaims were prominent merchants and public officers with numerous connections among powerful city citizens, many of whom were among their guardians, siblings, and relatives who came to their assistance in times of need. For example, when Michael Behaim (1510–1569) was orphaned at one year old, his cousin, Friederich VII Behaim, became the steward of his paternal inheritance. Friederich was an influential senator in the city, and he subsequently arranged Michael's apprenticeship with a merchant as far off as Milan, and then with another trader in Breslau. Throughout the years when Michael served as an apprentice, his cousin continued to supervise and offer assistance with money and advice whenever Michael applied for it. When Michael's sister, Margaretha, grew up and decided to leave their mother and stepfather, Michael approached Friederich and asked him "to take my sister into your care so that she might be honorably provided for."[19] Margaretha soon moved in with their cousin and was subsequently helped to a suitable match by her older brother and other friends.[20]

Michael pursued his long and arduous apprenticeship away from Nuremberg and family of birth. By 1532, when he finished his second apprenticeship, he was already laying foundations for his own business; he managed to repay some of his debts to his cousin, and then he set up on his own. All this was achieved through an intensive use of two sets of networks. The first included relatives on the side of his younger cousin's mother, who were powerful merchants in their own right (one of them an Italian merchant) and who secured an apprenticeship in Cracow for the younger cousin. The latter in due course formed business liaisons with his older cousin Michael. The second set of relations was formed through his own marriage, which Michael arranged on his own and without the interference or even knowledge of his family (including his older guardian and supporter, Friederich). This alliance brought him into the embrace of yet another family of some wealth and prominence in Breslau. When a couple of years later Michael and his young family returned to Nuremberg, in the late 1540s, he had not only acquired experience, skill, and wealth, but also critical contacts in Breslau, Cracow, and Nuremberg and an expanded set of connections among relatives, in-laws, older masters, and other merchants on whom he could count in his trading ventures within the business community in Nuremberg, Breslau, and elsewhere.[21]

TRADING TIES AND URBAN NEIGHBORHOODS

These communities of merchants intricately connected by blood ties, business contact, and urban office were indispensable to elite and middle-class families in growing commercial centers and smaller towns across northern, eastern, and western Europe, and increasingly in the colonies that were established overseas.[22] These communities formed networks of business in which economic interests, civil service, friendship, and sometimes religion could all become entwined, linking them in relations of trust, partnership, and the exchange of much-needed services, information, and mutual benefits and obligations. In early seventeenth-century Dorchester, the leading families—the Goulds, the Bushrods, the Whiteways—were united by their mercantile interests, the civic offices they shared, and their Puritan vision. They belonged to a group of people who migrated to Dorchester in the 1600s and then became supporters of the Puritan rector, John White, who established a godly reform in the town. The families intermarried, attended the ceremonies of birth, marriage, and death, and became godparents to one another. Some of them were also investors in economic ventures overseas (e.g., the Dorchester company, established in 1624).[23] As elsewhere, ties of trade and sociability were also consolidated and cemented through credit obligations, which deepened the bonds of exchange and the dependence of families on their networks, in towns no less than in the countryside.[24]

Some of these ties based on credit and sociability, marriage and kinship, economic interests, and local politics were focused in urban neighborhoods, where much interaction and assistance that was indispensable to households of all classes circulated. In fifteenth-century Florence, lineage and patron-client ties—without which the power structure and politics in the city were unthinkable—were enmeshed within the homes, neighborhoods, and districts to which these elite families belonged. Similar patterns of neighborhoods that maintained strong ties among patrician families also appear in other large towns. In London by the 1630s, Covent Garden formed a tight-knit piazza where wealthy migrants—merchants and gentry families—settled and came to know almost every occupant on the square's north and east sides. These families played multiple roles for one another as executors, witnesses in wills, godparents, and pallbearers, as well as investors and creditors in businesses; they helped each other with large loans, patronage networks, and occasionally with sizeable bequests.[25]

Among artisans and the poorer migrants who congregated in the suburbs of many towns, these ties and exchanges were particularly potent and intense. In many cities—Venice, Rome, Lille, Seville, London, and Paris—the clustering of certain trades in specific streets and parishes was evident, with neighborly and working ties overlapping and reinforcing interdependence and obligations for help. Neighborly forms of assistance were vital to the security and survival strategies of families—women and children in particular—as well as the sociability and sense of identity of working families. In some towns (e.g., Genoa, Ghent) neighborhood associations were formed to provide mutual aid in fighting fires, organizing the night watch, or arranging festivals and funerals. In Venice, the cult of the *guerre dei pugni* (wars of the fists) was organized by neighborhood squads whose fighting not only consolidated the identity of male youth but also the pride and sense of belonging of their neighborhoods.[26] Elsewhere in towns across Europe and colonial America, neighbors offered ample help that encompassed the offering of food and clothes, credit and alms, small favors, visiting and aiding the sick, nursing children, sheltering battered women, or settling disputes and intervening on behalf of apprentices who were abused by their masters. As court records in some towns (e.g., in post-Tridentine Venice and Nantes) reveal, neighbors' role alongside kin in condemning marital violence and helping women who were entrapped in troubled marriages and were victims of violence and abuse was critical in offering aid and advancing their petitions for separation at the courts.[27]

As previously mentioned, close-knit communities and neighborly spaces had a great potential for monitoring behavior and for intrusion, conflict, and dispute. Yet it must also be emphasized that these disputes were the inevitable outcome of—rather than aberrations from—ongoing exchanges between families who greatly relied on each other and who routinely harbored intense expectations for mutual assistance and help. Numerous types of material aid alongside a host of social and cultural goods (e.g., sociability or sense of identity) continued to be vigorously exchanged between neighbors in urban communities across the European continent and in America throughout the seventeenth and eighteenth centuries, and beyond.[28]

ASSOCIATIONS, CHARITY, AND POOR RELIEF

Among the most distinctive and vigorous social institutions that tied children and families to communities and to broader social networks was the host of associations, confraternities, and guilds that proliferated from late medieval times onwards. These confraternities attracted members of the working and middle-class ranks of rural and urban society and were intimately linked to the lives of all family members. Their role was spiritual as well as social and material, and they offered members worship and prayers alongside charitable gifts and conviviality. When members were sick, the confraternities helped to cover medical costs and provided pastoral care; upon a member's death, they covered funeral expenses and supplied objects for burial. Some historians indeed view the confraternal movement of late medieval and pre-Reformation times as constituting a sort of extended family that complemented blood ties or supplied such ties for individuals and families who lacked them.[29]

As the sixteenth century wore on, confraternities mushroomed, and the roles they played in the lives of families and in the upbringing of their children multiplied. They provided urban migrants and families the means to establish connections and to extend their ties to construct bonds and networks within the civic community; they organized worship and prayers as well as processions, plays, and music celebrations. There were female confraternities that promoted the piety and sociability of noble women, as well as youth confraternities—Catholic and even Jewish (in Florence)—that catered to the education and piety of children and the young. Especially marked was the expansive horizon of charitable giving and welfare provision that associations offered to the wider community. In Italy, the confraternities provided dowries, protected battered wives and widows, and became increasingly engaged in more institutional forms of aid and social control of the community at large, whether by founding and operating hospices and hospitals or by establishing poor houses and even prisons. In seventeenth-century Florence and Bologna, some confraternities took over the charge—in both fund-raising and management—of orphanages that had been established several decades earlier by lay private initiatives.[30]

In parts of Europe that became Protestant and where fraternal associations were abolished, varied forms of support were provided on an increasing scale through more traditional forms of association based on parish, locality, and guild. As the number of craft guilds grew across European cities—in Venice, Seville, Augsburg, Paris, and London—their contribution to the material and spiritual welfare of members and their families enhanced.[31] Municipal governments and sometimes the state initiated schemes for the relief of the poor that were subsequently administered by lay parochial authorities or the local church. The assistance offered through these novel schemes for relief of the poor was modest and not designed to substitute the help of family or kin. It consisted of no more than bread, clothes, meat, or very small amounts of money offered selectively and only to those deemed the respectable poor. Yet this type of offering still reinforced the community's obligations to its poor by entitling needy families to minimal aid, contributing to their safety nets while also tying the recipients—widows, orphans, the old, and the sick—in bonds of dependence with their communities and with those who were in charge of offering aid.[32]

Families became intricately tied into local communities not only as potential recipients of relief but also as alms givers, charity donors and benefactors, or else as administrators of relief programs and rate payers. With the exception of England, where schemes for the relief of the poor were based on compulsory taxes, relief programs relied heavily on voluntary giving and charitable works, the scale of which continued to expand over much of the period. Even in England, charitable giving persisted and grew as the system of obligatory taxes was being implemented, with charitable acts taking numerous forms, including private alms and donations to municipal governments or the church, communal collections, endowments, and testamentary bequests. The latter increasingly involved the endowment of public institutions that were sometimes bound up with the survival strategies of the families of the donors themselves, or with the prospects and fortunes of their children.

Endowed almshouses, hospitals, and orphanages could serve as shelters for the donors when they reached old age or for their offspring if they were left orphaned. In Amsterdam, a municipal orphanage that was established with a charitable bequest in 1523 offered aid to the children of citizens, and from 1579 onward to Calvinist citizens only. Members of the Calvinist elite continued to contribute donations and could expect that the orphaned children of their relatives, or their own offspring in the event of their deaths, would be taken in by the orphanage. In London, Christ's Hospital also received donations from citizens and from relatives of the orphans residing in their midst throughout the late sixteenth century and early decades of the seventeenth century.[33]

The increased participation of lay people in endowments and donations to institutions thus deepened the bonds of families in their communities, enhancing the webs of their obligations within the local community and sometimes beyond. Charitable offering also afforded donors a venue for exercising authority, whether in the selective distribution of assistance to the poor, or in instilling morality and penalizing the community's youth or the laboring poor. Alongside the founding of hospitals and schools, endowments and charitable donations were instrumental in the foundation and emergence of prisons and institutions for confinement, where the itinerant poor and those implicated in crime—many of them the unmarried young—were sent by local authorities and the courts.[34]

Charitable acts also became part of the conscious efforts of householders and families to establish themselves as the respectable members and leaders of their communities. By endowing institutions like orphanages and hospitals—widely perceived as great civic institutions—the founders and donors who continued to support these institutions consolidated their position and enhanced the honor and reputation of their families. In mid-seventeenth-century Turin, the Ospedale di Carita was founded and soon became one of the major charitable institutions of the city. It was a large poorhouse that offered bread to hundreds of families within its confines, and it became a major source of attraction to benefactors among leading and rising families, whose donations and gifts to the institution not only enlarged the city's resources but also empowered their own standing and prestige. By the 1660s, the first busts of benefactors began to appear on the premises, followed by statues and memorial tables that celebrated the honor of prominent benefactors and families by presenting their portraits and the family coats of arms. In England similar practices that offered honor and extended the reputation and prestige of dominant benefactors and their families were evident in guildhalls and hospitals, in London and in many provincial towns elsewhere.[35]

EARLY COLONIAL AMERICA

The ties that inextricably linked families with communities carried special tenor and force during the early phase of the colonization of America, where by the end of the decade of the Great Migration (the 1630s), some 70,000 Britons had already crossed the Atlantic. Immigrants to the New World included dissenting Puritans intent on building the so-called city upon a hill (about a third), alongside many others, especially young indentured servants (about a quarter). Upon arrival in America, these immigrants encountered harsh and particularly unstable environments. In the southern colonies of the Chesapeake in the 1630s, for example, males outnumbered females by six to one and mortality rates were appallingly high (possibly forty percent of new arrivals died within two years, mostly from malaria). Marriage and family life were precarious and brief, with children often being deprived of both of their parents at an early age. Under these circumstances the immigrants adapted by drawing on and reinforcing familial practices long experienced on the continent from where they had arrived. Networks and communities became an ever-critical resource that replaced those of the immediate family, with children habitually being left to the care of affines, step-relatives, friends, or neighbors. Informal associations with friends and neighbors continued to be vital in the lives of planters and their families, despite the measure of isolation that characterized life in the plantations, well into the mid- and late seventeenth century.[36]

In the northerly settlements, communities were more commonly established by whole families rather than by single males (at least sixty percent of travelers were accompanied by family members), and family units were more viable. Settlements in Massachusetts were more controlled and less dispersed than in the Chesapeake, and they consisted of small towns and villages, with churches forming a place of assembly that was sustained by shared belief and by the great experiment of building a godly community. Incorporating no class of great landlords like the planters in Virginia, the first generation of Puritans possessed a strong sense of community; in 1635, for example, they attempted to draw clear boundaries of communities by legislating that all houses be built within half a mile of their meeting house. Such conditions produced relatively cohesive communities that not only imposed a great deal of surveillance and a measure of stability, but also provided multiple forms of sociability, support, and exchange, exemplifying with particular vigor the patterns and links between families and communities that existed on the continent.[37]

CONCLUSIONS

State formation and patronage ties; markets and trade; urbanization and patterns of migratory movements in Europe and overseas: all these produced distinctive and intricate patterns of life cycle experiences—growing up, marital life, old age—that were deeply enmeshed within an expanding set of networks and institutions outside the immediate family. Encompassing kin, patrons, and friends, as well as neighbors, associations, and local institutions, these communities invariably imposed rules and norms that implied greater surveillance and regulation of domestic life. At the same time, such communities were vital resources that sustained families and contributed to their welfare and well-being as they moved through the life course, from marriage and the upbringing of children to old age. Rather than becoming isolated units, children and their families in the early modern era were increasingly and at times overwhelmingly bound with webs of broader relations and ties.

CHAPTER THREE

Economy

CORDELIA BEATTIE

The comments of one official, who visited London in 1496–1497 in the entourage of a Venetian ambassador, about the treatment of children in England are often cited in order that they can be challenged:

> The want of affection in the English is strongly manifested towards their children; for after having kept them at home till they arrive at the age of 7 or 9 years at the utmost, they put them out, both males and females, to hard service in the houses of other people, binding them generally for another 7 or 9 years. And these are called apprentices, and during that time they perform all the most menial offices; and few are born who are exempted from this fate, for every one, however rich he may be, sends away his children into the houses of others, whilst he, in return, receives those of strangers into his own. And on inquiring their reason for this severity, they answered that they did it in order that their children might learn better manners. But I, for my part, believe that they do it because they like to enjoy all their comforts themselves, and that they are better served by strangers than they would be by their own children. Besides which the English being great epicures, and very avaricious by nature, indulge in the most delicate fare themselves and give their household the coarsest bread, and beer, and cold meat baked on Sunday for the week, which, however, they allow them in great abundance. If they had their own children at

home, they would be obliged to give them the same food they made use of for themselves.[1]

Commentators are quick to point out that apprenticeships did not normally begin at age seven or nine in England at this date, nor did service, and that there is much evidence that English parents did love their children. But what else might we glean from this passage? We need to ask not only how representative is this picture of the practices in England at this time but also what was it that shocked the Venetian observer, *and* what did not? That is, what did he think was culturally unacceptable and acceptable?

The Venetian official appears to think that seven or nine is too young for a child to be sent away. He perhaps thinks that the work—"hard" and "menial"—is inappropriate given that this is something undertaken by the children of well-off parents. A later comment suggests that he is thinking here of those who became civic officials, rather than the aristocracy: "No one can be mayor or alderman of London, who has not been an apprentice in his youth; that is, who has not passed the seven or nine years in that hard service described before. Still the citizens of London are thought quite as highly of there, as the Venetian gentlemen are at Venice."[2] However, he does not object to children working per se; the alternative he visualizes to this system is one in which parents are served "by their own children." Was this what happened in Venetian circles circa 1500? He paints a picture of such children not working as hard ("they are better served by strangers"), and having to be given the same food as their parents—that is, being treated differently from the apprentice or servant. It is this hidden workforce that this chapter will try to get at, by considering the various practices in different countries, regions, and among different social groups over the period 1400–1650.

The focus here, then, is not the macroeconomy but the many microeconomies that existed, the economies in operation in each and every household. Much has already been written on the different roles played in households, from the large estates of the aristocracy to small peasant holdings, by husbands and wives and their apprentices and/or servants. The emphasis is rarely on children and their economic contributions, however. Children and their labor are most visible in the sources when agreements were made for them to go to work for others. Thus, service and apprenticeship will feature in this attempt to reconstruct the place of children in the world of work and its relationship to the family, but so too will the treatment of orphans and slaves. When trying to understand how families function, an analysis of those that have broken down or been rent apart is sometimes most revealing. Further, this discussion covers the period known as the age of exploration, and there is much evidence that the European forays into the New World led to the destruction of families and abuse of child labor, often in pursuit of profit.

PEASANT HOUSEHOLDS

In the preindustrial period, about 80 percent of the population lived in rural areas and so we would expect some diversity in the operation of peasant households. There would have been differences according to the size and wealth of the household, and what kind of farming they were engaged in, as to whether they did everything themselves or bought goods and services, and whether they hired labor or contracted themselves out. But if one looks at some of the literary sources there is an evocation of households that are not only largely self-sufficient but are made up chiefly of the labor of the husband and the wife. In one late fifteenth-century ballad, which takes the form of an argument between a married couple as to who does the most work, the husband goes off to plow, accompanied by a lad, whereas the wife has to juggle child care with multiple tasks, with no servant to help: milk the cows, make butter and cheese, look after the poultry, bake, brew, process flax, spin and card wool, prepare meals, and keep the house tidy. The husband in the poem comments that this is an exaggerated picture, as the wife only has to bake and brew once a fortnight, but the author perhaps deliberately made all her children young so that she has an additional burden as opposed to any help.[3]

Husbandry manuals also pile up the tasks that the married couple might do. John Fitzherbert's early sixteenth-century *Book of Husbandry* largely focuses on the husbandman, although there are occasional references to servants. The wife merits a separate section in which a daunting catalogue of her duties is given. These range from dressing the children and making three meals a day for the husband, children, and servants to, "in tyme of nede," helping her husband fill the dung cart, drive the plow, load hay, and ride to market.[4] However, the title woodcut for the 1530 and 1532 editions depicts a boy helping a plowman by goading the oxen (Figure 3.1), akin to the "lad" mentioned in the earlier ballad. Whether a son, servant, or hired youth, the boy in the image gives more prominence to the use of child labor than do the texts themselves. The unpaid labor of children probably enabled many households to survive and, for those who could afford to hire in labor, local youths were probably in most plentiful supply.

It is difficult enough to reconstruct the day-to-day lives of adult workers, let alone their children. Much of our evidence for the work of small children, particularly for northwestern Europe, comes from texts relating to work-related

FIGURE 3.1: *Boy Helping a Ploughman by Goading the Oxen*, title woodcut of John Fitzherbert, *Here begynneth a newe tracte or treatyse moost profytable for all husbandmen* ... (London: Rycharde Pynson, 1532). © The British Library Board (C.71.b.27). Image published with permission of ProQuest. Further reproduction is prohibited without permission.

accidents, either coroners' records or miracle collections. Barbara Hanawalt has argued, on the basis of various coroners' rolls from fourteenth- and early fifteenth-century England, that already by the age of two or three children were observing their parents work and emulating them, with girls involved in accidents that involved gathering food, drawing water, and working with pots, while boys watched their fathers cut wood or work at a mill. The compiler of the miracles of Henry VI tells how, on the last day of August 1481, Richard Queston took his grandson with him to his water mill in Westwell, near Canterbury; on this occasion the boy fell into some water and would have drowned but for the miraculous intervention of King Henry. In 1487 Joan Estmond of Somerset took her one-year-old daughter with her when she went to thresh grain, and again it is an appeal to Henry that saves the girl from choking on a head of coarse wheat.[5]

Hanawalt found "real chores" beginning for children at the age of six and gendered in their division. Boys might fish, herd, or look after horses, although these would be tasks rather than full-time occupations. The compiler of Henry VI's miracles recounts how in 1490 one John Searle, age eight, was gored by an ox in a village near Exeter, while helping his stepfather with the plowing by prodding the animals. He comments, though, that the boy "was not capable of rural business or household work, because of his small body and young age," which gives us further material for interpreting Fitzherbert's woodcut. Hanawalt argues that girls were more likely to be helping their mothers with all kinds of chores, such as fetching water, cooking, doing the laundry, and building fires, and that their work was closer to that of an adult female than was the case with boys, for whom age thirteen was perhaps more of a turning point in terms of what they were required to do.[6] We have already heard from Fitzherbert that adult females were expected to be involved in all kinds of rural work, if needed, and so it is unsurprising to see in an early sixteenth-century French manuscript that a young girl is depicted driving along a donkey (Figure 3.2).

FIGURE 3.2: *Young Girl Driving along a Donkey,* MS Douce 276, fol. 10r. © The Bodleian Library, University of Oxford, detail.

Those who have worked with southern European evidence, usually legal cases, have found a similar tendency for young children to help out with various rural tasks, although they have downplayed gender differences. David Vassberg found that female youths were involved in herding and shepherding in sixteenth-century Castile, even though this often entailed spending a night in the pasture, perhaps on an isolated mountain slope. He comments that this might have been a group activity and cites a case from 1569 in which a number of women from Codesal (Zamora) testify that as unmarried girls, one from the age of ten, they had herded their parents' cattle in the pastures of the area. Nevertheless, Samuel Cohn Jr. found that "young and unmarried girls in the village communities of early fifteenth-century Florence were often sexually violated while herding their sheep or other cattle in the long-distant march between summer and winter pastures (transhumance)—an occupation that historians have recently assumed was suitable only for 'rough and savage males.'" He gives the example of a six-and-a-half-year-old girl who was sodomized while tending sheep far from home on the high Apennine passes of the Romagna, en route to the southern Chianti, and apparently without family protection.[7]

It should be remembered that Cohn's criminal records are more likely to give an impression of work as a dangerous activity, in the same way that coroners' rolls do, whereas Vassberg's anecdotes were included more incidentally in lawsuits, for example, when a witness recounted childhood activities in order to establish his or her credentials. That said, Vassberg appears more skeptical of the testimony when a middle-aged widow from Codesal (Zamora) testified in 1569 that she had helped her father with his plowing for about ten years before she left home and married, and—like the recorder of Henry VI's miracles—sees the urging on of the animals as a task more suitable for teenaged boys. All these scenarios—of young girls looking after animals alone or in groups, of pastoral idylls and dangerous landscapes—are depicted in a range of cultural media. Fifteenth-century written versions of the life of St, Margaret refer to the fifteen-year-old girl keeping her nurse's sheep in the field every day, although not all note that she was in the company of other maidens. Visual representations generally show her alone, but one late fifteenth-century book of hours depicted her tending sheep, and spinning, among a large group of maidens (Figure 3.3). Castilian and German texts from the fifteenth century, drawing on the French *pastourelle* tradition of the thirteenth century, depict amorous knights coming across lone young women herding animals, although the mountain girl usually has a rougher image than the girl from the plains.[8]

Once children reached puberty it was sometimes common for them to leave home and to live and work in another person's household, although there is the

FIGURE 3.3: *St Margaret Tending Sheep*, and spinning, with a large group of maidens, miniature by Jean Fouquet, Louvre, Paris. © R.M.N/Thierry Le Mage.

occasional example of younger servants. One of Henry VI's miracles concerns a seven-year-old maid who fell into a well while collecting water, but again her young age is stressed and she is referred to as "ancillulam," a little maid.[9] Vassberg found examples of youths as young as ten leaving home to work as "mozos de soldada" (hired juvenile help) in sixteenth-century Castile, although he found fourteen or fifteen to be a more common age, an age when many had "reached adult statute, and ... [were] fully capable of sharing in hard physical labour."[10] While there are problems with the sources, with censuses under-reporting the transient and the unpropertied, Vassberg argues that "it does not seem too venturesome to suggest that at least one peasant family in ten had a hired youth," and he cites a case in which six out of twelve male peasants reported that they had worked in this way when teenagers. Ann Kussmaul has argued that in early modern England around 60 percent of young people (aged fifteen to twenty-four) were life cycle servants. Her sources only date from 1574 and her data set is heavily skewed to the period after 1650, but Jane Whittle's study of rural wills, together with household accounts, does suggest that service was widespread both geographically and socially throughout this period, although female servants were more common in pastoral than arable areas. Whittle also found that female servants were more likely to be employed if there were children under the age of six in the household, which suggests that women's work in this period was not easily compatible with childcare. We have already seen that accidents could happen when small children accompanied their caregivers to work. Servants might be paid to take over the childcare if the mother's labor elsewhere was more profitable to the household.[11]

Adolescents also migrated to towns and cities in search of work. While David Herlihy and Christine Klapisch-Zuber's study of the Florentine Catasto of 1427 found that the vast majority of migrants were men, they comment that female mobility was "pronounced, but difficult to ascertain" as census takers only made casual observation about such people because they were not liable to the head tax. They maintain that many girls of rural origin entered service in the city in order to earn a dowry, while others moved to different villages.[12] With the exception of elite households where male servants generally outnumbered female servants, other studies have suggested that servants in urban areas tended to be a combination of migrants, female, poor, and orphans.

URBAN HOUSEHOLDS

The dominant ideal of the urban household was that of a male-headed household in which the man worked at his craft, aided by his wife, children, apprentices, journeymen, and servants. The workshop would be adjoined to the living quarters, and the apprentices and servants would live in their master's household as quasi-children. However, one must again think of the diversity of households. Some household heads were engaged in trades where there was not enough work to occupy two adult workers, and not all households could afford to employ others; Cissie Fairchilds comments that because shoemakers were the most numerous artisans in many towns, most only made a meager living, and "their businesses were too small to employ a wife."[13] Other men might have relied on their wife's labor more; in 1647 a married couple in Wildberg, Germany, was fined for stretching a worsted weft on the Sabbath. And many female-headed households were too poor to hire domestic servants. Also, not all work was carried out in a domestic setting; in 1592 a mason's wife accused a Wildberg citizen of stealing a piece of masonry she had intended to build into a wall. Carol Loats found, in a study of apprenticeship contracts in sixteenth-century Paris, that 45 percent of wives were engaged in a distinctly different trade from that of their husbands; wives who worked in the same trade as their husbands or in a very closely related one made up only 24 percent. So one can question the pervasiveness of the family production unit, but the link between work and family remains important. Wage labor by men and women made it possible to marry and have a family, and either marketable goods were produced by the joint labor of spouses and their children or other dependants, or income from the couple's work inside and outside the home secured the livelihood of all.[14]

Wives had a further role in terms of buying the food, clothing, linen, and furniture that the household needed. This role also remained in those well-off households that did not need the wife to work for pay or alongside the husband. In the households of wealthy merchants, husbands often had to be away from home on business, and the surviving correspondence between husbands and wives demonstrates the key roles that wives played in economic purchases. For example, Balthasar Paumgartner, an affluent long-distance merchant based in sixteenth-century Nuremberg, largely corresponded with his wife Magdalena about her purchases for their household when he was away. He also briefed her on the goods he was shipping back so that she could prepare for their storage and distribution, thus revealing her role in his business.[15]

As in the countryside, children living in towns and cities were expected, from the age of six or seven, to undertake small chores, such as cleaning, cooking, and running errands, sometimes in exchange for pay. Louis Haas comments that getting small boys (the average age was ten) to act as messengers in Florence was one way of teaching them about business. In 1402 the thirteen-year-old Cosimo de' Medici was named head of the Medici's wool manufacturing firm, although an experienced manager would have carried out the actual administration. Similarly, in 1430 the eleven-year-old Antonio di Battista was named as *capomaestro*, alongside his father, on the cupola project for Florence's cathedral, although his participation was probably minimal. Other boys might be sent to learn from others, as apprentices, although not usually until late adolescence.[16]

In late sixteenth-century Kraków it appears to have been customary for poor Jewish girls to go into domestic service as early as age ten. However, daughters of the urban bourgeoisie were less likely to go into service unless their parents, or at least their fathers, had died; this seems to have been already the case in fifteenth-century Italy, for example, but represented a shift in England over the course of the fifteenth century. Daughters of tradesmen and master craftsmen in sixteenth-century Lyon, for example, tended to stay at home until marriage but might help with their father's trade. An agreement between master silk weavers, wimple makers, and button makers in 1561 stated that a "father can show [his art] to his daughter and the brother to his sister."[17] The 1570 Norwich census of the poor suggests that girls were much more easily fitted into the household economy of a textile town than were boys. Of those listed as aged six to twelve and still living in the parental home, over four fifths of the girls were working (described as spinning or knitting), compared with less than a third of the boys.[18]

In general it was the poor and the orphaned that started work at the youngest ages, and it is such groups for whom we have the most evidence mainly because institutions were often involved in finding them places to live and work. Studies of orphanages in a range of European cities suggest an emphasis on training and work when arranging adoptions, with some differences according to gender and social status. The Ospedale degli Innocenti in Florence (see fig. 6.3), founded by the city's silk guild and the commune at the behest of Francesco Datini in 1410, tended to combine adoption with apprenticeship or household service and usually deferred adoption until the age of five or six, particularly for boys, so that they were in a position to learn basic skills. In 1451, when the consuls of the silk guild agreed to give the six-year-old boy called Venturino to Giovanni di Fruosino, a childless cutler, the latter "promised to keep him and treat him just as if he were his own son, and to have him learn to read and write, and to do sums on the abacus, and then to place him at whatever trade he likes." The agreements concerning girls are less detailed about their training. For example, in 1450 Domenico d'Andrea Porcellani and his wife Mona Pipa adopted Angiola Innocente on the following terms: "that they wish to raise her as their own daughter, and to teach her all good manners and that trade at which she would be adept, in such a way as to lead her to honor."[19] The apprenticeship agreements for girls were usually temporary ones (e.g., in the silk trade where they were taught to throw, spin, and wash silk), and service was a more usual route.

That this was part of broader cultural mindset regarding male and female children is suggested by the title woodcut for Bartholomaeus Metlinger's *Regiment der jungen Kinder* ("On the Care of the Newborn Infant"), which was first printed in Augsburg in 1473 (see Figure 3.4). This was the first pediatric text to be printed in the vernacular, and it was the first of its kind to contain an illustration, but what is particularly interesting about the woodcut is that the newborn child is integrated into a domestic scene that suggests a gendered division of roles not just for the parents but also for the other children. The child's cot is placed at the mother's feet so that she can rock it while spinning with a distaff. The daughter sits next to her, perhaps learning how to spin from her mother as she both watches her and mirrors her hand movements. The father stands behind a table on the right, holding a book open and doing his accounts. The boy is seated on the right, in front of the table, and also holds a book, although he is reading.

FIGURE 3.4: *A Family at Work,* title woodcut from Bartholomaeus Metlinger, *Regiment der jungen Kinder* (Augsburg: Hanns Schauren, 1500). Courtesy of the National Library of Medicine.

In general, there was an equal demand for girls from the orphanage, despite the adoptive parents having to provide them with a dowry, perhaps because they provided those of modest means with a useful source of labor around the house for which they did not have to pay wages. In 1445 one Anellina was returned to the Ospedale degli Innocenti by a broker "because she seemed small and not suited to the needs of his household," and in 1453 Dorothea Innocente was returned at the age of seven by her first set of adoptive parents because "she seemed tired."[20] Sixteenth-century Italian orphanages tended to differ from their fifteenth-century antecedents in that while the latter had mainly taken in infants, perhaps only a few hours old, the former were more selective, taking in older children, often with a network of kin to whom they might return after receiving some education and training. Putting a child in such an orphanage might imply that they were seen as a drain on the family economy but it might also suggest that kin were more interested in the education of their children than in using them as cheap labor.[21]

In England, laws were passed in the late sixteenth century that gave justices of the peace and civic officials the power to bind as an apprentice the children of paupers and vagrants; in 1601 these powers were extended to parents overburdened with children. These children could be apprenticed between the ages of four and twenty, although eight was a common age. The arrangement was similar to modern-day fostering, in the sense that the surrogate parent agreed to provide the child with lodging, clothes, and food, but this person was being paid by the parish for providing training and the child was providing free labor, perhaps in a workshop or farm. There are examples of individuals across Europe making similar arrangements for their own kin. Such solutions were not always possible, though, and some poor children had to support themselves by doing odd jobs, begging, or stealing. This led to more severe solutions such as deportation to the colonies, to be put into service there (a practice we will come back to), or employment as cabin boys on merchant ships.[22]

The other children who were forced to work in the galleys were slaves. However, from the mid-fourteenth century domestic slavery underwent something of a resurgence in Mediterranean Europe, as a consequence of trading in the East. In the first half of the fifteenth century, the majority of the slaves bought for the main cities in north and central Italy were Russian, female, and young. The highest prices were paid for girls just past puberty, who were usually given domestic work to do.[23] In 1393 Francesco Datini, the Merchant of Prato, instructed his partner in Genoa to find him another slave:

> Pray buy me a little slave-girl, young and rustic, between eight and ten years old, and she must be of good stock, strong enough to bear much hard work, and of good health and temper, so that I may bring her up in my own way. I would have her only to wash the dishes and carry wood and bread to the oven, and work of that sort ... for I have another here who is a good slave, and can cook and serve well.[24]

The work Datini proposes for the slave child is no different from that which a child or young servant might be asked to do, but presumably he felt that this was cheaper in the long run than paying wages.

After the fall of Constantinople, the slave trade in Italy went into decline, and the smaller number of slaves in circulation tended to be Moors, Berbers, and black Africans. However, here the possession of black African slaves was more about social prestige and fascination with the exotic than economic motives, and such slaves were to be found largely at court or in the houses of very rich merchants. On May 1, 1491 Isabella d'Este asked her agent in Venice to procure a black girl ("una moreta") between the ages of one-and-a-half and four, and twice in early June reminded him of her request, emphasizing that the girl should be "as black as possible." This request and the girl's young age suggest that the slave was to be an accessory rather than a domestic worker. This was also the case in the Iberian Peninsula in the early fifteenth century, although as the slave trade increased even modest urban households in Portugal could afford an African slave. Figure 3.5, which is from an early sixteenth-century book of hours belonging to King D. Manuel of Portugal, depicts a young black boy serving a wealthy patrician and his family. But compare it with Figure 3.6, a court portrait of Juana of Austria, commissioned by her mother-in-law, queen Catherine, in 1553, in which a slave girl—a wedding gift from Juana's husband—is dressed as if as a page, and her role is to rest beneath Juana's right hand, as an oriental folding-fan sits under the left.[25]

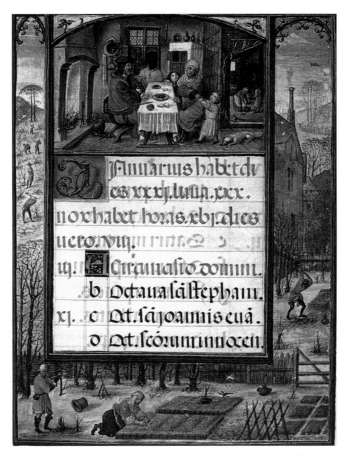

FIGURE 3.5: *Scene with a Young Black Slave Serving a Wealthy Patrician and His Family,* attributed to António de Holanda, book of hours belonging to King D. Manuel, 1517–1538. Museu Nacional de Arte Antiga, José Pessoa, Divisão de Documentação Fotográfica—Instituto dos Museus e da Conservção, I.P., detail.

FIGURE 3.6: *Portrait of Juana de Austria with Her Black Slave Girl,* Cristóvão de Morais, 1553, oil on canvas, Musées Royaux des Beaux Arts de Belgique, Brussels. ©IRPA-KIK, Brussels.

ARISTOCRATIC HOUSEHOLDS

Households served two key roles for elite families: they were public arenas in which a family could demonstrate its wealth through conspicuous consumption, and they greatly enlarged the family's patronage network by employing huge numbers of people of all social classes. A royal household might consist of several hundred members, a noble household could contain up to 200, and those of knights and clerical dignitaries would perhaps have a dozen or two, although so too could those of a successful merchant. Wives would still have played a crucial role in such large households and in the absences of their husbands were usually expected to take over household management. Again, letter collections are revealing, such as that pertaining to the Pastons, a fifteenth-century gentry family who owned an estate in Norfolk. Margaret Paston wrote many letters to her husband John Paston I, who spent much of his time London, and the main topics were domestic and business matters. In a letter written in 1448 she requested her husband to buy not only some good cloth so that she could have gowns made for the children, but also crossbows and poleaxes in case the manor house in Gresham was attacked.[26]

Child and juvenile labor was again a prominent feature, ranging from slaves to young nobles who spent time in the household of another family in order to gain training and patronage and who were partly supported by their own families. For example, the largest household in England was that of the king. In 1445, ordinances for its staffing mention sixty-two children spread across all departments: twelve henchmen and pages in attendance on the king and queen; seven choristers of the Chapel Royal; one boy in the counting-house; three boys in the great hall; and thirty-nine spread across the various departments of food and laundry, of which eight were in the kitchen, and the cellar, larder, and scullery employed four each. The so-called Black Book of Edward IV (1471–1472) said that the presence of child employees went back to at least the time of King Harthacnut (1040–1042) but that it was since the reign of Edward III (1327–1377) that boy assistants had proliferated. The henchmen and pages would certainly have been of noble rank and would have been dressed in the liveries of their lord, but it is likely that even the menial jobs would have been seen as desirable, as they offered board, lodging, clothing, and wages. For example, in 1511 Henry Percy, Earl of Northumberland, paid three pounds, six shillings, and eight pence for young, noble attendants, one pound and five shillings for chapel boys, and thirteen shillings and four pence for the boys in the working departments of the household, such as the kitchen, the scullery, and the stable.[27]

This picture looks very male, but the sixteenth-century royal palaces in Portugal, for example, were staffed by a large number of female and child slaves from their colonies. Catherine of Austria (1507–1578) preferred them to male slaves, and young, female slaves were given some formal training and education, with several sent to learn sewing and needlework at nearby convents. The female slaves responsible for the laundry were given a slave child by the name of Caterina to assist them. Although slaves who personally attended the queen and her female court were treated well—"almost as if they were freed maids of honour,"[28] according to Annmarie Jordan—they were still commodities and might be given away as gifts. Catherine's favorite lady, Mécia de Andrade, was rewarded with a small girl slave called Luçia in 1555.[29]

It is not that there were no female servants in English noble households, however. Kim Phillips has argued that historians have overlooked their presence because they were less likely to receive a wage or hold a position with an occupational title than were male servants. Girls might, like their brothers, be "boarded out." If they were well connected they could be taken into the royal household in their teens as maids of honor or even taken in as children to act as companions to the royal children; Lady Jane Grey joined Queen Katherine Parr's household at the age of nine, as a playmate for the future Edward VI. Young maidens in great households would have had limited duties, usually closely linked to the lady's person, such as helping with her dressing and toilette, carrying her train, and making her bed; in romance literature they also help disarm and robe knights. The Lisle letters reveal that Lady Lisle's teenaged daughter, Anne Bassett, when taken on as one of the Queen Jane Seymour's maids in 1537 (with a role akin to that of the king's yeoman-usher), was given a livery and a salary of ten pounds per annum, but her family had to cover all other costs, including providing her clothing and bedding.[30]

If a girl was of gentle status, and boarded in a household of similar status, the work might be more mundane: spinning, sewing, mending, keeping vegetable and herb gardens, and some cooking. All of this would have been good preparation for marriage. The diary of Lady Margaret Hoby (1599–1605) gives a detailed account of how this gentry wife spent her days: she worked in the kitchens, gardened, weighed and spun wool, sewed and embroidered, nursed ill staff and animals, and—in her husband's absence—kept accounts, paid the servants, and saw to matters in the fields and wood. Clearly there was much work to keep many occupied in such households, and therefore it is perhaps not surprising that John Paston I wrote to his wife on a number of occasions to complain that their son, John Paston II, was setting the servants a bad example by living in his parent's household but not contributing: "every poor man that has brought up his children to the age of twelve years expects then to be helped and profited by his children, and every gentleman that has good judgment expects that his kin and servants that live with him and at his cost should help him forward."[31]

AGE OF EXPLORATION, AGE OF EXPLOITATION

The Spanish *conquista* had a profound impact on indigenous families in Mesoamerica and the Andes. For those who survived the attacks and the arrival of new diseases, there was further disruption in the form of forced resettlement in the interests of supplying labor to new mines and building works, as well as working the land. A key policy after initial conquest was to grant a specific number of indigenous people to particular soldiers, who could make use of their labor in return for instructing them in the Spanish language and the Catholic faith and could exact an additional tribute in cash. This was then often followed by population counts, which served as an instrument of population relocation, and workers over the age of twelve were shifted from one area to another, and from one master to another. In the highlands of Peru, a forced draft was instituted in 1575, which made all male Indians between the ages of eighteen and fifty go to work in the silver mines for six months of the year. As most would have had to spend a further four months on the journey to Potsoi and back, some never returned to their communities. The results of such policies were communities, as well as individual families, left without the help of adult males at crucial points in the agricultural calendar.[32]

In the north of Peru, the draft was used to staff the textile mills, and here nine- or ten-year-old children could be called. The annual pay for children was 48 reals, whereas adults got 280 to 320 reals, although most would not see any of this money. Half was paid directly to their *corregidor* (the person who administered their area) and half was retained by the mill-owner for their maintenance. Failure to meet the quota on a single day could result in a fine sometimes equal to one year's pay, which meant that, as early as the 1630s, the system became one of debt servitude rather than conscripted labor and working conditions deteriorated further. The only positive to this form of work that Donald Wiedner could give was that "it did not separate families or present fatal occupational hazards," in contrast to the mining work.[33]

Some miners did take their families with them, though, and there is evidence of female and child labor in and around the mines. In the mining regions of the Andes, for example, older children worked outside the mine, picking up small pieces of silver that their mothers would then sell. But women, whether left in their home communities or accompanying their husbands to the mines, were often sexually abused by the Spanish. The result was a large mixed-race population, who were given their own identifying label as *mestizos*. In 1551, the Spanish city fathers of Cuzco, Peru, set up a nunnery for *mestizas*, with the expressed intent of "removing them from all communication with their mothers ... which was an impediment to instilling anything good in them."[34] Once "remedied," the intention was that the girls could go on to become professed nuns, marry Spanish men, or work as domestic servants in Spanish homes. However, already by the late 1560s it was becoming clear that the *mestizas,* like their brothers, would never be fully accepted in Spanish Cuzco. By the turn of the seventeenth century, the indigenous population also made similar attempts at improving the social and economic opportunities of their children. Some Indians chose to send their children, and orphans in their care, to live in colonial households, in the hope that it would lead to better life opportunities. There they might work as servants or, if their families could afford it, sons might be apprenticed to master craftsmen.[35]

Similar practices of using service, albeit indentured servitude, as a way of acculturating Indian children were also well established by the 1640s in New England. This approach was pioneered by men such as the Massachusetts Bay Colony missionary Daniel Gookin, who suggested that Indian children might be "procured" with "the free consent of their parents and relations" and then "placed in sober and christian families, as apprentices," in a trade if male, and in housewifery if female, although he noted that it might be difficult to persuade the parents of this plan, "for [Indians] are generally so indulgent to their children, that they are not easily persuaded to put them forth to the English."[36] However, many of the English colonies, such as Virginia and Barbados, found that they had to rely on labor from back home in order to run the labor-intensive tobacco and sugar plantations. For example, in 1611 the governor of Virginia asked the king to banish prisoners in English jails to the colony. Of course, some of the early settlers did opt for the chance at a better life in the New World. But many were poor, and their transportation costs had to be met; in the seventeenth century, one-half to two-thirds of those traveling to the English colonies signed agreements that bound their labor to those who paid the costs, labor which could be sold on. Indentured servitude only differed from slavery in that it had an end point, although masters had the power to change the end date as a punishment for a whole range of offences.

Initially, many English males set out alone; six men left London for every woman in 1635, for example. A so-called bridal boat of eligible women was sent to Virginia as early as 1620 in order to encourage family life in the colony; if the women married public tenants then their travel costs were paid by the company, but any other man had to pay off the costs of his new bride's transportation. In 1618 the Virginia Company asked the city to sponsor the transportation of 100 vagrant boys and girls between the ages of eight and sixteen who would be apprenticed to planters as laborers, a plan that suited both the colony's need for labor and the city's concern with street children. In London, homeless children were rounded up in the parishes and seventy-six "boys" and twenty-four "wenches" were shipped from Bridewell, with other shiploads following soon after. Pressure was put on parents in receipt of the poor law to let their children go. Very few of the hundreds of children transported to Virginia in the period 1618–1622 lived to become adults; of the 1618 group, half were dead within the year. Such high mortality rates were true of many of the early settlers, with disease, harsh working conditions, and Indian attacks being some of the causes.[37]

It seems, then, that the Venetian official visiting London in 1496–1497 and the native Americans in New England in the 1640s had something in common: they thought that the English treated the children in service in their households too harshly. Yet, while indentured servitude in the British colonies might have evolved from European practices of life cycle service and apprenticeship, in its application it came closer to the forms of slavery that various ethnic groups were already subjected to in parts of Europe. And, despite the Venetian official's skepticism that learning "better manners" was the real explanation for such "boarding out" practices, the skills and connections that a youth—peasant, artisan, gentle, or noble—acquired in another's household might be crucial to his or her future success, in terms of both work and marriage. It is perhaps less surprising, then, that some of the indigenous population who survived the Spanish *conquista* might have chosen to put their own children to work in the households of colonial families.

CHAPTER FOUR

Geography and the Environment

MARTA AJMAR-WOLLHEIM

Dating from the 1550s and set within the intimacy of their home in Vicenza, the portrait of the Valmarana family embodies early modern familial ideals (Figure 4.1).[1] The distinguished man of letters Giannalvise Valmarana and his wife, Isabella, present their children—four boys and four girls—arranged orderly from babyhood to adolescence. The parents' gentility is enhanced by their offspring, each of them exemplifying a different stage of childhood and its suitable occupations, and simultaneously conjuring up the journey from wilderness to civility that early modern concepts of upbringing often advocate. The eyes of the beholder are led from the naked baby sitting in his mother's lap, to the little boy riding a hobbyhorse, to the little girl with a dog, and finally to the older children holding educational books of various kinds, from music scores to literary or perhaps devotional texts. Both parents and children comply with contemporary notions of civility and with age and gender expectations in their dress, deportment, and attributes, which range from swords to jewelry. What can easily escape the modern viewer, accustomed to centuries of family portraiture, is the astonishing novelty of the subject matter depicted: the conjugal family. Almost a manifesto of the early modern household, with the mother visibly in charge of the youngest and the father casting a watchful eye on the entire group, this portrait exemplifies notions of family life as a powerful force

FIGURE 4.1: *The Valmarana Family,* Giovanni Antonio Fasolo, Italy, 1553–1554, oil on canvas, Civici Musei, Vicenza.

for civility and contentment. The group is presented as a nuclear unit, with no allusion to the extended family or to members of the larger household, such as servants. Through the total exclusion of the outdoor world, it also suggests that the natural family environment is domestic. But what is the relationship between this kind of family representation and actuality? What forces coalesced to produce such an overt display of the genteel family? Is such a genre geographically specific to Italy, or can we find it elsewhere? And what kind of material environment would such a family have inhabited?

Before tackling this complex set of issues, it is important to define the cultural, physical, and social parameters adopted for this chapter, which is heavily weighted toward the middle and upper classes and privileges the urban versus the rural context. Although these were clearly not the only milieus within which family life unfolded, they were the ones that attracted the greatest degree of attention in terms of early modern conceptualizations and those that have left behind the highest number of visual and material testimonies. All artifacts are cultural, says an old material culture adage, and here objects will be placed at the forefront to move from the realm of theory to that of actuality and explore the ways in which notions at the heart of the early modern family were put into practice and found material expressions. While it is undeniable that the wider world surrounding the family—from the neighborhood and parish to the village or city and beyond—played an important part in the life of the household, the immediate domestic environment will be at the center of this exploration, because it has a powerful impact on everyday life and because it is the direct, material expression of cultural constructions and myth-making processes surrounding the family.

DOMESTICITY BETWEEN THEORY AND PRACTICE

The period between 1400 and 1650 can be characterized as an age that saw the rise of a new culture of domesticity.[2] While this all-embracing claim certainly needs to be qualified in terms of its geographical, social, and cultural boundaries, it is hard to deny that domestic matters—from marriage to household management and child rearing—acquired great prominence on many cultural fronts during the early modern period. Within written culture, a plethora of new conduct books discussing household management celebrated with unparalleled conviction the joys, benefits, and long-term civilizing power of family life. From Leon Battista Alberti's *I libri della famiglia* (1430s) and Giacomo Lanteri's *Della economica* (1560) to Henry Peacham's *The Compleat Gentleman* (1622) or Jacob Cats' *Houwelyck* (1625), these texts placed marriage, children, and domesticity at the heart of social and individual identity. They combined instructions on the building of a house and the organization of its contents, with suggestions on how to find a wife, deal with servants, and bring up the children. The household was clearly perceived to be at the center of new concepts of civility and social standing, with the management of its material contents according to notions of morality, order, and well-being acquiring great significance.[3] Although the father was placed firmly at the top of the domestic hierarchy, the mother was assigned an important role in the everyday management and upkeep of the household and its contents.[4]

This process of theorization surrounding the household was paralleled by a visual culture promoting domesticity. At the core of it was, however, a moralized representation of the nuclear, patriarchal family as the social form par excellence, as testified by the shifting iconography of the Holy Family. From the mid-sixteenth century, Saints Anne and Elizabeth became more peripheral figures or were left out altogether, while greater emphasis was placed on Saint Joseph's role.[5] The domestic environment surrounding the Holy Family became increasingly polarized along gender lines too, often depicting Mary tending the child and Joseph engaged in higher occupations, such as reading. The interior acquired a novel prominence, now featuring the trappings of fashionable living, such as a carved fireplace, matching armchairs, sumptuous bed-hangings, crisp tablecloths and fine cradles. The morality of the Holy Family seemed to be going hand in hand with a comfortable and orderly domestic life.

This written and visual discourse is to some extent paralleled by actual social and economic developments involving the family. A deep engagement with household management, consumption, and private display develops during this period and is expressed in personal writings, from account books to correspondence and diaries, from inventories to wills.[6] Many aspects of family life—from everyday domestic expenditure to the assembling of a trousseau for a bride, from the acquisition of fashionable furnishings to the transmission of valuable objects to the next generation—are now documented in great detail. A rise in domestic consumption and levels of comfort is also detectable in many parts of Europe and North America among both the elites and the middle classes from the sixteenth century.[7] The quantity and variety of domestic possessions increases, leading to a greater investment in the social and cultural meanings of things and to a novel attention to the processes of acquisition, disposal, and transmission of objects. At the same time, while material possessions expand, the notion of family seems to narrow. Domestic bequests in rural England, for example, show a marked shift from a more open conception of the household in the fifteenth century, with bequests outside the family more common, to an increased tendency to bestow objects to members of one's close kin in the sixteenth century.[8]

DOMESTIC INTERIORS SPECIALIZE

The unstoppable advancement of specialization is one of the major forces at work in the early modern household, affecting the character and look of interior spaces and objects and informing every aspect of everyday family life.[9] Rooms multiply, their functions differentiate, and furniture and furnishings increase and become place specific. The sixteenth century is often referred to as the historical threshold for this gradual and partial, but momentous, shift from shared spaces to specific spaces, from socially more undifferentiated objects to objects of—and for—distinction. This also includes a shift from objects—and spaces—"used in essential human activities, which defined a community of common practice" to artifacts "indicative of a more mannered social existence."[10] In this move from inclusivity to social distinction, novelty and display played an important role, both being at the heart of this process of raising one's own status through material means. The spread of this phenomenon was not uniform, with cities and areas of greater prosperity being quicker at embracing change than were poorer rural areas.[11] Even in parts of the world—from the mountainous regions of Europe to the Puritan colonies of New England—far removed from the epicenters of this process, signs of its inception were visible by the early seventeenth century.[12]

A powerful new symbol of specialization and comfort was the fireplace. While the age-old open hearth generally presided over the hall (the shared space par excellence) the fireplace—a novel form first introduced in Italy in the eleventh century—could heat individual rooms, thus encouraging differentiation of usage. Leaning against the wall, the fireplace encouraged the establishment of a domestic hierarchy to secure greater closeness to heat. Thanks to the fireplace, in sixteenth-century Warwickshire some peasant homes could do away with the conventional two-room setting—with a kitchen and a large hall housing an open hearth, the smoke curing the bacon hanging from the roof—and replace it with the more genteel three-room model (kitchen, parlor, and bedroom) separating out cooking, living, and sleeping.[13] This process went hand in hand with the increased segregation of women (and servants if there were any) in the service areas, such as the kitchen, which in parts of Europe and New England were gradually moved to the rear of the house.[14] In the American colony of Plymouth the distinction between kitchen and parlor or "best room" emerged in the early seventeenth century, with the parlor housing all the best or most valuable possessions.[15] Throughout Europe and in the North American colonies, the fireplace enabled the creation of a loft, and thus of upper rooms, allowing couples to sleep separately from the children, grandparents, servants, or other household members.[16] The fireplace made smoke-free spaces possible and promoted genteel living, without losing the spiritualized appeal of the open fire as the focus of family gatherings and everyday activities. Coats of arms and the effigies of ancestors often appeared on the mantelpiece, while family portraits included it in the background, alongside another key symbol of familial unity, the dining table.

The dining table—with its associations to the Last Supper and allusion to the sharing of bread and wine that was often seen to constitute the essence of cohabitation—was another potent embodiment of early modern family life and domesticity.[17] The table was the arena in which secular notions of civility, such as etiquette, met devotional practices, such as the saying of grace before meals.[18] Assembling around the table, the household, including at times the servants, shared food, proximity and morality, embracing rituals reminiscent of the Last Supper. A new emphasis placed on child rearing during meal times is also attested to in a variety of written and visual sources of the early modern

FIGURE 4.2: *Ein schöne Tischzucht (A Beautiful Table Discipline)*, Moritz Wellhöfer, Germany, 1650–1670, woodcut hand-colored with stencils, British Museum, London. © The Trustees of the British Museum.

period.[19] In this important family ritual, while older children were expected to stand still by the table with their hands folded during prayer, younger children would sit on their mother's lap or, thanks to the high chair, would be able to participate, at least symbolically, as shown in this didactic print (Figure 4.2).

With the emergence of the individual table setting—demanding a separate plate, cutlery, and drinking glass for each diner—and of matching chairs gradually replacing traditional benches, the table became also a key locus for the display of novelty, good manners, and social distinction. While benches continued to feature in lower-class households well into the modern period, chairs gained a central role in early modern family life, and their popularity continued to increase.[20] From upholstered, decorative armchairs to birthing chairs, from austere desk chairs to children's high chairs and bare kitchen chairs for servants, chairs offered greater mobility and independence and could also fit countless specific demands and support a variety of domestic rituals and hierarchies. While "specialized" chairs embodied the individual demands of the household members, matching chairs exemplified the orderly organization of the house, as well as family unity and harmony.

CHILDREN IN THE HOUSE

From the moment of birth onward, children were engaged with objects and practices designed to shape them into healthy, well-behaved and virtuous individuals, so that they could embark on the different stages of life suitably equipped. Gaining popularity across Europe in innumerable variations from the fifteenth century onward, the visual theme of the ages of man and woman depicted graphically the process whereby the individual advanced through life by walking up steps representing different key ages and stages (Figure 6.1). The first stage often depicted a swaddled baby, sometimes in a cradle, the second a toddler tottering inside a walking frame or riding a hobbyhorse, while the third showed a pubescent child accompanied by an age and gender-appropriate attribute, such as a needlework pillow or a sword. From domestic spaces to images and objects, the material environment was seen as playing a pivotal role in the unfolding of child rearing.

What objects and practices constituted the material culture of early childhood and what set of beliefs accompanied it? An influential study by the sociologist Karin Calvert has depicted the early modern period in North America as the age of the "inchoate child," with much of the material culture aimed at infants seen as forcing "the young child to lie straight, stand straight, or walk erect."[21] Intent in reasserting the crucial boundaries separating mankind from animals, American parents were preoccupied with enforcing (physical and moral) uprightness in the child. In order to speed up children's participation into the adult world, parents strove to "create at least the semblance of adult appearance and behaviour" in children through the use of adultlike dress and of objects enabling them to be erect.[22] Although this approach provides a useful key for the reading of much early modern visual and material culture of childhood across the Atlantic divide, its tendency to read this historical period in terms of parents' unyielding strife to turn the child into a miniature adult is questionable. Calvert's analysis of the practice of swaddling the baby is a case in point. She presents it as a mark of parents' indifference to babies' discomfort and even safety, suggesting that the effect of swaddling was "an immobile little mummified package about the size and shape of a loaf of bread," more prone to choking and often left in its dirt for whole days.[23] As it will become clear from what follows, however, when this and other aspects of infants' care are examined within the context of the material culture of early childhood, a different reading can be offered.

Immediately after birth, and just after being bathed, babies would be swaddled (Figure 4.3). This time-honored practice involved wrapping the newborn with long linen (and sometimes woolen) bands from the feet upward. Swaddling was designed to keep the baby warm, protect it in the event of a fall and secure the diaper.[24] It was sanctioned by medical culture, since it was believed that swaddling could strengthen the spine and limbs and provide the baby with the correct anatomical shape, as well as be an antidote against rickets. It is clear, however, that these medical concerns were expected to go hand in hand with comfort, as suggested, for example, by the French doctor and royal surgeon Jacques Guillemeau. His treatise *The nursing of children* (1612), which enjoyed great popularity across Europe, suggested that it was important to refrain from excessively tight swaddling, recommending instead wrapping the baby loosely in bands of cloth.[25] To prevent diaper rashes, he

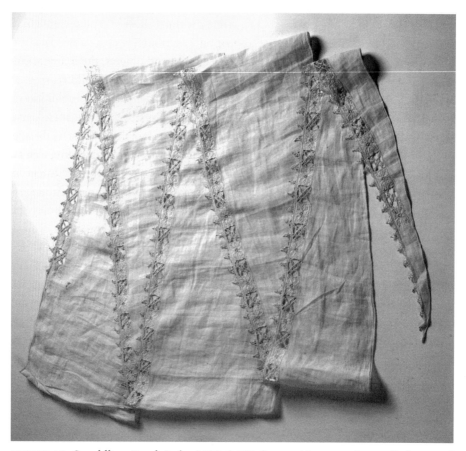

FIGURE 4.3: *Swaddling Band*, Italy, 1590–1600, linen with cutwork, needle lace, and embroidery, V&A Museum of Childhood, London.

prescribed cleaning the baby with water and a little wine as soon as "they have foul'd themselves."[26] Attention to this aspect of hygiene would also, no doubt, minimize foul smells. Sensitive to babies' physical development, he also suggested that at about six weeks little sleeves should be introduced so that the child could have "his armes and hands at liberty."[27] Far from being a practice serving exclusively parents' interests, therefore, swaddling would also make babies more comfortable and better able to participate in the familial world around them.

Cradles reinforce this picture of the material culture of early childhood as being dominated by concerns surrounding babies' safety, comfort, and inclusion within the life of the household. Cradles were the first item of furniture, and the first controlled microenvironment, experienced by infants. They constituted the object in which the baby would spend most of its time in the early months, and although they varied significantly in design and value—they could range from humble hammocks suspended from the ceilings by cords to elaborately carved rocking cradles with classicizing decoration—they were generally equipped with a set of key features designed to make them comfortable and secure. Endowed with mattress, pillow, and blankets, they included strings for strapping the baby, so that it could not easily fall out. Although their width could vary, everyday cradles were often relatively narrow, so as to prevent the baby from turning and thus reducing the risk of choking. For extra warmth, cradles could include in the foot a drawer designed to hold a hot brick.[28] At the head of the cradle an arch provided with coverlet would "keepe away the wind."[29] To reduce further the dangers of draught, cradles could be placed within "a little bed, the curteynes drawne round about it" and kept in a room neither too light nor too dark to encourage sleep.[30] In hot climates cradles could be adapted to protect the baby from the nuisance of insects. Made in colonial India probably for European consumption, the ebony rocking cradle depicted in Figure 4.4 is equipped with supports for a mosquito net. Most cradles would rock, as rocking was seen as soothing. Writing in 1607, the author of the *Institution of a young noble man* James Cleland advised that "as soon as [the baby] begines to crie" the nurse "should bear the child in her armes, or rock him in the cradle."[31]

Another object that would dominate the early years of childhood was the baby walker. In the early modern period the traditional design, which required the toddler to propel an open frame, was replaced by a model encircling the child and providing support on all sides (Figure 4.5). Like swaddling, baby walkers too have been seen as constricting objects forcing the child to stand and walk unreasonably early.[32] It is clear, however, that precautions were taken

FIGURE 4.4: *Rocking Cradle*, India, 1660–1680, Carved and pierced ebony, Victoria and Albert Museum, London.

to minimize the risks of dangerous falls, for example by padding the baby's head with a circular headgear known as "pudding" and securing the baby's waist with a belt to the middle of the frame (Figure 4.6).[33] Made by order, often by local craftsmen or even the family carpenter, baby walkers could be highly customized to suit the needs of the individual child.[34] Varying widely in style, look, and materials employed—ranging from wicker basket to finely carved and turned walnut or oak—baby walkers also embodied domestic innovation, fashionability, and civility, becoming an attribute of the genteel child. Fostering the child's participation in the life of the household, walking frames supported its drive for independence, self-development, and learning. By the sixteenth century, the baby walker had become a powerful symbol not only of childhood, but also of self-improvement. Playing ironically on this notion, a famous engraving

FIGURE 4.5: *Baby Walker,* Italy, sixteenth to seventeenth century, carved and turned walnut, Museo Bagatti Valsecchi, Milan.

by Baccio Bandinelli of 1538 depicted an old man in a walking frame, a banner above him announcing "I am still learning" ("Anchora Inparo") (Figure 4.7). An inscription at the bottom added a satirical note to the picture: "You should keep learning as long as you live. The old are twice children," combining poignantly the humanistic notion of perpetual self-improvement with the ancient concept of senility representing a second childhood.[35] Walking frames could also be seen as belonging to the child safety armory, which included other protective artifacts, such as talismans made of coral, traditionally worn by young children around the neck or as part of their rattles (Figure 4.6). Various amulets were believed to cast a protective layer over the vulnerable child, and jewelry often incorporated apotropaic elements.[36] Objects such as this bauble combined a wolf tooth—credited for relieving children from the troubles of teething and for freeing them from the fear of darkness—with bells to ward off evil (Figure 4.8).

High chairs (Figure 6.5) have also been seen as objects enforcing the early modern concern with speeding up child development, while also creating a barrier between the child and its environment.[37] Like cradles and walking

FIGURE 4.6: *Young Boy with Baby Walker and Red Coral Rattle,*
England, mid-seventeenth century, oil on canvas, Norwich Castle
Museum and Art Gallery.

frames, however, they can be read instead as artifacts combining comfort and
safety with participation, civility with a child's autonomy. High chairs adapted
to children's demands a genteel, new object—the chair. Often designed with
arm and foot rests for comfort and security, and equipped with soft furnishings,
high chairs allowed children to join in at the table, raising them to the same
level. Protection and safety were therefore universal concern for parents, and
were enforced through all means available—from artifacts designed to support
and ease every aspect of daily routine to accessories such as talismanic jewelry.

Did children inhabit specific spaces within the house? From fragmentary evidence it is possible to suggest that children would often be admitted to most rooms
and allowed to move around the house. In his diary, the seventeenth-century
clergyman Ralph Josselin recorded the developments of his infant children, for
example, "My little daughter Jane began to goe alone" at the age of one and "my

FIGURE 4.7: *Anchora Imparo*, Baccio Bandinelli, printed by Antonio Salamanca, Italy, 1538, engraving, Civica Raccolta delle Stampe Achille Bertarelli, Milan.

FIGURE 4.8: *Bauble,* Southern Germany, probably seventeenth century, silver gilt set with a wolf's tooth, Victoria and Albert Museum, London.

sonne Thomas now would walk up and downe the house of his owne accord," also pointing out that at thirteen months Thomas could close the parlor door.[38] Material traces of children's presence might be scattered throughout the house and suggest that they participated to many family rituals, although sometimes through some form of segregation: separate children's chairs and tables are recorded in the main dining room in Walton Hall in 1624.[39]

Although small children generally slept with their parents, as will be discussed later, some hybrid solutions were also available. In Venetian palaces the parental bedchamber would often house an alcove bed surmounted by a mezzanine room called the *sopraletto,* reachable via a hidden staircase.[40] The *sopraletto* would accommodate young children and their nurse, while ensuring constant supervision by the parents from the bed below. The increased specialization of space, however, fostered also the creation of rooms designed exclusively for children, known as nurseries. From the sixteenth century many English upperclass houses would have at least one nursery.[41] If comfort was considered of paramount importance in the furnishing of a nursery, the belief that children's rooms should be cheerful was often endorsed too. Nurseries featured paintings of landscapes, tapestries, and other hangings, curtains, and carpets.[42] The introduction of nurseries had also a tangible impact on the household, since it often involved hiring at least one nurse. In middle-class and poor households, however, children continued to sleep in the same room as their parents, if not the same bed. In the American colony of Plymouth, for example, ingenious solutions designed to maximize the use of floor space were often devised, with children sleeping on small trundle beds, which fitted under full-size beds and were pulled out only at night. It was also common for children to share the same bed with other children of both sexes, as we know from religious moralists criticizing the practice on the grounds of the dangers of promiscuity.[43]

GENDERED HOUSEHOLDS

Gender was a key factor within the life of household members from birth onward. This fact emerges very powerfully in seventeenth-century Dutch family portraiture. In the group portrait attributed to Michael Nouts (Figure 4.9),

FIGURE 4.9: *Family Portrait,* attributed to Michiel Nouts, Netherlands, circa 1655, oil on canvas, National Gallery, London.

an austere family is conventionally gathered around the table, suggesting unity and harmony, but is split along gender lines. Assembled around the mother and largely mirroring her attire are three girls, one carrying a doll dressed in a similar fashion as her toddler sister, foreshadowing the little girl's role as a mother. At the opposite side of the table, the father, engaged in writing, proudly points to his son, who holds a substantial book, another attribute of learning. The message couldn't be clearer: while the female members of the family are totally immersed in domesticity, the male ones are deemed worthy to pursue higher, intellectual ambitions.[44]

Little boys were more likely to survive than girls, since greater care was put in choosing a wet nurse and in taking care of their overall well-being.[45] From the earliest stages of education, too, boys occupied a privileged position in terms of time and resources employed. It was, however, with the onset of *pueritia,* at the age of six or seven, that gender became a key concern, demanding two different upbringing paradigms for boys and girls. This reflected the belief that each sex followed a natural path, as testified in this Dutch poem written by Jakob Cats in 1625 as part of his influential treatise on marriage (*Houwelyck*):

See how human nature
Is revealed in early youth!
The little girl plays with dolls,
The little boy shows more courage;
The little girl rocks the cradle,
The little boy beats the drum;
The little girl plays with small objects
That are useful in the kitchen;
The little boy plays with a harmless lance
Like rough men do.[46]

Spelling out gender division, this poem is accompanied by an engraving illustrating children's games (Figure 4.10). While a large, boisterous party of mostly boys parades in the square carrying weapons, drums, and other instruments, in the foreground a small, quiet group of girls, one of them carrying a baby, is engaged in supposedly female occupations, such as setting up a cradle and playing with dolls and surrounded by miniature domestic utensils and furnishings. Together, words and images present a depiction of childhood dominated by gender-specific activities, something that most early modern parents would feel compelled to embrace. This gender segregation represented the norm, becoming the dominant factor guiding children's upbringing and education. Boys were expected to enter into their father's orbit and follow male

FIGURE 4.10: *Kinderspel,* illustration from Jacob Cats, *Houwelyck* (first published in 1625), in *Alle de wercken, soo oude als nieuwe,* Amsterdam, 1700, The Warburg Institute, London.

pursuits, such as reading, writing, and drawing as well as energetic physical exercise and outdoor activities. Girls, on the other hand, would continue to stay within their mother's sphere and engage with real or pretend domestic activities, such as needlework and housework. They might learn to read and even have some musical training, but the ultimate goal of their upbringing would be motherhood and housewifery. While boys' existence would increasingly gravitate around the outside world, through schooling and apprenticeship, girls' lives generally would unfold indoors, within the home.

All aspects of material culture associated with children—from clothing to food and toys—conformed to this paradigm. Writing his advice book of *ricordanze*—a genre which often combined family memoirs and domestic record-keeping with moral and financial instructions—in the 1360s, but probably expressing views that kept their hold on society until much later, the Florentine merchant Paolo da Certaldo drew a clear distinction between the upbringing of little boys and little girls. A boy was to be fed and dressed well and schooled from the age of six or seven. A girl destined for marriage, by contrast, was more in need of good clothing than nutrition; domestic competence was crucial for her and was reliant on her mother's teachings; literacy was unnecessary.[47] The arena in which gender distinctions were most obviously performed was clothing. One of the events symbolizing the inset of *pueritia* for boys was being put into breeches, while girls would start wearing a bodice. Both items would imitate adults' dress. Moderation was to be exercised in the level of luxury and sophistication endowed to children's clothing, since expensive dress was only deemed appropriate for adults.

The belief in the relationship between toys and the adult a child would grow into was very rooted in early modern society and manifested itself clearly in the choice of toys given to boys and girls. In his *Bartholomew Fayre* of 1614, Ben Jonson summed it up through the dialogue between the hobbyhorse seller and a mother, in which the man asks: "What do you lack? What do you buy, pretty mistress? A fine hobbyhorse, to make your son a tilter? A drum to make him a soldier? A fiddle to make him a reveller?"[48] The sixteenth-century English schoolmaster Roger Asham wrote that the appropriate activities for a noble child were "to ride comely, to run far at the tilt or ring, to play at all weapons, to shoot far in bow and straight in gun."[49] This wide array of outdoor activities in which boys would be involved would account for the choice of certain toys—from model wooden ships to base-metal knights and soldiers to miniature guns. The following early seventeenth-century toy musket found in the river Thames retains its working lock that enables it to fire, thus bridging the gap between play and reality (Figure 4.11).

FIGURE 4.11: *Matchlock Toy Musket,* England, circa 1600, brass, Royal Armouries, Leeds.

The training of little girls was discussed in some detail in sixteenth-century conduct books. It initially revolved almost entirely around domestic matters, first through simulation and play, and subsequently through real responsibility. Educators such as Juan Luis Vives and Lodovico Dolce, for example, disapproved of the custom of presenting girls with dressed-up dolls, which were supposed to stir up their vanity. Instead, they recommend that "the tools needed for all household activities, reduced to miniature size and made, as we see them, of wood or various metals, should be put in a young girl's hands.... Familiarity with these objects will ensure that she will take delight in learning the name and the function of each of them."[50] Presumably she would also remember their use at the appropriate time. After this symbolic introduction to the material culture of the household, the process of learning by doing would continue, and the girl would be taught "how to decorate a room, make a bed, ensure that all household goods are arranged in order and in the appropriate place, so that the whole house will look as if it rejoices and abounds in happiness."[51] Miniature tableware, which would have served such didactic functions, alongside more playful ones, still survives. Ceramic crockery has been excavated in France, while lead-tin jugs, ewers, cups, and plates have been recovered in England dating from the fourteenth-century onward (Figure 4.12).[52] By the sixteenth century, miniature cauldron tripods and skillets strong enough to be actually used on the hearth were manufactured in England.[53] Even novelties, such as cupboards, appeared in toy form. An ornate cupboard inclusive of ewer and basin stamped from a flat sheet of alloy and ready to be assembled has recently emerged in London (Figure 4.13).[54] All of these artifacts testify to the belief in implementing through toys notions at

FIGURE 4.12: *Miniature Jug*, England, fifteenth
century, pewter, Museum of London.

the heart of early modern feminine domesticity, such as diligence and order.
The cupboard kit, however, with its inherent potential for children's active
creative engagement in the assemblage and use of the toy, brings up a largely
neglected aspect of children's material culture, that of agency.

One of the challenges inherent in a study of the material culture of children
is that historically it has only been interpreted by reference to adults. This
approach has led to the construction of a historical child devoid of agency
and action. Objects surrounding children—from furniture and clothing to
toys—have been read as manifestations of adults' actions and beliefs, the child
being left in a passive role. Even if objects such as toys may be given by adults
and embody an adult purpose, however, "they may also be used by children in
original ways," thus revealing crucial aspects of children's processes of learning
and socialization.[55] The production of meaning involved in the appropriation
of objects by children, however, is very hard to gain for historical periods that
have left very few testimonies by children's own hands. A promising line of
investigation resides within the artifacts *produced by children* that, even when

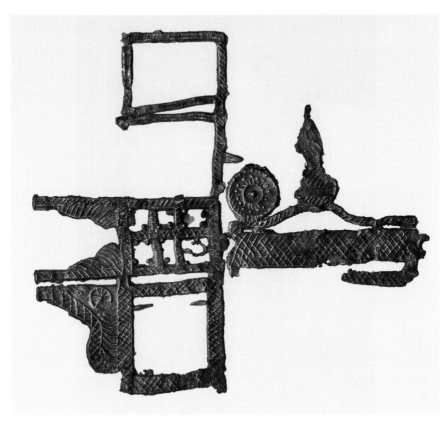

FIGURE 4.13: *Miniature Three-Dimensional Cupboard,* England, probably sixteenth century, alloy, Museum of London.

made under adult supervision, would nevertheless encapsulate a degree of children's agency. A fifteenth-century Scottish didactic poem highlights how children from the age of three to seven would begin to make things: "from gathering flowers, building houses with sticks, and using bread, stalks, sedges and rags to make a horse, ship, spear, sword or doll."[56] Boys involved in professional apprenticeships, for example, would have left considerable material evidence of their activities, from preliminary drawings to models of objects. The irreverent, laughing young boy portrayed by Giovanni Francesco Caroto (Figure 4.14) in the mid-sixteenth century holding in his hands a childish sketch of a human figure might allude to the practice of training children within artists' workshops and to their capricious creative output.

Largely excluded from formal apprenticeships, girls would have been involved in the manufacture of domestic objects, mostly textiles.[57] This

FIGURE 4.14: *Young Boy with His Drawing,* Giovanni
Francesco Caroto, Italy, 1500–1550, oil on panel, Museo
di Castelvecchio, Veron A.

multifaceted productive activity—ranging from small-scale weaving to sewing and embroidery—provided girls with opportunities not just for domestic
accomplishment, but also for self-improvement and even education. A girl's
use of thread could take many different forms, and by the sixteenth century
the various production and decoration techniques involved had assumed different cultural connotations, depending on the social milieus in which they
were practiced, the demands of fashion, and the economic rewards that
they could command. Sewing was traditionally associated with women of
all classes and carried strong ethical connotations. In his *Decor puellarum*
(1471) the friar Giovanni di Dio included sewing among the duties expected
of a virtuous girl—involving making both items of clothing for the whole

family and textiles for the home. He devoted considerable attention to describing the different types of desirable homemade textile goods, divided into clothing—such as shirts, doublets, socks, leather goods, and furs—and items for the house—including blankets and door hangings.[58] Lodovico Dolce, by contrast, simply remarked that "girls should at least be able to sew and embroider as required."[59] Needlework was unanimously presented by moralists as an activity embodying the essence of femininity. It was also, however, an occupation giving girls agency. In Dolce's dialogue, a female character, Dorothea, suggests that being able to sew belongs to women in the same way as being able to write belongs to men, thus alluding to its creative appeal. With its imaginative decorative patterns and fashionably attired figure of a girl, raising the issue of self-portraiture, the seventeenth-century Italian sampler signed in large capital letters by a Sienese girl, Giulia Piccolomini, conjures up this notion of self-expression through embroidery (Figure 4.15). After practicing on samplers, in seventeenth-century England girls between the ages of eleven and twelve demonstrated their achievements as embroiderers by decorating fine caskets covered with silk panels displaying subtle figurative needlework (Figures 4.16–4.17). Even if the imagery was often derived from printed sources, girls might exert their autonomy and taste in the choice of subjects, overall composition, color selection, and type of stitching. After the

FIGURE 4.15: *Sampler,* Giulia Piccolomini, Italy, 1600–1660, linen embroidered with linen and metal thread in satin stitch, Victoria and Albert Museum, London.

embroidered panels were fitted together by a cabinet-maker and equipped with miniature drawers, some secret, the object was reappropriated by girls who used them for storing personal possessions, such as miniature toys, jewelry, cosmetics, or private papers. Under the lid a mirror was often fitted to assist in beauty rituals. With doors that could be opened and shut, the finished product embraced contemporary notions of fashionable but virtuous femininity in its constant play between display and concealment. Placed on a chest or table, it poignantly embodies a child's ability to shape her own environment.

FIGURES 4.16 AND 4.17: *Casket,* England, 1650–1680, wood covered with panels of silk embroidery, protected with sheets of mica, held in place by metal braid, two views with doors shut and open, Victoria and Albert Museum, London.

FIGURES 4.16 AND 4.17: *Continued.*

CONCLUSION

The early modern period in Europe and North America arguably witnessed the rise of a new culture of domesticity: while domestic expenditure increased, the cultural, social, and moral importance of the household deepened. Greater emphasis was now placed on household management, and advice books multiplied. As interiors and their contents specialized and new features such as fireplaces or matching chairs entered the domestic area, social, and cultural aspirations took material form in the wide array of material possessions that assisted everyday life. Objects aimed at children—from cradles to baby walkers and highchairs—supported the sustained process of socialization of the young and their participation in household life, while also embracing contemporary notions of civility, fashionability, and novelty. Relatively rigid gender expectations shaped the range of objects and practices—from toys to physical exercise—seen as suitable for little girls and boys respectively, and as children grew the divide deepened. Even within this conventional framework, however, focusing on agency allows to explore the range of activities, from the making of toys to the manufacture of textiles, that put children center stage in the production of culture.

This far-reaching approach leaves many questions of geographical, social, and cultural specificity open for more in-depth investigations. Rather than clear-cut answers, material culture can provide stimulating platforms for further research.

CHAPTER FIVE

Education

ANNA BELLAVITIS

In the years from 1400 to 1650, with the invention of printing, which made available formerly undreamed opportunities for the spread of knowledge, educational theory and practice in Europe changed radically. The humanists questioned established educational methods, and their theories influenced teaching in colleges and universities. In the sixteenth and seventeenth centuries, religious reform movements were catalysts for the spread of literacy and the creation of new forms of schooling. This development affected women's education, sparking debate on what the objectives of schooling for girls should be. The purpose of most forms of education, at least those for boys, was to provide students with the skills required for making a living. An important new development was the founding of universities and colleges to educate those going into the service of the nation-states being formed. All these theoretical debates and new developments followed Europeans to the colonies, where they were often found in a more radical form than in their countries of origin, for they mingled with discussions about the need to convert indigenous peoples and with the colonists' search for an identity independent from their motherland. This chapter will follow the developments that took place, focusing on new approaches to learning that were to have far-reaching effects on educational systems throughout the Western world.

THE DEBATE ON EDUCATION

Starting in the fourteenth century and continuing throughout the fifteenth century, humanists stressed the importance of learning. The humanistic revolution rejected scholastic pedagogy and was based on the study of classical literature. The humanists sought to introduce new subjects into the curriculum and change the ways all subjects were taught, in particular the rote, mechanical learning typical of the late medieval period. Textbooks from which students were expected to learn by heart were replaced by the works of classical Latin and Greek authors. Physical punishment was rejected and replaced by example and dialogue between teachers and students. As the Florentine merchant Giovanni Rucellai wrote in 1450, children should be allowed to "jump and play," although within imposed limits and measures, and they should not be hit because this was contrary to human dignity.[1] The humanists rediscovered the educational potential of play, an activity that Christian moralists had condemned. Instead of whipping and whacking, they used talk and persuasion; instead of terror and praying, they encouraged joy and play. In reality, however, in their virulent attacks on the old scholastic educational methods, the humanists may have exaggerated the degree to which physical punishment had been used in schools.

Most of these new theories and programs, however, concerned men's education, and in most cases the education of the urban upper class, destined for government service. Both the philosophical and practical bases of education changed: its purpose came to be seen as that of forming good citizens, and the state became involved in providing instruction. A new educational model emerged, one that was radically different from the one embraced by the feudal nobility. Old chivalric values were becoming obsolete: fighting, hunting, and going to war were no longer regarded as the ideal occupations for the sons of the ruling class. As Pier Paolo Vergerio wrote in 1402, knowledge was the best gift a father could give his son. The new vision of children's education meant that parents, too, played a key role. According to Leon Battista Alberti (*Libri della famiglia*, 1437–1441), fathers, in particular, were responsible for encouraging the development of their children's natural capacities.[2]

The new ideas on education spread across Europe and were formalized and transformed into practical educational syllabuses by humanists such as Thomas More, Rudulphus Agricola, Juan-Luis Vivès, and especially Erasmus. Erasmus's *Ratio studii ac legendi interpretandique auctores* (1512) established a method for teaching boys age twelve to fifteen. Teachers were instructed to respect their students' freedom and individuality and base learning on understanding rather than memory. In the *Declamatio de pueris statim ac liberaliter instituendis* (1529), one of the most important Renaissance treatises on children's education, Erasmus extended these ideas to younger children, aged three to five. In this text he denounced the violence and ignorance of teachers and criticized parents who did not put enough care into choosing tutors for their children or refused to pay for their education. In 1530, his *Civilitas morum puerilium* introduced a new literary genre, which was soon to become successful throughout Europe: treatises establishing rules of behavior for children. These texts dealt with decency, clothing, play, eating, and sleeping, and some of their rules were very basic—for example, using a handkerchief rather than one's hand to blow one's nose. At the same time they showed attention to gestures and body control, and these concerns, as Norbert Elias has argued, can be regarded as crucial elements in a more general civilizing process. Erasmus's treatise was innovative because it was specifically written for children and not for adults and was intended for everyone, without distinction of class, nation, or profession (but not of gender!), for, as he wrote, "nobody chooses his father or country, but everybody can acquire qualities and manners."[3]

The debate on education continued almost everywhere in Europe in the following period, in the wake of religious reform. Education was seen by both Protestants and Catholics as an important means of creating a more disciplined society in the context of the confessionalization of Europe. There were, however, significant differences in approach. Humanistic education was theoretically intended for children of all ages and from all social classes. In practice, as it was devoted to the study of classical authors, its main objective was to educate upper-class urban males. Instead, Protestant reformers, whose objective was to give common people the opportunity to read religious texts in the vernacular, were more concerned with universal education. In fact, compulsory school attendance was first introduced in Protestant areas. In 1536 the General Council in Geneva decided to make elementary education mandatory on the same day it decided to embrace the Calvinist reformation.

In the sermon *Dass man Kinder zur Schulen Halten solle* (1530), Martin Luther explained that the opportunity to study to pursue a career in the church and in the government of the state should be open to all rather than being limited to a privileged few. More than enabling everyone to read the Bible on their own, what really interested Luther was the formation of new pastoral and administrative elites. In order to do this he redesigned the curriculum for vernacular schools while Melanchton did the same for Latin schools. Lutheran pedagogical principles also differed radically from humanistic ones on another point: Luther and Melanchton rejected the Aristotelian notion of infantile minds as tabulae rasae. Both believed instead that evil and sin were universal propensities from the youngest age.[4]

In Poland, all dissident churches promoted the education of the lesser nobility and the mercantile and artisan classes. One of the most important pedagogical writers in early modern Europe was John Amos Comenius, a Moravian pastor who escaped persecution and took refuge in Leszno, where he founded a college with ten classes in which not only the humanities but also natural philosophy and geography were taught. In his treatises (*Janua linguarum reserata*, 1631, and *Didactica Magna*, 1632), Comenius set forth his pedagogical principles, founded both on religious doctrine and the observation of nature and its laws. As the majority of the Moravian brothers were artisans, practical training was fundamental, and great importance was given to the proper learning of their mother tongue.[5]

While the Protestants were introducing new pedagogical methods, Catholic reformers, the Jesuits in particular, were pursuing their own educational revolution, whose objective was to promote faith, defend the Catholic Church against the Reformation, and undertake missionary work. Teaching was done in Latin. In the sixteenth century it was no longer universally accepted that Latin was to be preferred to the vernacular languages, therefore the Jesuits' choice was a conservative one. Although their decision was not surprising in the context of the Catholic Reformation, it involved selection based on social status: most students in the Jesuits' colleges came from upper-class families. The Jesuits' constitutions envisaged two types of institutions: colleges, in which the humanities, ancient languages, and religion would be taught; and universities, where the students would study philosophy, the natural sciences, and theology. The *Ratio atque institutio studiorum,* approved in two stages in 1586 and in 1599, defined in detail how schools should be divided into classes, the subjects and authors that were to be taught, and also established disciplinary principles and leisure-time activities. Theater had a very important role as an educational tool in Jesuit colleges. It was a so-called school of virtue and also a medium for teaching young men, especially those destined for a religious life, how to deal with the world in which they would live, work, and preach.[6]

The humanists and religious reformers of the early modern age, both Protestants and Catholics, were interested in increasing the spread of knowledge, but their reasons for doing so were often different, at times even diametrically opposed. The humanists, starting from the concept of human dignity, believed that we are not born human beings but instead reach our potential through education. The Protestants, who held that the Bible should be read by all, changed the way the purpose of education was conceived. If everyone needed at least to be able to read, and preferably to write as well, there had to be universal education. In response to the challenge posed by Protestantism, but also to train its own clerics, the Catholic church was obliged to adapt its educational institutions and invent new forms of schooling. How far, however, could this revolution in education go? In a period when almost every aspect of life was undergoing transformation, questions regarding how girls should be educated were also raised, framed in entirely new terms.

LA QUERELLE DES FEMMES: MEN DEBATE WOMEN'S ABILITIES

In the sixteenth and seventeenth centuries the issue of education for women was an aspect of the *querelle des femmes,* becoming part of a an ongoing debate about women's abilities in general. It came to the fore once again during the religious conflicts of the period, becoming one of the major concerns of religious reformers, Protestants and Catholics alike. At the beginning of the fifteenth century, Christine de Pizan had already raised the question of women's education. If girls received the same education as their male counterparts, she wrote in *La cité des dames,* they would become equally proficient in the arts and natural sciences. The issue was also dear to the humanists, who proclaimed the virtues of education and saw in it an essential element of human dignity. Hence, although More's Utopia is a patriarchal society, he made sure his daughters received good educations. In fact, his eldest daughter, Margaret Roper, translated Erasmus from Latin into English. Likewise, Leonardo Bruni, who dedicated his treatise *De studiis et literis* (1422–1429) to lady Battista Malatesta of Montefeltro, encouraged women to read the Latin poets, although he advised against their studying the natural sciences, mathematics, and geometry.

Both Protestant and Catholic reformers saw the purpose of women's education as ensuring that girls would become good Christian wives and mothers. Learning to read was therefore more important than learning to write, and in many cases it was the only form of education available to girls. In 1523 Juan-Luis Vives, Mary Tudor's preceptor, published the treatise *De institutione foeminae christianae*. In his view, girls should be encouraged to read the church fathers and selected classical authors such as Plato, Cicero, and Seneca under the guidance of some wise men, but they should not be allowed to read poetry and novellas. Vives accepted that girls should study classical literature but limited what they could read to authors who could transmit moral precepts. Nor did girls need to learn rhetoric, because their greatest virtues were silence and honesty. Slightly different opinions were expressed by Sabba Castiglione, who argued that girls should read Dante, Petrarch, and Boccaccio. Silvio Antoniano proposed specific programs for educating girls according to their social origins: poor girls needed only to be able to read prayer books; middle-class girls should be taught both to read and write; and the daughters of the nobility were also to learn arithmetic and how to keep household account books.[7] According to Johann Bugenhagen, who worked with Luther and Melanchton in determining what kind of education Lutheran children should be given, "girls need to learn only to read, and to hear explanations of the ten commandments, the creed and the Lord's prayer and some sacred stories that are suitable for girls, in order to exercise their memories.... Such they can learn in a year or at most two years.... Girls, moreover, shall go to school only one or at most two hours a day. The rest of the time they shall repeat their lessons at home, and also help their parents, observe them and learn to keep house."[8] The emergence of new patterns of education and new institutions in Protestant areas was also a consequence of the suppression of convents, where many daughters of the aristocracy had been educated. In London, the first boarding school for girls was founded in 1617. Girls were taught dancing, cooking, and how to govern a house, and also to write with neat, regular handwriting.

In Catholic Europe the concern for girls' education prompted the foundation of new religious orders that redefined women's roles. These orders were regarded with concern by the Catholic hierarchy. One of the most important was the secular order of the Ursulines, founded in Italy in 1535. After the Council of Trent, a papal brief imposed monastic vows and enclosure on the Ursulines, partly as a response to parents' complaints about the freedom supposedly enjoyed by their daughters in their schools, in spite of the fact that the Ursulines' rules stated that they would teach girls to escape impurity and heresy and to learn reading, writing, sewing, and all the arts that are convenient to women of honorable background.[9]

In England, Mary Ward founded a religious congregation of women, based on the Jesuit model, to educate women from both rich and poor families to become teachers. Ward subsequently established similar schools elsewhere in Europe, including the Habsburg territories and Rome. The students were given teaching, similar in many ways to the instruction boys received in Jesuit colleges, so that they could venture out into the world and become teachers themselves. They had to know Latin, and their mission was to instruct girls and young women of all classes in both day schools and boarding schools. In spite of the fact that this congregation, often called the "English Ladies," saw their teaching as contributing to a Catholic reconquest of Europe, Pope Urban VIII suppressed the order in 1631, writing that under the pretext of promoting the salvation of souls, they carried out many works that were the least suitable to their sex. Mary Ward went to Munich, where she continued to teach, but only "in those things that are fitting and in the manner customary among secular people in this land and thus they can earn their sustenance."[10]

Among the female voices who participated in the debate on women's education we find those of cloistered nuns. In the first half of the seventeenth century the Venetian nun Arcangela Tarabotti accused men of criticizing "the qualities of women's intelligence" while in fact, they "enviously deny to women the way to acquire an education, when even Socrates admitted that women's natural disposition and intellect allowed them to succeed as men do in any enterprise and doctrine."[11]

Protestants and Catholics agreed that the education girls received should be limited to the religious instruction that they as mothers would need to impart to their children. But not all girls were educated at home, as is often held. There was a need to equip girls to become teachers, which in turn meant that there needed to be places where they could receive instruction. Accepting the principle of education for women meant coming to grips with the larger question of what role women should have in society—in this case a society that was undergoing radical change.

EDUCATING CHILDREN AT HOME

Most early education was received in the household. Just by repeating prayers children learned to recognize the letters and began to read. The first rudiments of literacy were often imparted by mothers, like Bartolomea Rinieri, who in fifteenth-century Florence taught her son the psalter and the multiplication tables before he went to school at the age of seven. The role of the mother as the educator not only of her daughters but also of her sons, in their early years, was vital in upper- and middle-class families because fathers were frequently absent. According to contemporary treatises, fathers' involvement in their children's education should begin only when the latter reached the age of reason. In practice, however, there were fathers who took an interest in their children's early education. Around 1430, for example, the rich Florentine merchant Matteo Palmieri explained in the treatise *La vita civile* how it was possible to form letters with biscuits, fruit, or other food in order to help very young children learn the alphabet. Archaeological research has shown that a variety of educational toys, like alphabet bowls and abacuses, were in use. The publication, in sixteenth-century Venice, of books whose stated purpose was to assist parents to teach sons, daughters, and friends to read confirms that instruction was in fact often imparted at home.[12]

Although parents' expectations were different for girls and boys, in the fifteenth century, the urban upper classes began to take an interest in their daughters' education. In the case of Isotta Nogarola, a well-known writer and scholar, it was her widowed mother who decided to give Isotta and her sister Ginevra a humanistic education. However, while the older girl abandoned her studies when she married at the age of twenty-one, Isotta chose a solitary life that would enable her to continue to study. For the rest of her life, she lived almost totally secluded in her family home, in celibacy, exploring different humanistic genres in her writings.[13]

Young princes and princesses were often educated together in their early years. This was true at the Sforza's court, where in the fifteenth century, boys and girls learned grammar and Latin together, and also at the Portuguese and French courts. The future Henri II shared his preceptor with his sisters Elisabeth and Claude de Valois. At age five or six they were taught to read (prayer books and the holy scriptures) and write, after which they were divided and went to live in separate "households," one for the Dauphin and his brothers and one for the girls.[14]

Women played a key role in this early years phase. When King Louis XIII turned two, just after weaning, he began to be instructed in religion and piety by his governess. His physician Héroard trusted women who, he believed, were guided by their affection and were "much more suited than men to deal with children." At around six, Louis left this protective environment and went to live "with men." The Dauphin moved from Saint-Germain-en-Laye to the Louvre, where he could see his parents more often, although studies continued to follow a strict schedule. From six to seven in the morning, he was taught reading; at seven he started Latin, which was followed by grammar lessons from eight to ten. From ten to two he studied rhetoric and the natural sciences. The overall educational program included poetry, history, and other humanities, but the most important subjects were moral principles and religion. Besides teachers and tutors it was his father, the king, who was supposed to impart an education to his son and teach him how to fulfill his duties when he came to the throne.[15]

Merchants' sons were often initially educated by private tutors at home. Starting at the age of four, the Genoese Andrea Spinola was taught Italian and Latin by a tutor. At twelve, he could read Livy and had a master of *abbaco* (commercial mathematics) who taught him at home until he was seventeen. A boy whose father was a merchant could also learn through travel and practice. Matthäus Schwarz was only fifteen when he followed his father, who was traveling on business, from Augsburg to Munich. Widowed mothers, too, could take charge of their children's education. This was true in the case of Caterina Llull I Cabastida, a Catalonian widow who, in fifteenth-century Sicily, arranged for her children to be educated. She hired tutors to teach her daughter to read, write, and keep the account books of the family's mercantile company, and to teach her son to read, write, and dance, as was the custom among the aristocracy. The transmission of mercantile skills was largely a family affair. Boys learned by working alongside their fathers and uncles and then went into the family business. Yet, especially if he had brothers who would work in the family company, a merchant's son could also choose a different career, normally in medicine, law, or the church, which involved being educated outside the home.[16]

The fact that similar techniques were used in a number of fields in the artisan world was another reason why the training received at home, helping parents and other family members with their work, was precious. Even if the son then pursued an occupation different from his father's, the skills acquired in childhood could still be transferred to a range of related crafts.[17]

There was no clear distinction between learning and working in early modern towns and villages. In rural areas, very young boys and girls assisted their parents and relatives. They could help their mothers feed the family's chickens, ducks, and geese or pick fruit and gather vegetables and take care of the sheep. It was certainly normal, as John Paston wrote in 1465, for even very young children in poor families to help their parents. In this way they acquired the basic skills they would then develop and use as adults.

Early education was imparted within the family circle. Comenius institutionalized this first phase in the learning process, calling it "maternal school," an explicit recognition of the role mothers played in teaching their children. Yet in many instances, especially among the aristocracy, education at home continued until the child became an adult, thanks to the services of professional preceptors. It cannot be said that the educational institutions founded during this period were in competition with older practices of educating children at home. It would be more appropriate to speak of an increase of educational opportunities and of the ways through which children could learn.

APPRENTICESHIP AND EDUCATION
IN ANOTHER FAMILY

Social mobility could be favored when a child was sent to live with another family. For example, the fifteenth-century letters of the Paston family of Norfolk suggest that placing children, especially daughters, in other people's households could allow them to acquire an education through service and increase their prospects of making a good marriage. Sending children to another family in order to facilitate their assimilation in a higher class was common practice in the Iberian peninsula in the sixteenth century. Being educated outside the home conferred on a child the status of *criado,* a term that literally means "brought up" and that was applied to all children, male and female, who were either sent to live at court or had professional preceptors. Noble children could be sent to live in noble households of a higher social rank. Of these the highest was of course the royal court.[18]

At a lower social level, many children moved out of their family home in order to learn a trade by serving as an apprentice. According to the statutes of various trades from a number of European countries, apprentices were expected to be at least fourteen years old, although in practice they started at different ages. In Orléans, between 1440 and 1490, boys started their apprenticeship at an average age of fifteen and a half, but most were over sixteen. In London, the age of entry into apprenticeship rose to at least sixteen in the fifteenth century, although the majority of apprentices began at the age of eighteen. The reason for this age increase was that many of the elite guilds in London began to ask that apprentices had already acquired a basic education before starting their training. Therefore, boys often spent longer periods at school, while girls who often did not attend school entered service, or apprenticeship, at a younger age. Financial arrangements varied according to the craft and the length of time the apprenticeship lasted. At the end of their training period, apprentices could either pay for it or be paid by their master. In some places, such as in fifteenth-century Aix-en-Provence, apprenticeship contracts in which the youth's family pledged to pay the master became more frequent as a consequence of demographic growth.[19]

As well as learning a trade, boys and girls were sometimes taught to read and write in their master's house, especially in highly specialized crafts. By 1490, this had become the norm among London goldsmiths, and the practice even became compulsory with an ordinance the company issued in 1498. In reality there was often a gap between theory and practice. In some cases male apprentices were allowed to go to school once a week, while in other instances they learned to read and write on their own, in the evening after finishing their work; they received little help from their master, or even encountered the master's opposition.

Apprenticeship was the only prospect most abandoned or orphaned children had. In the Florentine foundling hospital (Ospedale degli Innocenti) in the fifteenth century, most deeds of adoption concerning boys ages five to ten specified permanent apprenticeship as part of the contract. There was considerable ambiguity in the terms used in these contracts, and in the case of orphans the boundaries between adoption, apprenticeship, and service were often blurred. The hospital also entrusted its children to merchants on a temporary basis, but the contract was normally limited to the agreement that they would be taught a trade and did not entail assurances that they would be taught to read and write, as was customary for nonorphan children. There was also considerable gender variation. While boys from the Valencia Colegio de los Ninos Huerfanos were placed in apprenticeship from twelve to fifteen years old, and for a period of five to eight years (until they were twenty, when they became of age according to the civic statutes), girls left the orphanage when they were much younger, around age six, and remained in apprenticeship or service for about twelve years. While far fewer nonorphan girls than boys served apprenticeships, it was a frequent practice for girls who had lost one or both of their parents to become apprentices, and it was virtually the norm when the child was motherless and there was no female figure in the family to ensure proper care and the transmission of specifically "female virtues."[20]

If some children left their families when they were apprenticed to craftspeople, others did this to attend school. Sometimes this did not involve moving to another house but simply going there during the day. In fifteenth-century Italian cities, many private tutors opened fee-paying schools in their homes, teaching vernacular grammar and *abbaco* (bookkeeping). In seventeenth-century England another form of schooling was the so-called dame school or reading school, run by women in their own homes for small children of both genders.

It has often been argued that it was more common for children to leave home at an early age in northern than in southern Europe. This custom was a contributing factor in the development of the precocious individualism found in the north of Europe. The evidence assembled by recent studies, however, invalidates this hypothesis and suggests that such a clear-cut geographical difference is hard to detect.

FROM PETTY SCHOOL TO UNIVERSITY

There was a network of primary schools in European towns and villages that dated back to the Middle Ages. In rural areas boys aged nine to twelve attended parish schools, where they were taught to read and, less frequently, to write by priests, who were often not much more educated than their pupils. There were additional options in cities, where two sorts of institutions had developed from the Latin schools run by cathedral chapters: parish petty schools, where children were taught the rudiments of Latin and learned to sing and participate in religious rituals, and *majores scholae,* colleges where Latin was taught at a more advanced level.

The demand for education and schooling increased all across Europe at the beginning of the sixteenth century as a consequence of Gutenberg's invention of movable type and the proliferation of books and printed texts that this brought about, and more generally as a result of increasing levels of literacy. In France, petty schools, paid for by local councils but still under the control of cathedral chapters, multiplied during the century. They were also open to girls. Because of the increased involvement of local authorities education became more and more a civic concern. Schools grew, and so did the number of teachers. In Paris, in 1357, there were fifty schoolmasters and twenty-five schoolmistresses, while in 1672 there were 166 school districts, each with a schoolmaster and schoolmistress. Moreover, schooling acquired new social meaning, and schools sought to teach children not only to be good Christians but also to obey magistrates.

In England, the greater responsibility taken by the government in education was also a consequence of the Reformation and the dissolution of the monasteries and chantries that ensued. However, most Tudor schools flourished not because they received support from the crown but thanks to wealthy benefactors, private schoolmasters, and fee-paying pupils.[21]

In fifteenth- and sixteenth-centuries Italian cities, schoolmasters teaching *abbaco* and reading and writing in the vernacular were an expanding professional group in comparison to teachers in Latin schools. The establishment of schools in this period was also a consequence of the development of Renaissance states. In Venice, for example, schools were created specifically to teach Latin and rhetoric to future state administrators.[22] Furthermore, in the wake of the religious reform movements that developed within the church, Italy saw the growth of schools for teaching Christian doctrine, open to both boys and girls aged five to fifteen. Pupils went to school only on Sunday and religious holidays, about eighty-five days a year. Boys and girls were taught separately by men and women teachers. They studied religion, reading, and writing. The church's attempt to control education went beyond these schools for Christian doctrine, and in the last twenty-five years of the sixteenth century new religious orders progressively took over secular schools.

Luther adopted the ancient classification, which divided childhood and youth into three periods (*infantia, pueritia, adolescentia*), and organized the schools in Protestant areas in three cycles of seven years each. In 1528

Melanchton's Latin-school syllabus, strongly influenced by humanist values, was adopted in all schools in Saxony. In the first year of *classis elementariorum* pupils learned the alphabet, reading, and the rudiments of Latin, but teaching took place in the vernacular, while in second grade they were introduced to the study of Latin syntax and the use of German in the classroom was reduced to a minimum. In their third year, pupils were expected to learn the rudiments of logic and the principles of rhetoric, considered indispensable both for future university studies and for possible careers in the professions. Boys were grouped according to their ability, and the best students were taught Greek and Hebrew.

The 1559 School Ordinance of Württemberg was based on the Latin-school syllabus devised by Melanchton but also established vernacular schools, as well as schools for the poor and schools for girls, in order to "carry youth from the elements through successive grades to the degree of education demanded for offices in the church and in the state."[23] While schools in rural hamlets and villages simply provided basic religious instruction to all children in the parish, the primary schools established in larger towns and in cities were organized into five classes, in preparation for university entrance. At all five levels, children were taught music, singing, and gymnastics, which were seen as a means of training impulsive young bodies into docility and the habit of self-discipline.

In 1559, Geneva magistrates approved John Calvin's *Ordre du Collège,* which organized the city's academy in two sections: a college, offering secondary and some primary education, and an academy, the forerunner of the University of Geneva, offering instruction in theology to male students. As for women's education, this consisted entirely of a few schools where girls from the neighborhood could receive some very basic instruction in reading the Bible and perhaps in writing and arithmetic.[24]

At the age of fourteen, and sometimes even earlier, a boy could go to university. One of the consequences of the birth of Renaissance states and of the process of confessionalization was the founding of new universities throughout Europe. In 1479, for example, King Christian I founded the University of Copenhagen, the first in a Scandinavian country, and a system of grants was set in place to attract students from poor families. In Castile, seventeen new universities were established between 1474 and 1620, and enrolments grew steadily, reaching a peak at the close of the sixteenth century. If we also take into account the many thousands of students studying the liberal arts and Latin in Jesuit colleges, as many as one fourth to one third of Castile's young noblemen may have received some form of university-level education.

In England, between 1560 and 1640, 2.5 percent of seventeen-year-olds entered university each year. In Castile, where students were admitted to university at the age of eighteen, the figure was 5.43 percent. We should bear in mind, however, that the majority of these students did not graduate. In the late sixteenth century, less than one third of those who enrolled completed their studies. For the majority, attending university was only meant to provide a general introduction to the disciplines needed to pursue a career in the legal profession or in the state administration.[25]

Many university students were geographically mobile. For example, in sixteenth-century Poland boys were taught Latin by local prelates and aristocrats to prepare them to be sent abroad and study the humanities at university, particularly in Padua, where Polish students were so numerous that they formed a "nation." These foreign students rarely passed examinations or obtained a degree. But completing the course of study was not the main aim of university education.

Even for members of peasant families, social advancement through education was possible. In fifteenth-century Tuscany, some students at the universities of Pisa and Florence came from small villages and well-off peasant families. Attending university enabled them to become schoolmasters, notaries, or doctors in cities or in their villages. We can find similar examples in other European countries. In Switzerland, Thomas Platter was a shepherd at the age of six who went on to become the Rector of the cathedral school in Basel, after long peregrinations in which he moved from one school to another with a group of fellow clerics. While his case is certainly exceptional, education in Renaissance Europe, even if acquired piecemeal and from various sources and institutions, could undoubtedly be a way to improve social status.[26]

EDUCATION IN THE
AMERICAN COLONIES

With the growth of the colonial empires, the debates about education and experimentation in teaching methods that were taking place in Europe came up against the need to assimilate other cultures and to evangelize.

Starting in the earliest years of colonization, schools and universities were established in Spanish colonies and religious orders developed specific methods for teaching Catholic doctrine to indigenous students. In sixteenth-century Mexico, Franciscan friars (later followed by Dominicans and Augustinians) used large visual images or theatrical representations of religious subjects. In order to cut children's ties with their traditional beliefs, from the ages of seven to fourteen they were lodged in colleges, where they could receive only rare visits from their families. Once they had learnt the catechism, they were taught to read, write, and sing in Latin. Girls, taught by nuns or lay sisters sent from Spain, were given only religious instruction.

In the Jesuit College of San Martin de Tepotzoltlan, there was also a secular school, where boys received some basic training in a craft before being placed in apprenticeship. At the college in Tlatelolco, the sons of the indigenous ruling class, ages twelve to fifteen, learned Latin grammar, rhetoric, history, geography, and literature, following the same curricula that was used in Spanish colleges for the sons of the nobility. These experiments lasted only until the beginning of the seventeenth century, after which the only instruction available to Mexican children was in the catechism.[27]

In seventeenth-century Peru, the Spanish authorities sought to control the indigenous population by encouraging children and youths to be brought up in cities by Spanish families. The practice of sending boys and girls to work in their *encomendero*'s house in the city close to the pueblo he controlled was common. Peruvian notables from villages near Lima sometimes brought orphaned children to the city and placed them with Spanish masters so they would learn a trade, while the sons and daughters of indigenous notables were often entrusted to a monastery or entered the houses of Spanish lawyers, notaries, and priests, where they received an education. Sometimes their families paid, while in other cases teaching was offered in exchange for the child's service. A child apprentice placed with an artisan did not normally receive any money during the first two years of his contract. Parents agreed to this because the prospect of becoming a journeyman gave these youths a better chance to earn a living in Spanish colonial society. Girls in Lima, barred from learning a trade, usually remained in their masters' houses until marriage, learning to clean, cook, and sew. They could then become seamstresses.[28]

One century later, the situation in North America's English and French colonies was roughly similar. According to their act of foundation (1639), the Ursulines in Québec, were to "teach savage girls in New France the Catholic religion, reading and, whenever possible, writing."[29] In the same years, the English Puritans founded schools for native American boys in New England. In 1652, a bilingual English schoolmaster opened a school in Noepe (Martha's Vineyard) in order to teach the Wampanoags to read and write, and the catechism. Even Harvard College, founded in 1636, was open to young native Americans, although only four of them matriculated before 1700.[30] Although Puritans were religious dissenters and not missionaries, and they had not come to the New World primarily to convert people, they saw education as a crucial element for the spiritual development of non-Christian children as well as their own children.

In New England specific laws were issued to regulate the education of the colonists' children. In 1642, a Massachusetts law empowered the colony's selectmen to monitor children's ability "to read & understand the principles of religion and the capitall lawes of this country."[31] In the same year, a New Haven, Connecticut law stated "that a free schoole shall be sett up in this towne." The schoolmaster was to "perfect male children in English, after they can reade in their New Testament or Bible, & to learne them to wright, & so bring them on to Latin as they are capeable & desire to proceede therein."[32] Children did not go to the town school for initial reading instruction, which they were supposed to receive either at home or in a dame school.

A 1650 law affecting the entire colony of Connecticut reproached parents and masters for being indulgent and negligent. A section of the 1656 Statutes of New Haven criticized parents and teachers who neglected the education of the children, male and female, in their care. They were called upon to ensure that children and apprentices should "attain at least so much, as to be able duly to read the scriptures, and other good and profitable printed Books in the English tongue, being their native Language, and in some competent measure, to understand the main grounds and principles of Christian Religion necessary to salvation."[33]

In every colony, the laws that made the teaching of reading mandatory preceded legislation that related to teaching children to write. Writing was not essential for salvation, but it was needed by those who wished to become ministers. The 1647 Massachusetts law on education (the "Old Satan Deluder Law"),[34] established schools that would enable a relatively small number of young men to learn Latin and eventually go to Harvard College. Latin grammar schools did not accept girls, since they were specifically designed to "instruct youth so farr as they may be fited for the university."[35] In fact, girls were also excluded from most town schools. When they were admitted, as they were in Hampton, for example, the law specified that only girls "capiable of learning should go to school."[36]

Religious instruction was central to education in the colonies. In both South and North America it was seen by the colonists also as a way to civilize savages, thereby justifying colonization. For the Puritans in New England, it was also one of the bases on which they founded their settlements. Like Protestant communities in Europe, the Puritans made schooling for boys compulsory, an extremely important development that it would take a further two centuries to actually accomplish. Schools in the Spanish colonies were founded by religious orders using methods similar to those used in Spain, and approximately thirty new universities were founded between 1538 and 1812. Until the eighteenth century indigenous students were allowed to enroll. Education in the colonies was marked by experimentation but beset by many of the contradictions inherent in Europe's educational systems at this time, often manifested in extreme forms overseas.

CONCLUSION

The revolution in education that took place in early modern Europe was initiated by humanist thinkers and their fierce attack on the way in which medieval schools and universities imparted knowledge. Their criticism propounded new ways of teaching and learning, both at home and in schools, and paved the way for further developments. At the end of the sixteenth century, their message was still valid, although their methods appeared rather elitist in a society where cultural expression was increasingly taking vernacular forms and seemed removed from the new scientific interests that were developing.

The growth of a state apparatus in the European countries created new opportunities for social mobility and hence the necessity to provide more people with higher education. Protestant and Catholic reformers saw education as essential. They reformed teaching methods and increased the availability of schooling, but they also assigned parents greater responsibility, especially in the religious education of their children. These new developments were carried to the rest of the world by the colonists, as were the debates and controversies about education in which Europeans were involved.

The transfer of educational responsibility from the family to institutions was clearly one of the major changes to take place in this period but was not in contradiction with the fact that learning at home remained an important part of the educational experience. Moreover, in this period, new learning opportunities were made possible mainly by the invention of the printing press. Thanks to Gutenberg, it became common for some people to have books at home and acquire some degree of literacy, although the process was a slow, unequal one, occurring more rapidly in cities than in rural areas, and involving men more than women.[37]

CHAPTER SIX

Life Cycle

PHILIPPA MADDERN
AND STEPHANIE TARBIN

Life cycle may seem a concept easily applicable to the period 1400–1650. It was well-known to contemporaries, through widespread Ages of "Man" texts and illustrations. Every adult had passed through physical stages of infancy, prepubescence, and adolescence. Families underwent cyclical change as couples married, produced children, and saw them leave home for work or their own marriage. What is left for historians but to detail these inevitable progressions?

Closer examination, however, disrupts these assumptions. A slew of cultural presuppositions inflected understandings of families, childhood, and transformations into adult life and produced varying treatments of children, adolescents, and critical life transitions. Geographic, social, and gender differences affected children's careers. Sizeable segments of the population never followed conventional life cycles. Hence this chapter, rather than seeking to establish an average life cycle for the period, aims to question the concept of early modern life cycle and to open to scrutiny the vast range of early modern understandings and experiences of growth, transition, career, and family.

EARLY MODERN CONCEPTS OF LIFE CYCLE:
THE AGES OF MAN TOPOS

By 1400, theoretical understandings of the human life cycle had been explained and represented for over a thousand years in the topos of the Ages of "Man."

Though variants of the scheme divided the life sequence into differing numbers of stages (from three to twelve age sequences), all represented human life as an inevitable progression from growth through an ideal age of adulthood to decline. Most drew on a common stock of images—the swaddled infant, the curly haired child playing with bat and ball or hobbyhorse, the sword-bearing young adult, the mature man with a purse, the balding elder with his crutch (Figure 6.1).[1] Literary and visual representations harmonized; a series of popular verses often accompanied the set of twelve age illustrations from 1500 onward, relating in detail the characteristics of each six-year period of life until a person's (presumed) death at age seventy-two. Children under six were said to have neither "strength" nor "courage." From seven to twelve, a child was "moost apt and redy/To receyue chastisement, nurture and lernynge." A youth up to age eighteen "without thought dooth his sporte and pleasure." By the sixth age, the perfect halfway stage, the adult achieves prudence; he "studyeth for to acquire rychesse/And taken awyfe to kepe his householde." Slow decline follows; by forty-two "his mygth fayleth euer." At sixty-six, he becomes "sekely

FIGURE 6.1: *The Nine Ages of Man,* Jorg de Breu, circa 1540, print. © The British Museum. Life cycle is here represented as a series of steps up and down; each male representative holds his appropriate attributes (note the hobbyhorse for the young child).

and colde," and should study "his soule helth." At seventy-two, Nature decrees "The tyme is come that he must go hym selue."[2]

Traits attributed to childhood were particularly consistent across centuries, regions, and genres. Images of swaddled babies and playing children appeared from the twelfth to the sixteenth centuries in England, Italy, France, Germany, and the Netherlands, in stained glass, fresco, and manuscript, and in works as diverse as books of hours, didactic poems, and encyclopedias of natural philosophy. Schoolboys aged six to twelve represented the second (or sometimes third) age of life in texts and sculptures from France, Italy, and Germany from the thirteenth to the sixteenth centuries.

Explanations of life cycle changes in physique and temperament in the period 1400–1650 were likewise long established. Theorists employed classical scientific and medical ideas of age-related characteristics. Each life stage was thought to be governed by the predominance of one of the four humors—blood, choler, bile, and phlegm—that together regulated bodily constitution. The four humors represented and were influenced by the four universal elements (air, fire, earth, and water) and symbolized the four seasons of the year. Traits of childhood such as growth, restlessness, and propensity for play and mischief were thus generally ascribed to a predominance of blood, a warm and wet humor associated with fluidity, change, and springtime. Young adulthood (*iuventus*) was marked by a predominance of choler (linked to fire and summer), whose dry heat produced boldness, strength, and aggression. Black bile, cold, dry, and autumnal, dominated middle age. Old age (*senium*) resulted from an excess of the cold and wet humor phlegm, associated with winter, water, and weakness.[3]

This model represented human life as literally cyclical, and the cycle as unquestionably natural. The elderly resembled children in their more fluid constitution, which inevitably produced similar incapacities: "olde men with blood that waxith coold, and children with blood that hetith nought, kannen but litil good," proclaimed the fifteenth-century translation of a popular medieval encyclopedia. Physiological processes would inevitably return the aged individual to a likeness of the childhood whence he began. Jorg de Breu's 1540 print of nine human life stages shows the ancient, at the last age of his life, fittingly embracing a baby (Figure 6.1).[4]

Though actual years assigned to childhood differed between texts, infancy was generally thought to last until about age six; childhood (*pueritia*) extended to about age fifteen. Yet whatever their ages, characteristics of children in this cycle were clear. Infants were helpless, speechless, tender; younger children were playful, carefree, and innocent—some texts associated the word *puer* (boy) with *puritas* (purity). From about age seven to about age fourteen the child was archetypally a student.[5]

A discourse so coherent and widespread suggests that early modern people held settled and well-articulated views of the human life cycle. Why, then, should we treat these texts with caution when assessing real early modern life cycles?

Put bluntly, Ages of "Man" images were probably never intended to depict real individuals. Instead, they commonly represented moral, theological, and didactic tropes. Hence to social historians they appear peculiarly unrepresentative. In most sequences, only upper-class males represent human life stages. A persistent association of adult behavior with the practice of aristocratic war, governance, and the attainment of riches effectively excluded both women and subordinate classes from achieving the adult stage of an ideal life cycle. In fifteenth-century seven-age cycles, both boys and girls appear playing in the first age. But by the second age, gender divisions appear: the boys study, and the girls spin. In succeeding images, boys and men move through life stages as scholars, fighters, and financiers; girls and women up to the fifth age are shown still spinning, as if they by-passed adulthood, transitioning directly from childhood to a subadult domesticity. Only at life's end did they rejoin the masculine cycle: both men and women are shown bedridden in old age. Again, humoral theory explained these divergences. Since women were by nature cooler and more fluid than men, the sexes were most alike at the age-extremes of youth and senility, when men were at their dampest stages.[6]

Arguably, early modern Europeans envisaged upper-class women as undergoing an entirely separate life cycle of fertility and decay, in which the moment of marriage (perhaps at age eighteen) represented the pinnacle. Hans Baldung Grien's early sixteenth-century *Seven Ages of Woman* (Figure 6.2) shows female development and status not in terms of activity and capacity but by changing hair and body shape, from the hairless, chubby infant and flat-chested young girl in plaits through the small-breasted maiden with flowing locks and the nubile bride in the center, to the matron and widow, breasts visibly sagging and hair neatly braided, and finally the haggard matriarch.[7]

Thus, studying Ages of "Man" sequences reveals ideals and medical theories of childhood. Children in the first stages of life were clearly conceptualized as, on the one hand, innocent, but on the other restless, unsettled, and fluid in demeanor and physical constitution. Yet using such ideals to detect real life cycles is misleading. They show stereotypes rather than realities, privilege male, rather than female, life experience, and represent upper-class, rather than ordinary, theories of life cycle.

FIGURE 6.2: *The Seven Ages of Woman*, Hans Baldung Grien, 1484–1545, oil on wood. © Museum der Bildenden Kuenste, Leipzig. In comparison with de Breu's vision (Figure 6.1), female life stages are represented more by changing body shape and hair style than by attributes of activities and capacities.

EXPERIENCES OF LIFE CYCLE, 1400–1650

The period 1400–1650 produced more practical and inclusive life stage markers, though they varied for children from different classes, centuries, and cultures. Parents, nurses, and teachers acted on beliefs about the appropriate treatment of children; legislators decided on ages of inheritance and legal and criminal liability; canonists regulated ages of marriage; and custom dictated actual marriage ages and the progression from childhood to work. What, then, do these institutions, actions, and genres say about real early modern children's life cycles?

Perhaps the most poignant divergence between theory and actuality lies in children's survival. Intent on depicting childhood as a time of growth, theorists neglected to note how often it was the time of death. Of 1,041 burials from around 950 to 1550 in the cemetery of St. Helen-on-the-Walls, York, twenty-seven percent were children, mostly aged between six and ten. Very few infant burials were detectable; the authors of the report considered that correcting for probable infant deaths would bring the proportion of children to "nearer 50% of the total."[8] Florentine *Books of the Dead* (1385–1430) classified over forty percent of 32,909 recorded deaths as infants or children. Family reconstructions from early modern English parish records yield decennial averages of infant deaths in the period 1580–1650 from 153.6 to 180 per 1,000 births.[9]

For survivors, life stage markers were less clear and invariant than Ages of "Man" depictions suggest. In this chapter, we consider four major indicators of life stage: the age of weaning, the age at which children were thought to acquire powers of reason and communication, the age at which children entered the world of adult work, either directly or as apprentices or servants (together with question of how long early modern children commonly spent living in their family of origin), and the age at which the transition to adulthood was thought to occur (including the ages of marriage). Each stage meant different things and took place at differing ages, depending on an individual's gender, wealth, status, and location. Not all life stages applied to everyone.

INFANCY AND WEANING

Early modern children's lives were conditioned by complex synergies between intractable biological factors and contingent cultural presuppositions. Children's weaning and early development is a case in point. Almost all early modern babies were highly dependent on breast-feeding. European and Middle Eastern theorists generally posited that children should be weaned at about eighteen months to two years of age.[10] Yet not all babies experienced the close bonding of breast-feeding from their mother, or even lived with their parents during this period. Infants as young as four months were offered solid foods, animal milk, or sugared water in feeding jugs or feeding horns.[11] Wet-nursing until about age two was common among aristocratic and artisanal families throughout Europe. Most wet-nursed children were sent away from their homes, returning only after weaning.[12]

Lower down the social scale, orphans and foundlings had to be wet-nursed if they were to survive. From the 1450s onward, hospital officials at Florence's foundling hospital, the Ospedale degli Innocenti, received babies "90 percent of whom were between three hours and three weeks old,"[13] had them wet-nursed at the hospital for an average of six to twelve days, then sent them out to wet nurses in the surrounding countryside. They returned, newly weaned, at 18–24 months (Figure 6.3). Though these children were presumably never a majority of any birth cohort, their numbers were significant. Admissions in 1465 amounted to 8.9 percent of the baptisms at the local church of San Giovanni. By the seventeenth century, the hospital took in 13.7 percent of the region's children.[14]

FIGURE 6.3: *The façade of the Ospedale degli Innocenti, Florence, designed by Filippo Brunelleschi, constructed 1424–1445.* Inset: detail of one of Andrea della Robbia's representations of swaddled foundlings with which the façade was decorated (circa 1463), photo. © Philippa Maddern (2009). Here arrangements were made to feed and care for orphans and foundlings at least during the years of early childhood, though children frequently moved between the orphanage and foster homes.

Some families maintained close long-term relationships with wet nurses. Mary Page nursed several children of Sir Simonds and Lady Anne d'Ewes, writing, in 1639, that she would be "exceeding glad . . . that your Ladyship might see your little ones," whom she affectionately described as "very well and merry."[15] In 1549–1550 Sir William Petre sent his newborn son to be nursed by Alice Humfrey, wife of a demesne farmer. Both parents visited the child, and Alice remained his nurse for several years after his weaning.[16] Yet for poorer children, breast-feeding could be curtailed, and change of caregivers frequent. Jane Vmfrey, a single woman apparently living with her mother, bore a child in March 1569, nursing it herself for two months. Parish officials then consigned it to a wet nurse. By Christmas the nine-month-old child was said to be weaned, and was transferred to the care of another poor couple. Three weeks later, unable or unwilling to keep it, they returned it, unceremoniously and against Jane's mother's advice, to Jane herself.[17]

Furthermore, wet-nursing involved more than a temporary transfer of one child between families. Each wet nurse's other child either underwent the psychological and physical traumas of sharing the nurturing breast, or was in turn displaced to a surrogate mother. The Petres paid for Alice Humfrey's baby to be breastfed by a woman in another village.[18] Poorer women might find themselves, ironically, temporarily wet-nursing their own babies. In 1450 a heavily pregnant slave came to Florence's Ospedale to give birth to her master's illegitimate child and subsequently to work for the hospital nursing other foundlings. Though she probably fed her own son, he was put out for adoption at age seven.[19] In 1545 in Kent, John Hobbye was ordered to pay three pence per week to maintain the bastard he had fathered with Alice Adamson, until "the Child shalbe wyned holly" (at a minimum age of fifteen months). He was then to take the child—but not Alice—into his own household.[20] Though these children were maternally breastfed, it was not the start of a lifelong mother-child relationship.

In sum, early modern people apparently appreciated the physical needs of neonates, and took care to provide infants with appropriate nursing. But they did not necessarily set a high priority on ensuring stability of care, or long-term child-caregiver bonding from breast-feeding.

Gender crucially influenced children's experiences, including their survival, from birth, but in different ways depending on geographical region. In Florence, 1445–1466, 56.4 percent of admissions to the foundling hospital were girls. Fewer girls than boys were subsequently reclaimed by their birth families (three percent versus ten percent, respectively), and more died within a year of admission (on average, 522 per 1,000 admissions versus 443 per 1,000 boys).[21] Yet sixteenth-century records from England's Christ's Hospital show fewer foundlings and opposite ratios among them of boys to girls. Foundlings composed only seventeen percent of admissions in the hospital's early years. Boys outnumbered girls three to two, probably because the hospital offered elementary and grammar schooling. Girls were more likely than boys to leave the hospital's care for that of relatives or fostering (twenty-one percent compared to eleven percent); and boys experienced slightly higher mortality rates than did girls (forty-nine percent of boys died by age twenty-one, compared to forty-six percent of girls).[22]

Childhood material culture suggests that developmental needs of babies and toddlers were tacitly understood and catered for. The plethora of paraphernalia available to middle-class parents in the fourteenth to sixteenth centuries included, for infants, cradles, swaddling clothes, rattles, teething corals, and feeding horns, and, for weanlings and toddlers, feeding dishes, walking frames, and (by the 1600s) high chairs (see Figures 6.4–6.5).[23] Yet writers differed over the length of the earliest stage of childhood. On the issue of speech development, for instance, the fifteenth-century translator of Bartolomaeus Anglicus's encyclopedia asserted that a child could not "speke nothir sowne his wordes profitabliche" until, by age seven, all the teeth were properly grown. Yet staff and clients at Florence's Ospedale apparently either expected children to begin talking very young, or classified babbling as speech.

FIGURE 6.4: *Education of Children*, Hans Weiditz, circa 1532, woodcut. © Bildarchiv Preussischer Kulturbesitz. Note the plethora of childhood equipment, including rattles and walking frames, available to middle-class families by the mid-sixteenth century.

FIGURE 6.5: *English high chair, 1642, York, UK, photo© Stephanie Tarbin*. Reproduced by kind permission of the Company of Merchant Adventurers of the City of York. Such specially designed furniture may have enabled young children to eat together with their families.

One foundling girl was judged to be "six months old or more, since she has begun to speak." Another, aged "about eighteen months" arrived with "her tongue-string cut because she stammered, and ... afterwards ... spoke badly." She was forthwith labeled "mute and crazy."[24]

THE SECOND AGE: SCHOOLING, THE DEVELOPMENT OF REASON, AND DRESS CODES

Such a description suggests that a supposed age of speech and reason could begin very young. In fact, most European and Middle Eastern theorists taught

that children developed powers of reasoned speech and thought at about age
seven, and could then profitably begin formal schooling. Islamic writers influential in the period 1400–1650 emphasized the importance of *tamyiz,* the
period at which seven-year-olds moved from the government of the senses to
intellectual apprehension, becoming able to discern good from evil. Hence, they
wrote, from this age children could be taught by logic, rather than by a system
of immediate rewards and punishments, and could be encouraged to perform
Islamic religious duties.[25] The Bartolomeus Anglicus translator likewise noted
that from seven to fourteen a child is "sette to lore vndir tutours."[26] However,
both Christian and Islamic writers tended tacitly to ignore girls in their treatments of the age of learning. In reality, schooling was not solely confined to
boys; Nicholas Orme found cases of school mistresses, and evidence of an
eight-year-old girl attending school, in fifteenth- to sixteenth-century England.
But they were apparently a minority in largely masculine schoolrooms.[27]

For early modern boys, schooling often entailed boarding away from home.[28]
But though some poor children received schooling through charity, most formal education was for the comparatively well-off. School age was therefore
not the almost universal life stage marker in the early modern world that it is
today. Furthermore, the age of starting school differed according to the class
or home of the child. In England, upper-class children were set to study well
before age six. Ordinances were drawn up for the education of Edward V in
1472, when he was under three. By 1659, Charles Hoole thought that four or
five was the usual school starting age in towns, though country children, forced
to travel to school or to board, might not start till age six or seven.[29]

For early modern English boys, the beginning of schooling could coincide
with gender-based dressing. Elite parents dressed both boys and girls in coats
or robes once they were mobile and out of swaddling clothes, but the fashion
for breeching boys around the age of six to eight years may have been linked to
their entry into formal education. Aristocratic girls, however, were sometimes
put into adult clothing much earlier. Lady Anne Clifford recorded her daughter
wearing her first whalebone bodice and velvet coat at the age of two years and
nine months.[30]

WORK AND DEPARTURE FROM
THE NATAL HOME

If schooling was an uncertain marker of the time when early modern children left home, the start of working life was even more so. The age at which
northwestern European boys and girls became apprentices or domestic servants

rose throughout the period 1400–1650. The average age for both girls and
boys in late medieval England and France was probably fifteen to sixteen,
and departure was in some cases delayed until age eighteen. Lengthy apprenticeships could see young men living as dependants in strangers' households
well into their twenties, in what Barbara Hanawalt shrewdly termed extended
"social puberty."[31] Such apprentices, together with Continental urban aristocrats, sometimes fostered group adolescent identity by forming notoriously
unruly and violent clubs, whose functions paradoxically included policing
familial order by punishing delinquent couples through charivari rituals. On
the darker side of such activities, Jacques Rossiaud found that in fifteenth-
century Dijon, eighty-five percent of perpetrators of gang rapes were "jeunes
fils," most aged eighteen to twenty-four.[32] Some historians argue that early
modern Italian confraternities for boys aged six to fourteen were attempts to
channel incipient gang misbehavior into holier and healthier pastimes or, in the
case of Savonarola's youth brigades, to oppose the dissolute violence of young
men with the socially purifying—though still violent—activities of boys.[33]

Children of the laboring classes, especially if orphaned, entered the workforce much younger than apprentices from well-off families. Foundling children
in Florence were commonly sent to service at six to eight years old. In England, Christ's Hospital apprenticed boys and girls from six or seven years of
age. Mean ages at apprenticeship for boys and girls in the 1563–1572 cohort
were respectively fourteen and thirteen, but many girls started work earlier;
thirty percent were apprenticed by age ten, compared to seven percent of boys.[34]
English statutes of 1536 and 1547 prescribed compulsory apprenticeships for
vagrant children between five and fourteen. The Elizabethan Poor Law (1601)
empowered local overseers of the poor to put to apprenticeship any child whose
parents could not maintain it. In Southampton, 1609–1650, over 870 poor
children were apprenticed. Of the ninety-five for whom an approximate age
was recorded, over half were between three and twelve.[35] For younger children, apparent apprenticeships might represent charitable adoption; a Salisbury
"Survey of the Poor" (1625) distinguished "working" from "small" children.
But families undertaking the expense of caring for young children evidently
expected compensation from their charges' labor. Agnes Harwood of Salisbury
was only six when she was apprenticed to a knitter—"her master to have the
work."[36] No doubt younger children performed lighter tasks. Thomas Shepard,
born in 1604 and later a colonist to Massachusetts, remembered being sent to
keep geese when he was three.[37] Yet early modern English children of the laboring classes were expected to be fully employed by age twelve. In 1616 John
Smith recommended the New England fisheries for providing "Imployment

for . . . fatherlesse children," contending that "hee is very idle that is past twelve yeares of age and cannot doe so much."[38]

Further down the social scale, some prepubescent children were forced into lonely vagrancy. John Reynoldes, aged ten in 1602, was apprehended by the Salisbury Justices of the Peace as a wandering beggar, "punished" (probably whipped), and given three days to travel to his Wiltshire birthplace.[39]

Throughout Europe, therefore, a child's birth status determined the age at which he or she left home and entered (or began to search for) work. This age could vary dramatically from three to eighteen years.

Nevertheless, theoreticians and social practitioners across Europe and the Middle East persistently identified ages six to seven and eleven to twelve as crucial developmental markers. Treatises defined age seven as the time when boys, at least, entered the age of reason and started their schooling. Poor and orphan children in both England and Florence were placed out to service at about seven. It was widely accepted that children under the age of twelve occupied themselves, where possible, in games and play. From the fifteenth century onward, mass-produced toys catered lavishly for these playful propensities.[40]

LEGAL CRITERIA FOR ENTERING ADULTHOOD

Nevertheless, in practice neither entry to work nor schooling marked an unmistakable transition toward adulthood for all children, and neither corresponded clearly with a stage of physical maturation. What then were the early modern marks of childhood's end? Even these varied widely. Laws provided several age-related criteria of adulthood. In late medieval England, boys (but not girls) over twelve years of age were expected to join tithings, neighborhood groups responsible for notifying criminal behavior to local legal sessions. Twelve was the age when both boys and girls became responsible in criminal charges. But different rulings determined when a child could outgrow guardianship or (if fatherless) inherit property. In common law, both boys and unmarried girls were free of wardship and could legally inherit a deceased parent's property at twenty-one. But a married girl, if fatherless, could inherit at sixteen, any guardianship of her property passing to her husband.[41] Manorial courts had different inheritance rules—"the usual ages of majority for both sons and daughters ranged from fifteen to twenty years."[42] Islamic legal treatises tended to define majority as occurring at about age fifteen, except for the Maliki tradition (eighteen), but a mother's right to custody of her children ended at age seven for boys, and age nine for girls.[43] At the other end of the age scale, Italian city-states such as Venice and Florence extended effective adolescence by legislating strict lower age limits—twenty-five, thirty, thirty-five, forty, or even forty-five—on such male adult rights as attending governing councils or holding important state offices.[44]

Finally, the canonical minimum age for marriage throughout Europe was fourteen for boys and twelve for girls, though children could make, or have made for them, contracts of future matrimony at younger ages. Marriages by future consent could be ratified or repudiated when the participants reached appropriate years and were also validated if the participants, at or after the due age, had sexual relations. Children themselves knew these rules: in 1522, Lawrence Staynfeld, seeking annulment of the contract he had made to Isabella Horsefalle when he was about eight, testified that ever since he turned fourteen he had wanted to repudiate the match.[45]

Thus depending on region and context, early modern children could apparently reach legal adulthood at any age between twelve and forty-five. But variations occurred between social practice and legal prescription. Some upper-class English will makers envisaged their underage children maturing gradually into inheritance. In 1421 Thomas Lovell directed his trustees to pay profits from some of his lands to his wife for the maintenance of their son John until he turned thirteen. The profits would then go to John himself until, at age twenty-one, he achieved full ownership.[46] Manorial courts relaxed inheritance rules in times of demographic stress. At Winslow, Buckinghamshire, the customary age of majority for men and women was, respectively, twenty and sixteen. Yet in the severe labor shortage following the Black Death most male heirs inherited their lands by ages sixteen to seventeen.[47]

AGES OF MARRIAGE AND TRANSITION
TO ADULTHOOD

Similarly, whatever canon law allowed, actual marriage ages of early modern men and women is a long-contested subject. Jan Hajnal's thesis that the marriage regimes of early modern Europe can be divided into a northwestern and a southeastern pattern, each with a distinctive life cycle scheme, has been widely accepted. Northwestern Europe, he posited, was characterized by comparatively late marriage ages (well into the twenties) for both sexes, a small age gap between partners, and neolocality on marriage; southeastern Europe saw a lower marriage age, especially for women, a consequent larger age gap between partners, and a greater prevalence of households where young couples lived with parents and in-laws. If so, life cycles and families in the two regions would differ dramatically. In the former, young people of both sexes would typically move from their parental home into apprenticeship, work, or domestic service, a life stage that would take them well into adulthood before they married and set up an independent home. Servanthood formed a significant life cycle component directly preceding marriage. In southeastern Europe, while boys and young men might serve an apprenticeship outside the home, most aristocratic girls would marry as teenagers, from their birth home, but the newlyweds might not become independent household heads for many years after.[48]

However, more recent research suggests that differences in participants' economic and social status produced variations in these patterns and confused regional categories. At first sight, analysis of marriages in Florence and its *contado* around 1427, as compared to the Cambridge Population Group's research in early modern England, confirms Hajnal's thesis. The mean marriage age for women in the Tuscan cities, 1427–1430, was 18.86; for men it was 27.85. Hence the average age difference between spouses was just over nine years. Analysis of 1,007 marriage licenses from Canterbury diocese, 1619–1660, shows the average age of the bridegrooms as 26.65, and of brides as a high 23.58, producing an average age difference of only 3.07 years. Yet economic and social factors inflected the data in both regions. In the Tuscan countryside, where marriage and children provided male peasants with much-needed agricultural labor, women's average marriage age was 19.28, and men's was 23.8, reducing the average age gap to 4.52 years.[49] In early modern England, contrary to orthodox belief, servants did marry, sometimes continuing to live in two separate households after their marriage. Of 417 cases of disputed marriages in English courts 1350–1500, 13.2 percent involved at least one domestic servant or apprentice. Such cases are easily overlooked, partly because servants tried to hide marriages from disapproving employers. In 1492 Richard Jelyf discovered that his live-in servant John Kendall had married Elizabeth Willy, a domestic in another London merchant's house, only by tracking the pair to a secret meeting place.[50] Though their ages are unknown, such couples may have married younger than has been supposed. For them, service was not a distinctly celibate life stage; and marriage was neither neolocal nor a step to adult independence.

Wealth also affected marital age, but differently in Italy compared to England. Urban male Florentines, concerned to make their way in business, married later than their rural contemporaries, and to younger women. English aristocrats, needing heirs to secure patrilineal landed inheritance, married younger than their contemporaries (average age 24.28), while their brides (average age 19.39) were hardly older than their Renaissance Florentine counterparts. Late medieval English land-owning heiresses were highly sought after and often married young. In a sample of fifty-three Yorkist and early Tudor aristocratic brides, forty-one were sixteen or under at marriage; twelve were twelve or under.[51]

Peter Laslett is inclined to dismiss early marriages as insignificant in both number and effect on the individuals' life cycles, arguing that recorded child marriages comprise only a tiny percentage of known cases and might not be confirmed until years after the promise. This interpretation, however, overlooks two important considerations.

First, the known number of underage marriages must be a minimum, since they were almost invariably recorded only when their breakdown initiated lengthy and expensive ecclesiastical inquisitions. Second, the sources suggest that early marriages could have important effects on the children involved. Orphaned children, married young, might find themselves living with parents-in-law, rather than parents, even if the marriage was never ratified. Around 1550 in Cheshire, when she was between nine and eleven, Constance Entwisell's father died. One of his neighbors took over his tenancy and had Constance married to his son. By her own account, she subsequently lived in her father-in-law's house for ten years, though the marriage was never confirmed. Furthermore, divorce litigation was expensive; to amass sufficient resources to invalidate early marriages, some young people were forced into service. Joan Leyland and Rafe Whittall married when they were eleven but never subsequently agreed to confirm the match. Joan's father, explaining a seven-year delay in seeking the annulment, said that Joan "was poor, and had no money; and nowe she hath gotten somewhat in Seruice and . . . spendes hit in triall of the Lawe." For Joan the supposedly normative sequence of childhood, adolescence in service, marriage, and the formation of her own household, was transmuted into childhood marriage, life in her father's household, and adolescence or young adulthood in service, leading to annulment.[52]

Since child marriages could be ratified by sexual congress, subsequent negotiations sometimes referred to the age at which children matured sexually. Infrequent references suggest that though twelve and fourteen were accepted as the legal ages of marriage, contemporaries believed young couples might not reach sexual maturity until around age sixteen. Lady Margaret Rowecliffe went through a form of marriage at age four, and ratified it at age twelve. But the bridegroom's father guaranteed that the couple "should not ligg togeder til she came to the age XVI years." Court officials recognized mismatches between canonical ascription of maturity and physical development. In 1563, Roger Massy was just over the canonical age of fourteen. The

Chester diocesan court annulled his marriage to Jane Sommer, celebrated six years previously, because Roger claimed that he never slept with Jane "nor yet knows what love meanes"—"as is clear by the look of his body" the court crisply noted.[53]

Equally, physical development was only one marker of adulthood; behavior also influenced perceptions of age, as the 1425 case of Katherine Northfolk's disputed entry into religion reveals. Katherine was alleged to have made her profession as a nun under duress, before she turned twelve. Marion Bocher, a fellow nun, testified that she believed Katherine to be over twelve at the time because her demeanor showed her "wise enough ... to be twenty."[54]

Katherine's case raises a further complication in early modern life cycles: the prevalence in pre-Reformation Europe and post-Reformation Catholic nations of lifetime religious celibates, who officially never took part in some of the so-called normal life stages—marriage, household formation, and child rearing. Their numbers could be large; according to one estimate, there were 33,000 priests, monks, and nuns in England in 1500. The ages at which people entered these alternate lifestyles varied considerably. Full ordination to the priesthood was limited to men aged twenty-four or over.[55] The canonical age for entry into a religious house, pre- and post-Reformation, was officially sixteen, but practice varied between different dioceses and orders. Some bishops (as in the Northfolk case) apparently allowed professions after age twelve. Some Franciscan and Dominican houses, despite prohibitions of general chapters, admitted novices as young as five and fifteen respectively, though an English royal ordinance (1366) prohibited any order of friars from accepting a child under fourteen without parents' or guardians' consent. In pre-Reformation England, most girls apparently entered the novitiate between fifteen and seventeen; most youths were professed at ages eighteen to twenty. But some were much younger; the last prior of the Ipswich Carmelite priory joined at age twelve.[56]

Thus at about ages fifteen to twenty-four, when many well-off people moved between apprenticeships and marriage, a sizeable minority of the population chose a very different life path, obviating official household formation and family life. Unofficial clerical households, however, may not have been uncommon. Priests were regularly cited in pre-Reformation English church courts for adultery or fornication; some cases seem to reflect marriagelike arrangements. In 1481 John York, a Yorkshire vicar, was suspended from sacral duties for having "long" kept Joan Chernok "as his concubine." How children of such relationships were brought up is almost unknown. Some, presumably, were boarded out, like the "Rector of Tuddenham's little son" recorded in Norwich priory boarding accounts in 1430.[57]

THE NEW WORLD

Throughout the early modern world, observers of the young correlated many factors—bodily development, legal standing, social and religious roles, behavior and responsibilities, habits and preoccupations, capacity for work or learning, and marital status (potential or actual)—when determining the limits of childhood, adolescence, and adulthood. Europeans made such judgments even of indigenous races encountered in the New World from the 1500s onward. Henry Spelman, himself only fourteen when he sailed to Virginia in 1609, was sent to live for a year with the Powhatans and noticed that only "wemen and young boyes" played a certain type of football, "the men never." William Strachey remembered Pocahontas, at about age eleven, teaching her male contemporaries in the English fort at Virginia to turn cartwheels; and observed that Powhatan girls went naked until age twelve, but then "put on a kind of semicintum leathren apron . . . and are very shamefac'd to be seene bare" (Figure 6.6).[58]

Yet American indigenous children followed many different life cycles, often unacceptable to Europeans, though for varying reasons. Aztec children underwent induction into adult religious rituals very early (aged two to seven), and were thereafter subjected to harsh discipline. Some, selected from babyhood, were sacrificed to the god Tlaloc. Conversely, Paul le Jeune was dismayed to find that seventeenth-century Algonquians, considering young children incapable of taking responsibility for wrongdoing, refused to "allow [a child] to be chastised." "How much trouble this will give us in carrying out our plans of teaching the young!" he worried.[59]

Demographic and social factors also differentiated conditions for European children in the Americas from those in their homelands. In New England 1620–1649 the proportion of the population aged between five and twenty-four was significantly higher than in England, and the number of elderly people was almost invisibly small. Intent on putting the "superfluous multitude" of poor European children to work in the labor-starved North American colonies, Dutch and English companies, 1619–1645, encouraged, and even sometimes forced, children to emigrate into apprenticeships in New York and Virginia. Even in less-coercive New England, the average age of unattached minor immigrants in 1621–1649 was 14.3 for boys and 14 for girls.[60] Such children underwent a sudden and radical separation from relatives and familiar locales but maintained a state of strictly controlled dependence.

FIGURE 6.6: *An Indian Woman and Child of Pomeiooc in Virginia,* John White, 1585, watercolor over graphite. © The British Museum. This picture of an Algonquian girl and her mother shows well the different dress styles between children and adults. Note that the girl holds a European-dressed doll, reflecting either the early transfer of cultural objects between Europeans and indigenous American children, or the artist's adherence to the European topos of the child at play.

Yet economic and religious factors could act paradoxically both to curtail, and to delay, the end of childhood. Because labor was scarce and land cheap, apprenticeships in practice might be curtailed. Young women especially achieved marriage and independent family life younger than their European contemporaries. Dutch apprenticeships in New York, 1645, were limited to less than "six or seven years" for girls who married before their term expired.[61] The *median* age at marriage for female New Englanders

1630–1639 was eighteen.[62] Religious motivations led to changes in some childhood life cycle markers. Puritan stress on pious education encouraged parents to teach children to study scripture and adopt adult routines of prayer and examination of conscience from their earliest years. Yet strict filial obedience was expected to continue into young adulthood. According to a 1646 Massachusetts ordinance, insubordinate sons who had reached "sufficient years of understanding, viz. sixteen," were to be delivered to the magistrates and put to death.[63]

Attempts to convert indigenous peoples to Christianity and (in New England) to ensure a Christian upbringing for all may also have made childhood schooling in the New World a more nearly universal phenomenon than in Europe. New England towns legislated in the 1640s for schools to be available to all. In 1512 Ferdinand of Spain ordered that all sons of Hispaniolan Indians under thirteen be "handed over" to Franciscan friars for four years' religious instruction.[64] In 1609, Virginia company officials were authorized to kidnap indigenous children to teach them Christianity.[65]

CONCLUSIONS

The complex experiences of children emphasized, and were produced by, radical inconsistencies in household formation and life cycle across the early modern world. Simple, supposedly standard, cycles of household formation and disintegration—beginning with the marriage of two young adults; enlarging with the arrival of children; diminishing at their departure as adolescents for apprenticeships, domestic service, or other forms of work; and finally shrinking to a single widow or widower—may have been the exception rather than the rule. In Europe, poor children left their birth homes very young. Comparatively high death rates among young adults left many orphans housed in institutions, with step-families, or with unrelated adults who might stand to them in the triple relationship of employers, educators, and substitute parents. Remarriage of widows/widowers produced blended families but also sent children into unrelated households. As a consequence of death, annulment, remarriage, and the constant flux of servants from household to household, the size and structure of individual household groupings could change quickly.

Family groupings meant different things according to region, wealth, and context. In fifteenth-century Tuscany, plutocrats grew up in patriarchally ruled agnatic groups of eleven to twenty-five inhabitants, so populous that they comprised less than 1 percent of all households yet housed 10.8 percent of the population. But the most frequently encountered domestic unit housed two people, and eighteen percent of urban households were one-person only. Simultaneously the city contained institutional families. The Ospedale degli Innocenti constantly represented itself as a family, although it combined a community of caregivers subject to a quasi-monastic profession with a large and mobile population of unrelated children floating between institutional care, wet-nursing, and apprenticeship or adoption.[66] In the Americas, 1500–1650, Puritans strove to enforce strict familial discipline on their children into young adulthood, yet simultaneously lone adolescents were shipped from Europe to the colonies to form a large class of unrelated and sometimes unruly workers and apprentices.

Some common themes emerge. Life cycles of the poor and the rich differed greatly, at almost all times and places, as did the life courses of girls and boys. Upper-class men's life cycles, particularly those of inheriting sons, might form a simple archway—childhood growth and education leading to power, wealth, and responsibility as a household head, with a corresponding decline from all three in old age. But women's life cycles were more complex; European women often elided schooling, achieved an early adulthood in marriage, gained full ownership of property only at widowhood, and relinquished it again (possibly) in second or subsequent marriages. Lifetime singletons, religious or other, added further diversity. Even in Protestant England, at least twenty percent of the population never married.[67]

In short, to depict early modern childhood as a well-defined stage in a single common life cycle is to underestimate drastically the variety of early modern children's experiences. Children grew up in, outside, and between nuclear families (their own and others). They followed varying pathways into adult worlds of work, property holding, and (sometimes) marriage. Markers of the change from childhood to adulthood included, but were not limited to, physical development, changes in dress and behavior, development of legal rights and responsibilities, understanding of religious duties, ability to work, the right to marry, and the control of an independent household. Not all children would achieve all stages, and the ages at which they were attained varied widely according to culture, status, wealth, gender, and custom. Life cycle was a flexible and multivalent concept; childhood almost equally so.

CHAPTER SEVEN

The State

JULIE HARDWICK

The family was highly politicized in the early modern world, both as a unit and in terms of the roles and expectations of each family member, whether husband, wife, or child. From the Ottoman empire though the European countries to the colonies of North and South America, as states sought to centralize and increase their powers, the family was a central focus as subject, object, and agent. Although the ambitions of early modern governments usually far exceeded their practical regulatory capacity, they made many—but not all—aspects of family life the focus of expansive rhetoric and legislation.

In doing so, they made the establishment of strong families a centerpiece of national state building and of imperial expansion, political projects that were often riven with rank and race imperatives. To the ruling elites who sought to enhance state power, stable, orderly families would guarantee political strength, economic productivity, and cultural morality. Most early modern communities wanted strong families too, although their ideas of what that meant and how to achieve it could differ significantly from those expressed by central authorities.

This chapter explores some of the key characteristics of the relationship between states, families, and children in the early modern Western world. It examines the critical role of families in political rhetoric, the many ways in which states sought to regulate different aspects of family life, and the lived experience of expansive state ambition for early modern families. While patterns varied across Europe, and of course in colonial rather than metro-politan regions, important common themes existed, such as the regulation of marriage formation, of illicit sexual activity, of family violence, of children's legal standing, and of the increasing role of the state in the lives of families and children. Historians have long argued for a transformation of family and childhood during the early modern centuries, at least since the classic and much-debated interventions of Phillipe Ariès and Lawrence Stone, which, however erroneous in the specifics, in many ways founded the fields of the histories of childhood and of family. It is only in the last decade or so, however, that the centrality of the state as a key dynamic in these fields has become a critical topic for historians' attention.

STATES AND FAMILIES

What was the state in the early modern West? In recent decades, historians have rethought the dynamics of early modern state formation in efforts to explore what actually happened in the wavering progression of early modern governance whose on-the-ground limitations stood in such stark contrast to the extraordinarily ambitious claims of its rhetoric. This revision, with its focus on symbiotic collaboration and the varied participation of many social groups from elites downward, in studies like Steve Hindle's exploration of the administration of the Poor Law in early modern England or Ulrike Strasser's work on the regulation of sexuality in Munich under Emperor Maximilian, has remade our understanding of how states worked.[1] The traditional conception of a top-down state as a matter of institutions or ministers or bureaucrats has been transformed by these elaborations of the complex, multitiered, diversely peopled apparatuses of early modern states, by the focus on governance and authority as process, and by the recognition that the early modern state was a claim to authority as much as a concrete reality. In all aspects of this more complex view of the state, families were central in political theory, in bureaucratic initiative, and in the haphazard process of state making on the ground.

Families, and to a significant but lesser degree children, were at the center of much early modern political rhetoric, whether this involved speeches, treatises, or the preambles to laws. In famous and oft-repeated framings, monarchs, political theorists, and authors of legislation who sought to clarify the nature of authority were quick to compare the power of rulers to that of husbands or fathers in ways that sought to naturalize their claims. King James I of England (who also ruled Scotland as James VI) simultaneously positioned himself explicitly both as "the Father," whose "fatherly duty is bound to care for the nourishing, education, and virtuous government of his children even as the King is bound to care for all his subjects," and as a spouse: "I am the

Husband and the whole Isle is my lawful Wife." Jean Bodin, one of the most important political theorists of the era, deployed similar language. He noted that, "The right and power to command is not by nature given to any except the Father who is the True Image of the great and almighty God, the Father of all Things ... a well governed family is the true reflection of the Republic and domestic power resembles sovereign power ... when families are well governed the Republic will be fine ... The right and power to command is not by nature given to any except the father."[2]

The centrality of the correlation between marriage, family, and political order was worked out in many formats. In France, the preamble to Louis XIV's 1666 marriage edict that offered tax exemptions to fathers of ten or more living children noted that "marriages are the fecund sources from which the strength and greatness of the state derive."[3] Even female monarchs appropriated the language of family to justify and legitimize their power. Elizabeth I of England, the most famous, used the marital language of sovereign and subject in describing her marriage to her kingdom: "I have already joined myself in Marriage to a Husband, namely, the Kingdom of England." Political writers at the time likewise adapted the familial model for a female monarch. Thomas Norton described her in 1569, for example, as "the most loving Mother and nurse of all her good subjects ... the husband of the commonwealth, married to the realm."[4] In ascribing his female ruler as the husband of their kingdom, Norton encapsulated how deeply embedded the gendered relationship between authority and power was at the level of state and family. Yet these examples also demonstrate how parental as well as conjugal binaries framed political imaginaries, with children as well as wives rhetorically positioned as subjects, and parents as well as husbands situated as household monarchs.

Indeed, for early modern elites, whose views such statements in fact expressed, families were regarded as integral to the strength of the state and thus also as potent potential threats to a state if family members did not conform to contemporary expectations about appropriate roles. This equation of strong families with potent states and disorderly families with weak ones created an imperative for new regulation of families, ushering in a raft of family legislation across the early modern world from the middle of the sixteenth century.

STATE REGULATION OF FAMILY LIFE

The regulation of many family matters became a secular rather than ecclesiastical matter across Europe from the early sixteenth century in a remarkable shift that strikingly expanded the role of the state in family life. Lay courts took over from ecclesiastical courts in the legal handling of many matters relating to household life, from domestic violence to sexual infractions. Although the jurisdictional change was striking in many newly Protestant areas from the 1520s, in line with Protestant beliefs that marriage was a contract rather than sacrament, Catholic states also quickly embraced the expansion of civil supervision of marriage and other domestic matters. In many Protestant regions, new civil courts known as "marriage courts" were established to regulate marriage as a secular contract, but throughout Protestant and Catholic Europe, marriage as a legal construct became a civil rather than canonical field. Through the passage of new laws and their treatment in royal legal systems, early modern states vastly expanded their reach into the lives of families and children. If sex became a crime rather than a sin, family life became a political as much as religious matter.

Governments were especially interested in managing marriage formation more effectively, that is, controlling who could marry whom. Traditionally, the Catholic Church had allowed people to marry with the consent of the two future spouses and with few caveats besides. Early modern governments, Protestant and Catholic, who took over regulation of marriage from the sixteenth century, instead emphasized publicity (for instance, in requiring the calling of banns in the home parish church of the spouses-to-be before the wedding) and parental consent as the new keys to marriage. In this area, states, extended families, and communities all shared a stake in making marriages as a means of fostering what they perceived to be appropriate social stability, although the specifics of what was deemed appropriate depended in part on the particulars of local situations as well as broader early modern trends. In France, what Sarah Hanley has termed the "family-state compact" produced an alliance between the monarchy and elite families to the mutual benefit of both as enhanced royal authority was secured in part by the support of noble families who saw their own ability to control their patrimonial property and reputation through enhanced legal powers over their children. In Munich, German middle-class burghers established a marriage license bureau that required would-be spouses to certify their economic stability, hoping to secure marriage as a privilege of the propertied and discourage poor individuals from imprudent, impoverished unions.[5]

Colonial authorities regulated gender and family matters as a tool for social engineering too, often as a means to crystallize racial hierarchies. In 1643, for example, the Virginia Assembly made a key distinction between white and black women, categorizing the latter as "tithables" whose labor in the fields gave them a productive—and taxable—capacity equivalent to men, whereas white women's legal identity remained consumed by coverture under that of their fathers or husbands, and assumed that their labor would take place in the household rather than field. Whatever the legal fiction entailed in this distinction, the outcome had important consequences—white masters paid tithes on their white male laborers as well as male and female enslaved Afro-Virginians. For the father or husbands of free black women, however, the costs of tithes on their female kin could be prohibitive. And black women's field work became a source of stigma in a racializing colonial society. Other laws followed to build on and consolidate these distinctions. In 1662, slavery became an inheritable condition through mothers, so the children born to enslaved women automatically became slaves. By the late seventeenth century, the Virginia Assembly forbade intermarriage between Europeans and free or enslaved Africans. All of these regulations served to manage spouses and children in ways that clarified racial hierarchies and secured the superiority of white Virginians.[6]

The dissolution of marriages as well as their formation was a critical matter for early modern states, whether Protestant or Catholic. The Protestant reinterpretation of marriage as a contract allowed for its dissolution, introducing divorce as a new possibility. One of the great cause célèbres of the early sixteenth century, English monarch Henry VIII's pursuit of a divorce from the Spanish princess Catherine of Aragon, became the stuff of legend and placed the new possibility at the forefront of early modern political as well as theological attention in the 1520s. John Calvin, in his writing and as leader of the city of Geneva, strongly supported the possibility of divorce in principle and in individual cases in the 1540s. Protestant regions throughout Europe legalized divorce, a revolutionary change in the legal status of marriage. In principle, wives in regions from British America to various German territories could sue for divorce on grounds such as cruelty, impotence, and adultery. Yet in practice, few divorces were sought and even fewer granted. Divorce remained very rare until at least the late eighteenth century and largely limited to elite men. This Protestant remaking of marriage as a contract open to renegotiation rather than sacrament for which there could be no temporal dissolution was an important part of a long process by which modern ideas about marriage came to replace medieval ones, but it was a long, slow process before dissolution of marriage became a meaningful possibility for most Europeans.[7]

Catholic countries did not embrace divorce, even as a legal possibility, but the possibility of separations of person and property or of separate property that the medieval Catholic church had offered on similar grounds to divorce continued to exist. These separations were available only to wives. The legal standard for separations of person and property (which permitted wives to live in separate households from their husbands but did not permit remarriage) was life-threatening violence, while the legal standard for separations of property (which in practice gave wives control over future earnings and inheritance) was household-threatening financial disarray. Sometimes, as in France, jurisdiction over separations, like so many other family matters, moved to the state's legal system, and sometimes, as in Venice, it remained an ecclesiastical matter. Although requests for separations of person and property—the proximate equivalent of divorce—were rare, unhappy wives far more commonly sought separate property, and this avenue provided a flexible resource that they could use to discipline husbands who were physically abusive or whose drinking and gambling (usually categorized as "debauchery") exceeded community norms, using the justification that these behaviors threatened the financial stability of their households. Separations in Catholic territories provided women with a means to renegotiate the terms of an unsatisfactory partnership, whether on the basis of securing the right to administer their own property or (much less commonly) to live separately, and perhaps even more importantly with the often valuable negotiating chip of a threat to initiate legal proceedings against their husbands with all the subsequent costs litigation could entail. Ironically, Protestant commitment to divorce may have made any separation more difficult to secure than it was in Catholic countries, although both came to handle the matter most often as a civil and secular matter.[8]

States also sought to police sexuality outside of marriage, an obvious source of instability in terms of the moral threat of illicit sexuality, the economic burden unwed and impoverished mothers placed on communities, and the disorder with which bastard children were associated. European demographic patterns contained a striking disjuncture—illegitimacy rates were very low, often less than three percent, but rates of premarital conception were very high, upward of thirty percent in many parts of Europe. These figures indicate (among other things) that while premarital sex was widespread, most out-of-wedlock pregnancies ended in marriage, an outcome rooted in community expectations as well as religious sensibilities.

Despite these low rates of illegitimacy that persisted until the eighteenth century, when out-of-wedlock births rapidly became more common, illegitimacy became a powerful signifier of disorder for early modern states, and they sought to manage illegitimacy in various ways: through disciplining unmarried women, through new attention to infanticide, and through efforts to manage foundlings. Early modern governments generally paid little attention to premarital conception as long as the babies were born to a married couple, no matter how little time couples had been married before becoming parents. Occasional efforts to introduce more punitive policies toward premarital conception itself, like the wave of prosecutions of spouses for fornication in England in the late seventeenth century if their babies were born within nine months of marriage, were extraordinary rather than the norm. For early modern governments, marriage was the key to stability—authorities generally asked no questions, and communities were unconcerned as long as babies were legitimate when they were born.

However, a wave of new laws and increasing prosecution of fornication for extramarital sex sought to stigmatize unwed motherhood. New laws were passed in many countries that required single women who were pregnant to register their pregnancies with local authorities, initiatives designed both to discipline sexually active single women and to deter the crime of infanticide, which was legally defined to include concealment of pregnancy as well as murder of a newborn.

Infanticide became a focus of criminal prosecution throughout the West, and in some areas far more women were executed for infanticide than the far better known example of witchcraft prosecution. In what historian Alfred Soman has called an "infanticide craze," eleven times as many women were tried for infanticide as witchcraft in the Parisian region in the seventeenth century. This ratio may not have held true elsewhere in Europe, as witchcraft prosecution levels were relatively low in France, but throughout the early modern world, states fixated on the problem of infanticide. In France, the establishment of a law outlawing infanticide in 1557, defined as concealment of pregnancy as well as child murder, was followed within a decade by a rapid rise in prosecutions that lasted until a precipitous decline began in the 1680s. Other countries followed suit in subsequent decades. In France and elsewhere, the trajectory of infanticide prosecution closely followed—or as in the French case may have led—the parallel path of witchcraft prosecution. Through the late sixteenth and seventeenth century, punishments for infanticide were usually severe: women found guilty were executed, sometimes in particularly gruesome fashion. While the increase in the number of prosecutions may well have been the effect of more surveillance, some historians think that the stigmatization of single motherhood also had the consequence of increasing actual infanticides.[9]

The concerns about illegitimacy loomed large in the colonies too, where they became intermingled with dynamics of labor and race as well as other kinds of social order. In seventeenth-century British North America, as in most of Europe, illegitimacy rates were low, although the rates of premarital conception are unclear. Very fragmentary records have made it difficult for historians of early American to draw definitive conclusions about seventeenth-century illegitimacy, but differences between the colonies are suggestive about the significance of local context in attitudes toward sex outside the family. In Connecticut, for example, punishment for illegitimacy framed it as a sin. In contrast, in the Chesapeake, where almost all data is drawn from employers suing pregnant servants in court, the concern of authorities about illegitimacy focused primarily on the loss of labor.

Unlike Europe or British America, illegitimacy rates were very high throughout colonial Latin America, with thirty percent or more of births out of wedlock. Many of these reflected the practice of living in long-term consensual unions, a custom more common in the Latin American world for a variety of reasons, including long-term concubinage and high rates of mixed-race partnerships. Colonial Latin American communities also continued to emphasize the significance of the free choices of spouses in contrast to the general increasing emphasis elsewhere on parental consent to marriage. These factors indicate some of the important ways in which patterns of family and childhood in the Hispanic Atlantic world were quite different than those broadly common to continental Europe or the British north Atlantic.[10]

States also invested new energy in managing the increasing numbers of abandoned or orphaned children, whether illegitimate or legitimate, although in practice the implementation was often left to local authorities. Many Italian city-states had established foundling hospitals during the Renaissance, but such projects became widespread in northwestern Europe in the early modern centuries. Like the orphanages of Augsburg in Germany, for example, or of Amsterdam, such projects were often overlaid with charitable and religious associations, but in sharp contrast to the medieval period, they were under secular rather than ecclesiastical control. In Paris, the language of the royal chartering of the Foundling Hospital in 1670 indicated the importance of population concern in motivating the government to bring the thirty-year-old institution under the state's wing, hoping that its graduates would become soldiers, artisans, or colonists. The Foundling Hospital was explicitly associated with the recently founded general hospital where beggars, prostitutes and the insane were incarcerated. Other cities likewise combined the care of children with the care of other instable elements of the population. They hoped to keep children off the streets and to train them as productive, moral subjects. In Venice, for instance, boys were apprenticed as sailors, providing the state with a critical workforce as well as providing the children with a livelihood. Girls were often taught to sew to prepare them to work in the textile manufactures that were expanding across Europe. In England, the Elizabethan Poor Laws of the 1570s and especially the 1590s sought to create a comprehensive public welfare policy out of varied local practices, with laws that required, for example, orphans to be placed in institutions or apprenticed and poor families to receive relief either in institutions or through alms, depending on their status and abilities. Yet as in other countries, the implementation of state policy in this regard rested on local initiatives, in the English case on parish officers and justices of the peace, with wide variation from county to county in compliance and conformity. Across colonial Latin America, the legal abandonment of children was sanctioned as an alternative to infanticide, and civil authorities established orphanages and foundling hospitals to take in legitimate as well as illegitimate children.

While Christian charity certainly had a role in these endeavors, the desire of state authorities to promote order and regulate population by managing impoverished children was clear. The institutional setting was coded as familial, with monarchs or city leaders as the surrogate fathers, institutions providing the families that foundlings as well as other indigent poor apparently lacked, and the small residents were frequently rhetorically identified as children of the state.[11] In this matter, as in many others, states depended on the cooperation of local elites to enact the policies they found desirable.

These anxieties about reproduction were related to larger concerns of states about social reproduction as population became clearly linked to national power. Early modern political theorists of the state, such as Jean Bodin and Thomas Hobbes, clearly connected the strength of a state to the size of its population, correlating that to the number of people available to fight wars, pay taxes, or produce goods, and saw the family as the natural site of population management. Although most efforts to enumerate population through censuses only began in the eighteenth century, starting in the early sixteenth century, states began to require parish clergy to keep track of births, deaths, and marriages in registers, inadvertently creating what would become an invaluable source for the history of the family and childhood in subsequent centuries. In France, for instance, an edict in 1539 required priests to provide copies of their records to secular authorities, and a 1668 edict established the requirement for priests to keep double copies of the registers. In England, a similar requirement was made in 1538, and in Scotland in 1616. As with many of the ambitions of early modern states, observation of these requirements varied enormously (as indicated in England, by the 1597 reiteration of the requirement with the addition of penalties for failures to do so). These initiatives certainly had complex roots, with the transition from oral to written culture and the contestation over ecclesiastical or lay control, for example, as two influences besides the growing reach of the state. However, as with regard to marriage, these measures marked states asserting a civil interest in family matters that had previously been the concern of the church. By the nineteenth century, this process was completed when civil registration of children was required through the West regardless of church baptism.

While these efforts by authorities problematized the situation of unmarried women, a similar powerful rhetoric and new laws in many ways sought to enhance the power of husband and fathers. In England, wives who killed husbands were charged not with murder but with petty treason in a remarkable expression of the embedded relationship between family and state. Pronatalist legislation in France targeted fathers for the incentives and rewards offered to large families as if mothers were incidental in the reproduction of the target of ten living children. The criminalization of extramarital sex, and especially women who participated in it, defined licit sex as the preserve of married men. While historian Holly Brewer's assertion that the early modern centuries saw the invention of the power of fathers seems to be too strong in view of the age-old roots of patriarchy, undoubtedly she points to the important ways in which the powers of husbands and fathers became a central feature of the political landscape.

States used laws to differentiate the position of children as well as that of wives and fathers within families, and states' political efforts to create stable families and use the language of family to political effect had varying consequences for children. There had been no consensus over the age of legal majority, that is, the age at which people became independent legal actors, in the medieval world, with legal majority rules varying by time, region, and legal capacity sought. Subsequently, in the premodern West, children legally married, served as jurors, were elected as members of Parliament, worked as apprentices or servants, and fulfilled many other roles that seem jarring to modern observers.

Two apparently conflicting evolutions are evident in the early modern period amid the hodgepodge of varying applications of legal minority. New laws clarified and extended the period of legal dependency associated with childhood by, for example, increasing the age of legal majority. In Spain, children became legal minors until they reached the age of twenty-five (although many specifics complicated this category: children could be engaged at seven, make wills at ten, be tried for crimes at ten and a half, and a boy could become a monk at sixteen, a lawyer at eighteen, and a judge at twenty). In France, young men remained minors until they were thirty, and young women until they were twenty-five, following new legislation in the late sixteenth century. Such developments often went hand in hand with new regulations about marriage. Parental consent, for instance, became an important new feature of early modern marriage for anyone under the age of legal majority, and so legal minors (even men and women in their twenties) could not marry without their parents' consent.[12]

Yet this pattern of extending legal minorities contrasted with states' efforts to delineate specific disabilities of childhood, especially in terms of political practice. Over the course of the seventeenth century, efforts to prohibit the practice of children being elected or appointed to various offices spread in England and colonial British America. New laws were introduced, for example, in the British colonies and in England that established twenty-one as the age for voting or holding many positions. Bianca Premo has argued that in the Spanish colonies, the status of legal minor was transformed into a much more fluid category, in which age was only one factor, in a process that—by the eighteenth century—also transformed the state's role as protector and guardian of many of its subjects. Minors in Spanish colonial society came to include all native inhabitants as well as slaves and Europeans under twenty-five. These redefinitions refined racial hierarchies, but the management of the civil cases around the protection of minors spurred the growth of colonial bureaucracies, placing the Spanish colonial state as the explicit guardian of a far larger proportion of the population than was the case in Europe.[13]

States played a critical role in the appointment of guardians for the many early modern children who lost one or both parents, and this process highlighted the role of the state in the management of children, families, and gendered authority in families. When mothers died, fathers remained of course the legal guardian of their children as they had been and no legal proceeding took place. When fathers died, however, mothers did not automatically replace them as guardians of the children, even though as widows women gained many of the legal rights associated with head of household status that fathers and husbands usually enjoyed, such as the rights to make contracts or appear in court in their own names. In these instances, courts appointed guardians for children. Regional practice seems to have varied quite substantially, with mothers often being appointed in some parts of Spain for instance and rarely in Nantes and other French cities. However, whatever the practice, in all cases mothers' access to their children and ability to manage their children's property was subject to the approval of judges who consulted with male kin—that is, mothers might become guardians if their conduct and reputation fit with local assumptions about appropriately gendered behavior.[14]

While the focus on families that European states pursued in their colonial projects had much in common with metropolitan emphases as we have

seen, children arguably played a far more important role as political subjects
in the colonies than in Europe itself, and the impact of state policies in this
period (as opposed to later) was greater for colonial children than for their
metropolitan counterparts. Colonial historiography has demonstrated the significance children—like wives and husbands/fathers—as figures in the cases
and consequences of state-building for Europe's far-flung new empires. As
Premo has recently argued, colonial children were critical targets of attention for early modern governments as future loyal subjects and as exploit-
able labor as well as potential taxpayers and soldiers. The Portuguese state
offered dowries to orphan girls who agreed to relocate to its colonies. The
thousands of Indians who migrated in the Andes after Spanish colonization,
include a high proportion of children. As Teresa Vergara's work on Lima
shows, Spanish authorities sought to control the impact of this migration and
shape the imperial future by encouraging the children to live with Spanish
families (some enslaved, some as servants) so they might better learn how to
be useful subjects and servants of empire.[15] All Indians became legal minors
in the Spanish empire, a practice that vastly expanded the category. While
this expansion might seem at first glance to have infantilized all indigenous
peoples, it also offered them legal avenues as well as regulation. While children appeared unevenly on the radar screens of early modern governments,
who paid virtually no attention to issues like child abuse, for instance (which
became a major concern of European states only from the nineteenth century
onward), they were indispensable subjects as early modern states pursued
their expansive ambitions, both metropolitan and colonial.

The emphasis on coerced labor was perhaps at the center of colonial
policies that affected children, and this is what differentiated state policy and
practice in the colonies from their domestic agendas. In Spanish and British
America, the creation of a variety of forced labor systems affected European,
indigenous, and African children in different ways. The forced labor tribute
in the Andes (called the *repartimiento de la mita*) led to massive migration
of indigenous peoples. Many children were placed as servants or in schools
and convents with people of different castes, or grew up as outsiders in ethnic
communities that were not their own. In British America, indentured servants,
almost all of whom were young people, provided essential labor for the new
colonies. Just as importantly, many European children who were born to free
families were bound out to strangers as pauper apprentices and spent their
childhoods in conditions of legal servitude.[16]

The laws European states and colonial authorities introduced to ensure the
enslavement of Africans had important implications for children as well as

their parents. The status of slavery was inherited through mothers, as we have seen. Slave marriages had no legal standing. Thus slave children legally lacked fathers or last names. There was no legal right to inheritance of property. In all these ways, the energy that European authorities devoted to the creation of powerfully hierarchical families at home and overseas was reversed in their many counter efforts to dissolve family order among the enslaved Africans on whose labor the fortunes of the new imperial states profited.

FAMILIES AND THE STATE

Not only were families and children important as subjects and as objects of state attention, but states also became an increasingly important resource for families in the early modern period. In the gap between the desires of state authorities, their ability to enact their wishes, and individual experience, legal process was a key link. Royal law courts were a primary expression of the state in most localities, both European and colonial. However, the extent of direct control by central authorities varied enormously, with judges often having wide latitude to rule as they saw fit. Moreover, in the complex, overlapping, crazy patch-work quilt of jurisdictions that characterized the early modern world, the new laws that early modern governments passed jostled with or sometimes directly conflicted with other law codes—municipal, customary, canon, or commercial. If the criminalization of illicit sexuality, especially young female sexuality, is highly visible to historians and a significant indicator of the desire of states to manage their subjects, the extraordinary increase in civil litigation—that is, of private individuals going to court to settle personal disputes—was equally transformative in remaking family-state relations.[17]

The gap between legal prescription and social practice is well known, and the experiences of single women who found themselves pregnant offer a timely reminder of the complexity of establishing the relationship between state intent, community attitudes, and grassroots impact. In France, for example, the requirement of unwed mothers to notify a public official about their pregnancies, one of the best-known examples of state discipline of female extramarital sexuality, seems to have been honored more in the breach than the observance, at least until the eighteenth century. Many single women had one or even multiple babies without registering their conditions. While prosecutions for infanticide certainly increased dramatically in the seventeenth century, these remained highly selective, as did all other forms of early modern criminality, given the shortage of on-the-ground state resources. The only in-fanticides we know about are "unsuccessful" ones—that is, where the baby's body was discovered or where the community decided to bring events to the notice of authorities. It is unclear, and probably impossible to know, how many single mothers were able to dispose of their newborns without discovery (perhaps with the help of the infants' fathers or other relatives) or how many times neighbors just turned the other way rather than report suspicious circumstances. While the heightened anxiety of states about infanticide is clear, the attitudes of communities were complex, and the responses of family and neighbors depended in large part on the status and circumstances of the mother rather than the fact of infanticide.[18]

In terms of children and families, the relationship with the state through local courts created a variety of conflicting dynamics and made for very complicated, often kaleidoscopic outcomes that are difficult to simplify in any meaningful way. Certainly, early modern states tried to regulate and discipline family life in key ways, as we have seen. Yet families and individual members of families could also use the legal system to bring the authority and interest of the state to bear on problems that states themselves expressed little initiative in. That is, the early modern state, through its law courts, provided a resource for families, for spouses, and much less often for children. Two very different examples of the ways in which the relationships of states and families through the legal system were symbiotic as well as disciplinary are provided by the handling of domestic violence in France and the manumission of slave children in colonial Latin America. In the early modern world, states sought to increase their roles in family life, but families also increasingly used the courts in ways that invited the state to take a greater role in remedying household difficulties and managing challenges. Early modern men and women increasingly discovered how useful courts could be in navigating their family lives.

In France, as in other European countries, husbands and fathers were legally entitled to discipline their wives, their children, and other household members. The virtual complete lack of criminal prosecution of any domestic violence short of murder seems to confirm the perception that states had no interest in family violence. Yet wives often used civil litigation to complain about husbands' abusive behavior, and judges in royal courts brought the authority of the state to the disciplining of men whose actions were judged to have exceeded the legal standard for household discipline. In this way, repeated decisions in royal courts endorsed the consensus in local communities about the parameters of husbands' prerogatives and the extent of their obligations, even while continuing to emphasize the gendered hierarchies at the center of family life.[19]

A similar dynamic in terms of family members using the authority of the state through its courts for their own immediate purposes and to large, long-term effect is evident in a quite different context: the manumission of slave children in the American colonies. In colonial Latin American countries, both slave masters and enslaved parents freed slave children using the legal process of manumission in huge numbers. Catholic slave owners in pursuit of salvation in late life were often motivated to manumit their slaves, and enslaved parents who were able to save money—often from their own earnings as artisans or traders—used the legal option of manumission to change the chattel status their children had inherited. Historians have argued that this practice was a critical element in the creation of a large proportion of free people of color in Latin America, undoubtedly not a goal that colonial states had in mind as their other efforts to entrench racial hierarchies indicated.[20]

Even young, single, pregnant women, the most obvious targets of state's commitment to police disorder and to create orderly families, found the civil system—and the state's commitment to stable households—a potential tool to use in their favor. More single women probably used the legal system proactively in their favor to sue reluctant suitors for breach of marriage promises, especially if they were pregnant, than submitted themselves to the disciplinary supervision of authorities by registering their extramarital pregnancies (at least until the eighteenth century, when a variety of factors changed the dynamics of single pregnancies). In the French city of Lyon, for instance, the court files labeled "pregnancy declarations" primarily included suits by young women or their parents against alleged wayward fathers who often found themselves detained by the court while the accusations were investigated—or sometimes until they agreed to marry the female complainant. In these ways, local courts—the nominal, at least, on-the-ground embodiments of states—showed intense concern for young men's extramarital sexual activity as well as that of young women.[21]

Children's ability to utilize the potential of the state's resources for their own ends was far more limited than that of families, wives, or single mothers, and indeed the day-to-day life of children was largely of little concern to states, and children had little ability to pursue their own issues in courts. Children were far less able than adults to use the civil system to their advantage, in part because the property issues that often provided the wedge for adults (as, for example, in the ability of battered women to use a threat to property—whether of their persons or households—as a justification for a civil procedure against their husbands) did not exist in the same way for children. Criminal prosecutions rarely involved children as either the accused or the victims. Most cases in which children did appear as victims in courts occurred when they were subject to abuse by someone other than their parents, but in practice violence against children—whoever the perpetrator—continued to be handled primarily by communities rather than as a subject for state intervention through the judicial process.

Children were occasionally participants as accused and accusers in those most famous of all state-sanctioned early modern criminal prosecutions: trials for witchcraft. Children could attain positions of unusual prominence as accusers in witchcraft allegations, as in the case of the Salem witchcraft panic in New England in 1692. As could be the case with husbands of alleged witches, children were sometimes presumed guilty through family association. Brian Levack notes the example of the children of a Saxon magician who were summarily executed after their father was found guilty. Generally, however, children were prosecuted as witches only in large-scale outbreaks and toward the end of investigations. Of the 160 witches executed in Würzburg between 1627 and 1629, over twenty-five percent were children and all such executions occurred toward the end of the hunt. Levack argues, in fact, that this pattern means that the emergence of children among the prosecuted often coincides with the end of witchcraft prosecution in particular areas across Europe.[22]

The historicization of child abuse is still in its infancy as it were, and—as in the case of wife beating—behavior categorized as abusive has been defined in different ways in different historical circumstances, but clearly Western states paid little attention to child abuse before the late eighteenth century, and consequently it has been difficult for historians to recover such information. Authorities—and communities—appear to have made clear distinctions between the level of force that was appropriate between spouses and the apparently far greater range that was deemed within acceptable limits between parents and children. At any rate, early modern states were invested in family violence primarily in terms of wife beating, with the physical abuse of children only slowly becoming problematized for states in the later eighteenth century.[23]

The history of the sexual abuse of children is likewise made challenging by the concerns of early modern authorities. Incest prosecutions were rare, and in any case not protective of children. Early modern beliefs interpreted incest as unnatural and monstrous rather than as family abuse, so both the girl and male perpetrator were regarded as guilty—in fact, young women were charged with incest as well as the fathers, stepfathers, fathers-in-law, brothers, and cousins who committed the acts. When Barbara Reiser, for example identified her father as the father of her baby during her labor in Wüttemberg in 1655, they were both tried and both were punished with banishment from the city.[24] Yet because authorities focused on the abuse of girls by older men, we know little about the abuse of boys, which presumably also existed.

CONCLUSIONS

The early modern expansion of state interest in families and children was a complicated matter, involving far more diverse dynamics than a simple disciplinary extension of regulation into household life. States became more involved in family life, not only as a matter of political motivation, but because household members and communities increasingly sought to use the legal system to manage familial disputes and to negotiate appropriate behavior, especially in terms of spouses and sexuality, for their own purposes. While the new laws introduced were important measures of an early modern sea change in the relationship between states and families, the very limited practical capacities of governments makes it critical to consider carefully the gap between the rhetoric and fantastical ambition of early modern states and the lived experience of families and children. The two were certainly related, as the constant deployment of familial language to valorize and legitimize—or challenge—particular forms of government authority would have a long resonance and impact right up to the family values debates that are central to Western democracies in the early twenty-first century. Yet the uneven privileging of the rights and obligations of family members, whether husbands, wives, or children, could be contested, endorsed, or indeed welcomed as early modern men and women increasingly elected to use the legal system that in so many ways gave the early modern state a meaningful contact point with its subjects as a key instrument to manage family life.

CHAPTER EIGHT

Faith and Religion

SILVIA EVANGELISTI

The early modern Western household was regarded as one of the primary contexts for experiencing religion, ensuring the transmission and continuity of faith. This was the case in Christian as well as in other contemporary cultures and confessions. The major religious changes that occurred in Europe in this period—above all the Protestant and Catholic reformations in the sixteenth century—made the family increasingly the focus of devotion and teachings, as well as the object of public discourses and regulations. In Europe and its colonies, adults and children of both sexes and class were important targets in the process of confessionalization set in motion by religious reformers and rulers. This process affected both Catholic and Protestant regions, becoming a fundamental step in early modern state building, even though theological differences divided the two confessions.[1] This chapter will discuss how religious practices and discourses played a role in shaping early modern understandings of childhood and family life, and the impact of the religious reforms on them. Since religion was deeply embedded in private and public life, this chapter will focus on both the domestic context and the religious and charitable institutions that, although distinct from the family, interacted with it. The chapter will also show how the religious realm offered a variety of roles within the community to individuals of all ages, both adults and children.

DEVOTIONS AT HOME

The domestic environment had its own religious routine and provided the basic setting for a number of ritual activities. Prayers were said at meal times and festivities, and saints were invoked for protection, for curing illnesses, and for aiding child birth. Celebrations of life cycles, from birth and baptism to marriage and mourning, required the participation of at least part of the family, and were often associated with the preparation of food to be consumed in the house. Multiple religious meanings were attached to the actual use of the domestic space. Late medieval biographies of female saints tell of holy women who turned their houses into a quasi-monastic spaces. They chose to live in reclusion and prayer and to be confined to their own bedchamber, which was sometimes defined a "cell."[2] Variations on these narrative motives remained part of the hagiographical tradition throughout the early modern period. The seventeenth-century Mexican saint Maria de San José described her childhood in her autobiography and drew on a threatening apparition of the devil, whom she confronted one day, on the staircase of her house next to her mother's chamber.[3] The not-so-implicit message suggested by episodes of this sort was that God, or the Devil, might be approachable directly from home, at any stage of life, particularly for exceptional individuals on their way to sanctity.

Although it is not always easy to trace ordinary religious experiences within the home, scholars have used material and visual evidence to explore the devotional and sacred meaning of the house. The presence within the house of objects and spaces associated with religious functions does not tell us a lot about the ways in which people used them. But it does tell us something about the meanings attributed to them. Holy images, for example, might be used to seek religious verification. Charged with spiritual authority, these images, and the behavior that they evoked, marked points of the house that were then believed to be closer to the divine. Devotional images might also have been seen as providers of supernatural protection over the household. Alternatively, they might simply have been regarded as decorative objects.[4] Their presence certainly suggests that people wanted their houses to evoke contemplation and worship for those who inhabited or visited them. Similarly, the dedicated sacred spaces for domestic praying, furnished with holy objects, recalled the idea of a pious and devoted household, whether these spaces were actually used for spiritual purposes by the dwellers or not. In the fifteenth and early sixteenth centuries, some English gentry mansions included domestic chapels where masses could be performed by priests.[5] In the same period, in Spain,

aristocratic families built palaces that were connected through passageways
to the chapel of monasteries and convents that were under their protection.
These architectonic devices allowed patrons to listen to the services celebrated
in the chapel or to gain visual access to the altar while praying from their
own dwellings.[6] In Renaissance Europe, some noble and wealthy homes featured altars that created formal liturgical settings where services could be celebrated, insofar as permission was granted by the authorities. Domestic altars
remained in place well after the restrictions introduced by the Roman ecclesiastical authorities in the second half of the sixteenth century, which prohibited the celebration of masses outside the church. These examples attest to
the popularity of homely devotion, in particular among the wealthy groups.[7]
They also indicate that the domestic space was both an expression of piety
and a representation of it, which located the family in a community of believ-
ers, reinforcing its social links and collective identity.[8] Moreover, the space
of the house was open to multiple uses and could be adapted according to
specific sacred and profane occasions. Objects and spaces associated with religious meanings, for instance, could serve for nonreligious purposes. Cosimo
de' Medici used the private chapel located in his Florentine palace as a study
and for receiving distinguished guests. Conversely, pieces of furniture, such as
portable altars or folding tables covered with altar cloths, could transform the
domestic space into an area suffused with religious meaning.[9]

   If research on the materiality of domestic devotion has more often focused
on the elites, there is scope for a more inclusive social spectrum. The idea
of the household as a religious body was acknowledged across different
social groups. Indeed, the circulation of holy images and gadgets in domestic
environments was not limited to the wealthy and noble families, and items
of religious significance were found in the houses of middle-class people and
artisans too. Visual representations of less wealthy or poor domestic interiors
support this point. They feature images of humble dwellings with an open
fire, where a small image of the Virgin and the Child is clearly visible on
the wall in proximity to the bed (Figure 8.1).[10] The increased circulation of
images, objects, and styles that has been observed in the early modern period
has been seen as an indicator per se of the standardization of domestic devotional culture, which did not exclusively concern patrician groups. In Venice,
for example, the presence in the home of images of the Virgin, and the Virgin
and the Child, increased during the fifteenth century, and went from one or
two in each dwelling to more than two in the following century, and preference was given to Byzantine-style Madonnas often listed in notarial records
and inventories.[11]

FIGURE 8.1: *Interior of a Poor Household,* Bologna, late sixteenth century, attributed to Annibale Carracci, drawing, whereabouts unknown.

Domestic materiality offers clues also about reformed family religiosity. Perhaps even more than Catholics, Protestants regarded the family as the place to experience religion, and they encouraged domestic forms of devotion. Protestants, unlike Catholics, did not associate religious life with celibacy, and the minister and the father were united in the same person. Fathers and male householders were like "bishops in their own homes."[12] They had to supervise the spiritual as well as the physical well-being of the house church and instruct their children in the right belief. Although Protestants were suspicious of religious images, they allowed them in their houses (and in inns and taverns), and even in their churches, which sometimes displayed biblical pictures and inscriptions. Small woodcut Christs and pictures of the Virgin continued to be part of the visual apparatus of the house, at least in the century following the adoption of Protestantism. Protestant domestic culture was also deeply influenced by the new religious attitudes. English house walls, for example, featured painted psalm verses and cloths with edifying sayings that were adapted to the new needs of the reformed family. In rich homes, printed wallpapers combining images and biblical words might be used to line wooden furniture. Lines from psalms, and simple sayings like "Fear the Lord" or "Obey the prince," were reproduced on the walls, and on wall cloths, sending spiritual and emotional messages to the dwellers of different ages (Figure 8.2). These messages could be memorized and recited aloud with prayers. Householders were encouraged to use pious and rather affordable broadsheets, reading and explaining them to all family members.[13] Religious images concentrated in particular points of the domestic space. In English and Scottish aristocratic mansions, the fireplace—a sacred and symbolic point of the house—was decorated with religious scenes that might help contemplation and meditation. Furthermore, some Protestant houses, like Catholic houses, included chapels for reformed worshipping, which might be fully part of the house rather than being separate from it.

FIGURE 8.2: *Family of Hans Conrad Bodmer, Landvogt zu Greifensee and Burgmeister of Zurich,* Zurich, 1643, attributed to Heinrich Sulzer, oil on canvas, Schweizerisches Landesmuseum (Dep. 3721). Photo: Dr Paul Hess.

These chapels fostered continuity between domestic and spiritual realms and a collective identification with the new faith.[14]

FATHERS, MOTHERS, AND DOMESTIC RELIGIOUS INSTRUCTION

One of the recurrent motifs in early modern literature of advice on the family, in Catholic as well as Protestant areas, is how to create a Christian family. That is, how could the head of the household ensure that his spouse, children, and servants received appropriate religious education and learnt to behave accordingly? All family members were called on to play their own part in the making of the Christian household and society. Fathers were held responsible for the discipline and spiritual development of their children. Mothers shared the burden under the guidance of their husbands and reached their children through persuasion and affective words. Therefore, both parents were expected to contribute to their family's spiritual well-being and were held responsible for it. Scholars who most recently examined paternal and maternal models in the education and spiritual development of children, underlined how, in practice, such roles were closely intertwined with ideas of femininity and masculinity.

Mothers were seen as particularly skilled in educating children because of their persuasive role, which differed from paternal authority. The French Jesuit Jean Cordier maintained that maternal affection was particularly "industrious" and successful for educational purposes. According to Cordier, the loving and emotional relationship that the mother, more than the father, established with her children, allowed her to educate them and shape their spirit according to the best of all virtues. Her teachings were imparted with less authority and "violence" than were the father's and would thus be better received by her children. Therefore mothers could "operate much more [effectively] than men in the education of their children."[15] The active role played by mothers in their children's spiritual instruction concentrated on the very early phase of the child's life. The maternal role was physiological and associated with bodily and reproductive functions: conception, gestation, birth, and nursing. Mothers should teach their offspring "to eat, to drink, to walk about … to be adorned with clothing' and to speak. Above all they should teach them to keep their devotion and discern good from evil."[16] As the American poet Ann Bradstreet wrote, with reference to the instruction of her eight children (1659), "I taught what was good, and what was ill, what would save life, and what would kill."[17] Indeed, mothers were encouraged to impart the first rudiments of Christian principles to the young boys and girls of the house, to read them edifying stories, and to teach catechism. A number of authors of pedagogical texts, from antiquity to the early modern age, identified the period up to seven years of age as the time when children were almost completely in the care of women (an idea that seems to have somehow survived into modernity). Seven was also the age of discretion or reason according to the Roman Catholic Church, and the time when children might be ready to take the first communion. After seven, the education of boys should be transferred into the male hands of the private tutor, the father, or the master—regarded as a more appropriate presence than the soft education imparted by the mother. In practice, girls remained even later under maternal influence; more rarely they were educated at home by their fathers or sent off to a convent school.

Maternal monopoly in early education of children should not be overstated, as it may have varied according to faith, as well as gender. Medieval Jewish fathers, for instance, took direct responsibility in the rearing of their young male children, below seven years old, whom they started in Hebrew and the Jewish tradition.[18] Interesting speculations have been made regarding Protestant regions, where men were publicly called to account for failing to discipline their children in their spiritual needs. In John Calvin's Geneva, in the years that immediately followed the Reformation, fathers were exhorted to ensure that all family members were properly baptized, that their children regularly attended catechism, and that they behaved properly in church. Indeed, man's duty to God was to ensure the propagation and continuity of the new faith, starting with his own family. Even if women could also be called to account, men were held primarily responsible for the entire family's religious education, and were more often summoned to report before the consistory.[19]

This early learning process, in which mothers and fathers were to participate, relied on orality and images and largely appealed to senses and emotions, since these were regarded as particularly relevant to religious learning and experience. To this extent, the history of childhood and religious education reveals interesting connections with the history of emotions, which have been little explored. Reference to emotions was made by several authors of texts on the education of children, including when religious education was discussed. In the very beginning of the fifteenth century, Giovanni Dominici discussed the rules for good domestic governing and children's religious development, which for him—a Dominican friar and then the archbishop of Ragusa—could not be separated from Christian family life. In order to create religious sentiments in young children and educate them in the love of God, he recommended first of all the use in the house of holy images appropriate to the children's age. Because children learned through senses, more than adults, images that were perceived through sight fostered unwritten and immediate didactic messages, allowing spiritual teachings to be understood by all family members irrespectively of their level of literacy.[20] Children should find in them sources of inspiration and examples to imitate. Pictures of young saints of both sexes embodied the holy virtues, portraits of the Virgin and the Child evoked the importance of the intimate mother-child relation, and the representation of the slaughter of the innocents induced fear of war and weapons. Children should be taken to the church, in particular if no pictures are available in the house; there, by engaging in devotional acts in imitation of Christian piety they could learn about true religious sentiments. Play also fostered religious learning and moral values. Boys and girls should amuse themselves by making and decorating their own small domestic altars, making candles and garlands of flowers to adorn them at festivities. Boys should imitate the movements and gestures of priests. Children were also advised to dress plainly and simply like the first church fathers, their clothing deprived of vanities. All five senses were important for reaching God. Sight and touch perceived nature and the creatures of God. Hearing captured the commands from God. Smell taught not to fear poverty, illnesses, and physical decline and stimulated the desire to serve the poor and the sick. Taste served for penitence in order to reach spiritual elevation. Dominici therefore employed a broad notion of learning that encompassed literacy and included gestures, speech, and feelings about the characters enacted during playing activities. This was an idea of learning found in later authors of pedagogical works, in particular Comenius, who underlined the educational role of imitative playing as a means for spiritual development, and the moral and spiritual value of the intimate and emotional bond between mother and child. A precursor of modern pedagogy, as well as the author of one of the first illustrated schoolbooks for children, *Orbis Pictus* (*The World in Pictures*), Comenius was widely known in his age, and translations of his work circulated in Europe and America, where he became very influential amongst the Puritans of New England. He advised mothers to teach children the postures of devotion: to kneel, to fold hands, to say little prayers. If these advices were put into practice, the house would be a "workshop of the holy spirit."[21]

The emphasis on the direct participation of the family in the spiritual improvement of their children, and the transmission of Christian behavior, was particularly relevant in an age of religious upheavals and can be traced by looking at the production and circulation of books for domestic religious instruction. Since childhood was seen as a critical phase for the formation of a Christian society, religious education was one of the bywords of the Protestant and Catholic reformations and a fundamental aspect of confessionalization on both sides.[22] With the progressive definition of religious differences—including those among the reformed confessions—members of the various churches increasingly saw the necessity to channel religious efforts of the young and encouraged domestic instruction of children in order to stimulate and reinforce their faith.[23] In Tudor and Stuart England and the colonies, handbooks and sermons containing instructions to mothers on their children's education became extremely popular, and a great number of books of catechism were printed in English. In Italy, handbooks for instructing those who were less likely to go to school, and women, also enjoyed great success. These handbooks promised rapid and successful results, including learning to read in "two months."[24] Their abundance and presence in postmortem inventories, including those of women, suggests that they reached the domestic world and probably served their purpose.

If on the one hand religious education within the household has been seen as a means to enhanced family cohesion, it also revealed the inherent limits of parental authority and the possibility of family conflicts. Indeed, individual choices regarding faith often clashed with parental authority. Historians have shown that in the wake of the Protestant Reformation, for instance, cases are known of monks and nuns who left their monasteries and convents, on the grounds of forced monasticism, or who refused to leave the convent on order of their families, on the grounds of their true faith. These cases make reference to the difficult balance between obedience and acknowledgment of parental authority and obedience to God.[25] Martin Luther himself had experienced this conflict in his youth, when he had decided to abandon university studies in law in order to join a monastic order against the will of his father. Later in his life he drew on this episode and used it to speculate on the theme of parental authority, maintaining that parents should recognize the supreme authority of God and the strength of the love of God that might be stronger than the love children had for their parents.[26]

OUTSIDE THE HOME

Schools, charitable institutions, and monastic houses provided the setting for religious experience outside the family and carried on the educational and devotional trajectory that had begun within it. In looking at the meaning and function of these institutions, we need to ask what they offered children and what they could provide that the family did not. It has to be considered, however, that in late medieval and Renaissance Europe, people received little religious instruction. Few parish schools taught basic doctrine, as in England, for example, and only some Italian school texts included prayers. But, prior to the sixteenth century, religious education was not regularly imparted to children and was mainly reserved for the elite, and those who would become clergymen. Following the Protestant and Catholic reformations, confessional education became a priority, and religious knowledge was increasingly introduced in primary school programs. Schools in France, Germany, Italy, and Spain took charge of instructing children in the Christian faith, which they included in their curriculum together with reading and, less often, writing skills. Specific religious schools, like Sunday schools, concentrated on spiritual and religious instruction. Protestants believed that early access to the scriptures should be available both at home and outside. Catechism and the expert supervision of pastors would be fundamental for a better understanding of the word of God. In Catholic countries, schools of Christian doctrine were organized by confraternities and mainly catered to less wealthy children. Boys and girls were taught (separately) the basics of religious education by means of catechism texts and by chanting and memorizing the prayers. Texts included the main prayers like the Pater Noster and Hail Mary, the Ten Commandments, and the seven works of mercy, together with a set of questions on the main sins. An adult, or a clergyman, would ask questions to the child, who, in turn, was supposed to provide answers learned by heart. Visual support in the form of pictures helped clarify the key messages.[27] Basic religious instruction was also available from charitable institutions, such as orphanages and foundling hospitals, which sought to impose bodily as well as spiritual discipline on young boys and girls. The children living in the civic orphanage of seventeenth-century Amsterdam were given a copy of the Bible, a gift that they would take with them on their eventual departure and return to the outside world. A sign of the received religious education, the Bible was part of the pious image that the institution wanted to project outside and was allegedly the mark of its attempt to train good Christians, although it is unlikely that many children would acquire the ability to read it.[28]

The education imparted by institutions aimed at ensuring social order and discipline and improving children's spiritual and social behavior in order to make them better members of the community. In the words of the citizens of Seville (1548), the newly created house for the instruction of Christian doctrine had brought "fewer thieves ... less disease and contagious illness, and more doctrine and better example amongst the poor."[29] Regulations regarding schools and religious education also responded to the need to prevent heresies. Particularly in mixed areas, like Spain, where the presence of *conversos* (Jews and Muslims converted to Christianity) was more significant than in other parts of Europe, the royal authorities attempted to establish a tight control on teachers, excluding from teaching professions all *conversos* and all those with ancestors who had been brought before the Inquisition.[30]

Much of the religious instruction provided by institutions was only available for children in cities. In Italy, for example, schools of Christian doctrine remained a city-based reality. In the countryside, the lack of religious instruction registered by the church authorities shows that the church did not always succeed in effectively reaching peasant families, some of whom remained ignorant of the precepts of religion.

In Catholic Europe, monastic houses offered boys and girls the opportunity to lead a total religious existence in a kind of symbolic, alternative family. Monasteries and convents mainly hosted the children of the elites and rich middling sorts, who entered to be educated as boarders and might remain to take the vows. Within the monastic community they were instructed in religious knowledge and received education that in some cases supplemented that already imparted by their families. The libraries of monasteries, and to a lesser extent those of convents, included theological texts and books of devotional literature in Latin and vernacular, showing the extent to which monastic houses, and in particular male ones, provided a good level of religious education and generally more opportunity for intellectual development. Convent education was much more oriented toward the type of domestic knowledge that was deemed appropriate for women. Rarely, the instruction that women received in nunneries went beyond devotional and domestic concerns to include literature, music, and the visual arts.[31] Class and gender are crucial divides for assessing the educational opportunities offered by religious institutions. While boys might choose among multiple options, from private preceptors, the university, or Jesuits colleges, girls faced a much narrower range of options. Since girls attended schools but in smaller numbers than boys, they were able to receive private tuition in their fathers' homes or enter the convent.[32] As far as gender is concerned, the foundation of new female active orders in the wake of the Catholic reformation introduced new educational opportunities to women, as a number of these, like the Ursulines or the English Ladies, were teaching orders. These new organizations reached a broader section of the society and were open to a wider variety of social groups, which also included artisan families. They also contributed to reinforcing Catholic welfare initiatives, since some of them, such as the Daughters of Charity, performed basic charitable services for the poor, the dying, and the orphans.[33]

COLONIAL CONTEXTS

The religious instruction of children outside the family became particularly relevant for the making of the new European frontiers beyond the continent, in the Asian and American contexts. True, as scholars have underlined, the history of early colonialism and the missionary enterprise is deeply linked to episodes of forced conversions, servitude, and violence, which saw the active participation of missionaries. However, scholars have also learned a great deal about childhood and the experience of religion from the study of missionary work.

Most missionary organizations operated outside Europe on behalf of kings and political rulers, as well as the pope. In the attempt to bring new souls to Christianity and to salvation, their main aim was to educate, or civilize, non-Christians, imposing ideas of Christian monogamy and domesticity. Children were their preferred targets since they could more easily be molded and guided toward the right faith and way of life. Appropriately instructed in the word of God, young boys and girls would take back to their families their new faith, possibly generating new conversions among their relatives or within their own future families. They therefore represented a great hope for developing colonial societies and played a crucial role in any program of Christianization.[34] Missionary writings, letters, and reports regarding their work refer to children as the missionaries' frequent interlocutors and recipients of their teaching activities. The report written around the 1630 by the Franciscan Alonso Benavides—a Portuguese friar and the head of a Franciscan expedition supported by the Spanish monarchy in New Mexico—contains detailed descriptions of the friars' encounters and interaction with Indians from different nations. Here Indian children appear as a recognizable component of the audience of the friars' preaching, together with Indian mothers who came to listen to the friars' words, holding their babies in their arms (Figure 8.3).[35] Children also represented the objects and beneficiaries of healing miracles performed by the missionaries with the aid of crosses and rosaries. Successful miracles would openly show the magnitude of God, thus paving the way for multiple, voluntary conversions. Visual representations of missionaries at work clearly allude to the importance of children in the making of new Christian societies. A canvas illustrating the life of the Spanish Jesuit Francis Xavier features him preaching in Goa, before an audience of men, women, and children from different ethic backgrounds (Figure 8.4).[36]

Missionaries gave priority to elementary religious education and simple catechism. They emphasized the recitation of prayers and the gesture of the sign of the cross, and taught their pupils useful skills and European lifestyle and manners. French Jesuits and Ursulines based in Canada, for example, took special care in teaching Indian boys and girls to make sure that they behaved

FIGURE 8.3: *The Mystic Maria de Agreda Preaching to the Indians of New Mexico,* print, frontispiece of *Tanto que se Sacó* ... (Madrid, 1631, repr. 1730). Photo: author.

FIGURE 8.4: *St. Francis Xavier Preaching in Goa,* Lisbon, circa 1619, André Reinoso, oil on canvas, Santa Casa da Misericórdia de Lisboa/Museu de Sao Roque (inv. 96). Photo: Júlio Marques.

and dressed in French style. In order to achieve successful conversions of adults and children, missionaries sought to exploit the cultural continuities that existed between their own culture and that of the people whom they sought to convert, in the hope of bridging the gap between them. On the one hand, missionaries devoted their work to the education of children and hosted them in their monasteries, and convents, or taught them in classes organized outside churches. Most of these children had already been instructed in their own non-Christian religion, either at home by their parents or in local schools.[37] On the other hand, missionaries acknowledged that the colonial context posed new challenges, particularly the problem of overcoming linguistic barriers. In Spanish and French America, Franciscans, Jesuits, and Ursulines learned the native languages, sometimes directly from the children who were in their charge. They compiled dictionaries and translated catechism, prayers, and religious songs. Above all, they created texts that reproduced some of the narrative and visual motives that might be familiar to their audience. Catechisms published in sixteenth-century Mexico, for instance, followed in part the style and structure of Aztec didactic speeches, or contained colored images to explain Bible stories that sought to imitate the aesthetic and symbols of pre-Hispanic culture. Theatrical pieces were composed in Náhuatl and performed using live animals, real trees, and costumes, after the fashion of pre-Hispanic Aztec performances, so that the Indian audience might recognize some tracts of their own cultural background.[38]

But in spite of all efforts, the spiritual conquest of sixteenth- and early seventeenth-century America proved quite difficult. It was not easy to persuade the Indians to abandon their religion and devotional practices for an externally imposed faith. As the Jesuit Paul Le Jeune wrote in 1633, pondering his own experience in Canada, conversions might be reversible, particularly if they were not backed up by Christian marriages and families. According to Le Jeune, Indian "boys ... when they marry Savage girls or women accustomed to wandering into the woods, will, as their husbands, be compelled to follow them and thus fall back into barbarism, or to leave them, another way full of danger." On the contrary, "a little savage girl comfortably settled and married to some Frenchman or Christian Savage, would be a powerful check upon some of her wandering countrymen."[39] An echo to Le Jeune's fear can be found in the words of Marie de l'Incarnation, the first Ursuline to set foot in Canada, in 1639. In spite of the Ursulines' success in making their convent in Montreal a pole of attraction for native girls by developing devotional and learning activities, the young Indians educated there could not resist the temptation to run off into the wild, "like squirrels," and rejoin their families, thus nullifying the work patiently done by the nuns.[40]

The experience of the Puritans of New England offers yet another angle for looking at children and religion in the colonial world. Originally a group of religious dissenters from England, Puritans proposed an elaborate body of thought on family and childhood. They accorded to education a primary role in the spiritual development of individuals of all ages. Relying on the Augustinian notion of original sin and infant depravity, according to which children were born in sin and with a predisposition to selfishness, they believed that children needed to be faced with discipline and education from an early age. Indeed good conduct and godly behavior started within the household. Puritans had not moved to America with the primary purpose of converting non-Christians, but they did dedicate some effort to the evangelization of the Indians, who they saw as a crucial colonizing force. Indian children living in praying towns, as the Christian villages of New England were known, became the targets of their religious teachings and colonizing aims. The Hertfordshire-born John Eliot, and the author of the first American Bible translated into Algonquin, ministered to the Indians of Massachusetts. In reporting the progress of his work he observed the Indians' willingness to get to know God, something that even children as young as three years old expressed the desire to do. In practice, however, the Puritan concern for children's spiritual development was subjected to some form of ethnic discrimination. The Christianization of Indian children often consisted of removing them from their families and placing them into service in Anglo-American homes. Here they might assimilate Christian faith and the European lifestyle while providing a precious source of labor for the colonizers.[41]

PUBLIC RITUALS AND SPIRITUAL MEDIATION

Religion offered opportunities for participation in forms of collective and associative life. A variety of groups—from informal groups of children to more formalized association of young males, such as the French abbeys or the Catholic confraternities—actively participated in urban rituals and festivities, as well as in religious fights and episodes of ritual violence.[42] Examples from fifteenth- and sixteenth-century Europe attest to the role played by these groups as symbolic mediators of political, social, and religious conflicts within the city. In years of religious upheavals, groups of children from different cities were involved in violent attacks against reformed citizens, for example in France in the 1560s. For their part, children from Huguenot families organized assaults on churches, interrupting services to shout slogans against priests, circulating broadsheets against the celebration of the mass, and destroying holy images. In Catholic countries, disasters such as earthquakes, waves of plague, or Turkish incursions were met with public responses invoking the protection and mercy of God for the benefit of the city. Civic authorities responded by organizing penitential processions and public flagellations with the visible participation of children.[43]

To a certain extent, the reasons children performed such a public and intercessory role also lay in their religious and sacred status. According to a tradition rooted in the Bible, children's innocence and absence of experience of the world afforded them the privilege of hearing the voice of God. They were endowed with wisdom, spoke the truth, and acted as protectors of the community. The sacred status of children was revealed by their separated, often advanced place in public religious celebrations, which gave them equivalent status to women, men, nobility, and the clergy. Less favorably, children were also considered to be the victims of diabolical possession, as some known cases of witchcraft attest. In a sense, diabolical possession can be seen as the negative side of the condition of divine grace.[44]

Perhaps one of the most interesting aspects in the discussion of the sacred meaning of childhood revolves around child saints and godly children. These charismatic children were found in Catholic as well as Protestant Europe, from the Middle Ages to the seventeenth and eighteenth centuries. Saints were a completely familiar presence in Christian cultures. Hagiographical narratives dedicated great attention to saints' childhoods, focusing on those signs of divine perfection that prefigured their holiness: deep devotion, early visions, and the desire to escape parental control and to follow the divine call. Child saints, however, were more than future saints; they acquired the recognized status of sainthood at a very young age.[45] In the sixteenth and seventeenth centuries, we encounter a number of these holy children who publicly professed their faith in God, possessed prophetic and thaumaturgic power or, more simply, gained moral respect among their contemporaries. They denounced the sins and immoralities of their times, and exhorted their listeners to repent. Their fame rapidly spread through pamphlets and street ballads, though it was often quick to disappear. Scholars have underlined that the lives of these exceptional individuals attest to the status that adults accorded to children and the authority they gained within their communities, with the obvious collaboration, and manipulation, of relatives, acquaintances, and clerics. The English example of the sixteen-year-old Sarah Wright, whose twenty-three speeches of Grace were recorded on paper by a Baptist independent minister, and published in 1647, attests of the resonance that the prophetic power of a girl might gain in the community around her. Indeed, as her fame grew, her audience did too, and lords, ladies, local gentry, as well as servants, paid visits to her house, where she received and spoke to people with a linen cloth covering her eyes.[46] The book containing her speeches was reprinted seven times, all in the second half of the seventeenth century. Although other English cases of child prophets suggest that local political developments, and religious tensions within the community, might free up space for children's prophetic voices to be heard, they also suggest something else. Prophetic experiences may have represented socially acceptable means to gain public attention, since children, like women, could not access more conventional means of communication—like print and the pulpit.[47] Furthermore, prophecy may also have been a response, and a psychological reaction, that temporarily lifted children from a state of dependence. Their charisma freed them, even if just for a brief period of time, from submission to adult authority and even from class subordination, given that among these exceptional children there were also some from less wealthy backgrounds.

CONCLUSIONS

Religion penetrated the intimate realm of the household and left its signs on the home through the display of holy images and the creation of dedicated devotional spaces. Religious life and education were experienced in schools and the various institutions in which people of different age spent parts of their lives, and public civic life provided multiple occasions for participation in collective devotion. Class, gender, and ethnicity played crucial parts as elements of discrimination for shaping people's experience of religion, in old Europe as much as in the New World. The religious perspective adopted in this chapter invites some general speculations on the nature of childhood. The child was educated first within the household, under the guidance and authority of parents and tutors, and then outside it, or was dutifully instructed and maybe converted to Christianity by willing missionaries. This same child might turn into a source of divine knowledge, truth, and spiritual authority, by means of the charismatic experience. It is possible, therefore, to identify at least two different notions of childhood that were rooted in Christian cultures. Far from being exclusively a period of training and discipline, childhood was, as it has been suggested, also a holy and "innately prophetic" state.[48]

CHAPTER NINE

Health and Science

SUSAN BROOMHALL

Knowledge about the body and the natural world was to inform the under-standing and experience of childhood and family life in unassuming but impor-tant ways in the early modern period. Scholars have looked to developments in science and medicine as explanations for shifting forms of affectivity within family relationships. The study of the child as an object of scholarly scientific interest is one example. Demographic transitions, changing access to medical care from varied providers, and new therapies have also been analyzed to under-stand early modern family and childhood experiences. In reverse, researchers are increasingly attentive to the ways in which memories and meanings of childhood and family influenced how forms of knowledge about the body and natural world were constructed, and thus what practices and treatments were appropriate. Indeed, recent analyses reveal how significantly early modern science and health were governed by notions of domestic relationships and models of family organization.

STUDYING THE CHILD

It has been suggested that children were the focus of an emergent scientific interest in the early modern period that was distinct from gynecological knowl-edge and adult ailments. Certainly the economic exigencies of print demanded new and distinctive material, encouraging the development of a specific litera-ture concerning children from a wide range of authors including physicians, surgeons, midwives, educators, and laypeople. By contrast, contemporary Jewish medical texts did not distinguish childhood and adolescence as meaningful categories, perhaps as a result of the comparatively young age of adulthood and marriage in the Jewish tradition. Nevertheless, the volume of texts produced about health and healing generally suggests a widespread desire among early modern Christian, Jewish, and Muslim populations to protect and preserve loved ones. Most people probably learned natural and bodily knowledge from fellow family members, neighbors, midwives, traveling practitioners, and perhaps surgeons, but printed texts were rendering some aspects of university medicine accessible to first a Latinate, then progressively vernacular, readership. Furthermore, illustrations of herbs, surgical techniques, or distillation procedures brought aspects of university knowledge to an ever broader, perhaps even illiterate, public.

Early modern clinical discussion of the pathology of childhood diseases remained embedded in classical and Arabic medical traditions. Paolo Bagellardo's 1472 *Libellus de aegritudinibus et remediis infantium* compiled the first printed collection of childhood diseases, mostly from the views of Arabic physicians. Cornelius Roelans, a physician from Mechlin, drew from both medieval as well as ancient sources in his *Liber de aegritudinibus infantium*, printed in the mid-1480s. Pierre Tolet's 1538 *Opusculum Recens Natum de morbis puerorum* preferred Greek authors, signaling his alignment with the Hellenist revival within Renaissance medicine. However, the 1544 *Regimen infantium* of Gabriel Miron also added his experiences as a royal physician. Girolamo Mercuriale's 1583 *De Morbis Puerorum* reflected this growing trend of including personal observations, and even dissention, to the classical medical authorities. By the seventeenth century, the empirical observations of contemporary physicians were creating new subjects of study, such as Daniel Whistler's 1645 *De morbo puerili Anglorum quem patrio idiomate indigenae vocant the Rickets*.

A concurrent increase in vernacular pediatric texts by physicians promoted a wider readership for works focused on practical therapies. Eucharius Rösslin's 1513 *Den Swangern frawen und hebammen Rosgarten* circulated in multiple languages and many editions. While Luis Lobera de Ávila's 1551 *Libro del Regimiento de la Salud y de la Esterilidad de los hombres y mugeres y de las Enfermedades de les niños* helped to disseminate the work of earlier Arabic physicians and his learned contemporaries, Thomas Phayer insisted in his 1545 *Boke of Children* on revealing only information that was not the purview of midwives and other practitioners. Women were identified explicitly as a primary readership for such texts, opening up a broader range of caregivers to whom these could be marketed. In his 1565 *Cinq livres de la maniere de nourrir et gouverner les enfants des leur naissance,* the French physician Simon de Vallambert argued vigorously to his female readers that children could be protected from common diseases by good health care practices and that they were morally worth saving. Georgius Pictorius' 1576 *Frawenzimmer* merged treatment of common childhood illnesses together with a range of topics intended to interest women, such as cosmetic and beauty regimens.

Rising literacy rates among both practitioners and potential readers gradually changed the nature of infant care and childhood health discussions in print. It was not only readers who were increasingly drawn from beyond the university, but also authors with different forms of expertise. The verses of the Freiburg priest Heinrich von Louffenburg on the care of infants and children were published in Augsburg in 1491. Increasingly, an author's claim to experience allowed new practitioners to record their occupational expertise. The Basle surgeon Felix Würtz was one of the first authors to treat orthopedics in his 1563 *Practica der Wundartzney,* having witnessed the problems arising from swaddling too tightly. The French royal midwife, Louise Bourgeois, published the first vernacular discussion of a midwife's knowledge in her 1609 *Observations diverse sur la sterilité, perte de fruict, foecondité, accouchements et maladies des Femmes et Enfants nouveaux naix.*

The preoccupations and debates found in such texts provide insights into the ways in which gestation, infancy, childhood, and family life were understood. Although fetuses were not considered human in religious and legal texts until their form was recognizable as such, they were of interest in the medical imagination as soon as they were conceived. Roelans's discussion of fetal life sparked scientific examination of human life only days after conception. The fetus in utero was also a focus of the work of Gabrielis de Zerbis, who, in his 1537 *Anatomia Infantis,* used a study of fetuses aborted at different stages to chart uterine development. These studies visualized the life of the child in utero, which had previously been visible only through the growing belly until the moment of birth, in its own terms. Through natural as well as supernatural knowledge, uterine development was marked as a phase in which the positive and negative behavior of family members could have critical implications.

The question of whether women released seed during sex and to what purpose it was used in conception was also widely debated across the early modern world. Within the medical sources of the Ottoman Middle East, both male and female seed were seen to be necessary to conception. Abdallah Ibn al-Tayyib al-'Iraqi, writing in the 1630s, was not convinced by the monogenesis model emerging in Western Europe, which held that only men produced semen.[1] The latter view would have far-reaching consequences in both popular culture and British and North American legal systems, where it became important in the rejection of accusations of rape in cases in which conception had occurred. Interpreting Leviticus, the physician and biblical commentator Obadiah ben Jacob Sforno concluded that ovarian seed was critical only to the formation of female offspring.[2] However, following humoral theory, Ottoman sources like many in the West indicated instead that the key element for producing a male fetus was vital heat.[3] Ovarian seed played no role: females were simply the result of lack of heat.

Matters of profound importance to non-Christian Europeans have received little attention within early modern pediatric scholarship. For Jews and Muslims, circumcision was not simply a cultural and religious but also a complex medical issue. It was generally regarded as a praiseworthy health practice in Muslim sources where it was perceived as an Arab custom.[4] Prior to circumcision, a male infant was understood in Jewish culture to be at particular spiritual and physical risk. Indeed, in Jewish German communities, the ceremony of the *vakhnakht*, in which friends and family gathered around the child through the night before circumcision, was designed to protect the child from danger.[5] The physical transformation of the male infant body through circumcision thus performed a protective role. However, the obligation to circumcise in Judaism led to further medical discussions. Talmudic and rabbinical sources forbade the circumcision of a son whose two elder brothers had died following the procedure. The physician and Talmudist Moses Maimonides had earlier recognized in the *Mishneh Torah* that hemophilia was transmitted through the maternal heritage, but Yosef ben Ephraim Caro in his sixteenth-century commentary on Maimonides, the *Shuchan Aruch*, argued that circumcision should also be delayed for the sons of a father whose previous sons had bled to death, until their strength was established.[6]

Among the most common pediatric issues with which contemporary Christian medical texts wrestled was the matter of maternal and mercenary breast-feeding. For most physicians, maternal breast-feeding was both a moral and medical matter. The majority favored the practice to promote bonding between mother and child as well as in fulfillment of her moral responsibilities. However, most were realistic that many families, particularly those of the elite to whom their works were frequently addressed, would employ a wet nurse and therefore gave extensive advice on the choice of such women. Selection was critical, for contemporaries believed that physical and moral characteristics could be transmitted from wet nurse to child. Wet nurses for elite Spanish families, for example, were carefully selected to transmit ethnic and moral characteristics consistent with the purity of their blood. A father was advised to prevent a wife who was not Christian from feeding their child, lest she should transmit her faith.[7] Theories of transmission were shared by Muslim theorists, and in Shari'a law children fed by the same woman were considered blood relatives in view of shared attributes endowed by their nurse.[8]

Faith also defined the terms in which nursing was debated. Contemporaries across the religious spectrum shared a preference for maternal feeding, citing religious exemplars, rather than medical reasons. The Catholic Scevole de Sainte Marthe's 1584 *Paedotrophiae* and Protestant Countess of Lincoln's 1622 *Countess of Lincolnes Nurserie* both exhorted women not to reject their maternal duty. Lincoln had been overruled in the care of her own eighteen children but encouraged other women to insist forcefully on their Christian duty. The Virgin Mary was of course frequently depicted in Catholic and Counter-Reformation art and literature as a model for maternal breast-feeding. By the early seventeenth century, women who did not feed their own children were explicitly criticized by Spanish texts such as in physician Juan Gutiérrez de Godoy's 1629 work aiming "to show that women of good health are obliged to feed their children at their own breast."[9]

Opinion as to the age at which a child ought to be weaned from the breast varied greatly. Mercuriale's 1552 *Nomothesaurus seu ratio lactandi infantes* suggested continuation until the child was two-and-a-half years old and chastised those modern mothers who introduced pap to their infants as early as the third month.[10] While Florentine *ricordanze*, or family chronicles, suggested it was fathers who took responsibility for the decision to wean, the Spanish archbishop Antonio de Guevara in the 1529 *Relox de Príncipes* debated whether it was the duty of mothers or fathers to decide nursing and care of a child.[11] The English clergyman Ralph Josselin carefully noted in his diary the dates at which his children were weaned but gave little indication whose decision it was. In practice, evidence for length of breast-feeding suggests Mercuriale's admonitions were largely unwarranted. In the fifteenth-century wet-nursing system of Montpellier town council, children, mostly newborns at the time their wet-nursing was commenced, were breastfed for about twenty-one months.[12] The records of the fifteenth-century Ospedale degli Innocenti in Florence suggest standard practice was to wean foundling charges between eighteen and twenty-four months.[13] The average age at which weaning was commenced was 18.7 months for those wealthy Florentine families whose *ricordanze* remain to be studied.[14] In the Castilian village of Villabáñez, thirty-three months was the average interval between children in families with more than four children in the late sixteenth century, suggestive of similar maternal breastfeeding patterns that may have been economically advantageous to families.[15]

THE IMPACT OF DISEASE AND MORTALITY ON FAMILY AND CHILDHOOD EXPERIENCES

Among the most profound impacts on family experience in the early modern period was disease. Illness took an enormous toll on families, particularly on children. Perhaps half of all fifteenth-century Florentine children had died by age ten.[16] Current evidence suggests that the average size of early modern families across the life cycle was relatively small. Study of the 1427–1430 Florentine documents from the *catasto,* a census of the population for administrative and taxation purposes, reveals an average size of 3.9 people per urban household and 4.7 in rural ones.[17] The study of *libri de ricordanze* reveals just how many more children were born (and lost) to elite families, in which the relentless pattern of youthful marriage, wet-nursing, and almost annual pregnancy took its toll on women. Even the poorest families, known to us through their interactions with hospitals and poor relief bureaus, show only two to three living children per family.[18] Although Michele Savonarola noted smallpox and measles as the most prevalent killers of children, medical writers focused primarily on gastrointestinal and respiratory diseases in their pediatric tracts.[19] Within the Ospedale degli Innocenti in Florence, communicable diseases, along with accidents, were recorded as the most common causes of child mortality. In the sixteenth- and seventeenth-century English Bills of Mortality, early infancy (chrisomes) was itself listed as a category of death. The Florentine Ospedale recorded twenty-seven to thirty-two percent mortality rates in its initial years of operation in 1445–1447, with chances of survival greatly increasing after the first year of life.[20] Sixteenth-century data for Christ's Hospital in London indicates relatively low mortality among its inmates, although they were notably older than the newborns of the Ospedale.[21] In later sixteenth-century Tours, the death rate among pauper infants at wet-nurse may have been as low as seventeen percent.[22] Children of the Florentine elite (often wet-nursed with less wealthy families) experienced only marginally better rates of survival than those raised within institutions.[23] Early modern natural and medical knowledge offered little defense to the ravages of widespread communicable diseases.

Crises periods in which yearly mortality was ten percent higher than the norm were, however, a different phenomenon that could affect families in particular ways. Harvest failure, grain prices, even political and cultural practices could have devastating effects on the accessibility of food, leading to famine. Levies by the Spanish in New Mexico on both the crops and labor of Pueblo Indians left those communities unable to produce sufficient food.[24] Malnourished poor families and children were more susceptible to disease, making it difficult for historians to connect famine directly to increased mortality. They were also more inclined to migration in search of subsistence, encouraging contemporary perceptions linking the poor to disease with important consequences for the development of poor-relief policy. Famine and plague were experienced successively in many parts of Europe, the latter provoking continual episodes of mortality crises across early modern Europe. At least five waves of the plague in London between 1563 and 1665 each killed a fifth of the city's total population. Felix Platter's records of plague cases in Basle from 1609 to 1611 show a mortality rate of 61.9 percent, and 30 percent of the Venetian population was lost to the plague in 1630–1631.[25] German parish records between 1560 and 1640 suggest that plague waves were rarely restricted by differing economic, social, and cultural interactions between towns.[26] Rates of death from plague within families and their dependents were likely high, especially in areas where quarantine enclosed entire households on suspicion of a single case. Such social practices make plague's patterns of mortality and spread difficult to ascertain. Plague also affected expressions of what it was to be a family. Because of municipal restrictions on personal liberty, London families were unable to enact the usual rites of mourning, organizing burials, and participating in funeral processions. In some cities, Paris and Florence among them, suspected victims of the plague were not permitted to be buried in churches, much to the distress of those with personal and familial connections to particular sites.[27]

Mortality crises on a massive scale appear even more starkly in the colonization of the Americas. Communities of indigenous families were obliterated through diseases such as smallpox and measles carried to biologically virgin soils and their comparatively genetically homogenous populations. In the absence of quantitative data, scholars' estimates of the total degree of population devastation have been highly controversial. Debate about both high and low pre-Columbian population estimates have been arguably underpinned by theories of indigenous racial and cultural inferiority or of Western exploitation. Pre-Columbian populations were already exposed to a wide variety of diseases, and the tendency toward increased living density and more sedentary lifestyles was already raising morbidity and mortality rates.[28] Nevertheless, eyewitness accounts of explorers, traders, missionaries, and the oral traditions of the aboriginal peoples demonstrate the enormity of the impact of European biological presence in the Americas. Fertility reduction as well as increased mortality exacerbated aboriginal population decline. Cultural and social destruction of Indian family structures followed swiftly in the wake of colonialism. The removal of children, and missionaries' encouragement of marriage between First Nations people and Europeans to create Christian *métis* populations, acted to breed out aboriginal genetic heritage.

Indigenous populations did respond to the new diseases and family dynamics they experienced. In the 1630s, for example, Iroquois depopulation was met by forcible integration of captives stolen from Huron enemies into Iroquois families as replacements for dead relatives.[29] However, cultural expectations of comfort and care among kin, requiring that relatives should gather round the ill, enabled the spread of infections. With the elderly, particularly susceptible to disease and malnutrition caused by European invasions, was also lost the collective heritage of therapies even for local illnesses that had traditionally passed from one generation to the next. For some groups, engaging with Europeans meant shifting from subsistence or farming activities to those profitable in the new economy of exchange. Lost cultural memory of traditional survival techniques, as well as reliance on Europeans for food, left them highly vulnerable.

For Europeans, the perceived physical weakness of indigenous populations was in part responsible for the introduction of Africans as slaves. The high resistance of Africans to illnesses such as malaria and yellow fever was significant in the Caribbean. Populations progressively shifted to small numbers of European men, separated from their own families, but enacting a form of paternalism over larger numbers of African American slaves on plantations, which contrasted with the colonial migration of both sexes and of entire families to North American settlements.[30] Contemporaries such as Richard Ligon, writing of a visit to Barbados in 1647, did not consider either the West Indies or the southern colonies of what would later form part of the United States to be healthy for permanent European settlement. By contrast, records from colonial New England suggest comparable or lower mortality rates to contemporary England, and high fertility rates in populations with very low proportions of never-married individuals.[31] The soils of the northeastern region enabled the stable production of familiar crops without the same pressures of population, prices, and politics experienced in Europe.

While information about the demography and even the health conditions of slave populations is abundant in trading records, little documentation exists about marital and familial relationships between slaves. The family life of slaves in the Americas was jeopardized by high mortality rates, particularly in the first years after arrival, as well as lack of recognition by Europeans who critiqued the practice of polygyny as evidence of African promiscuity. Even when slave owners invoked such beliefs for their own sexual benefit, slave fertility typically remained low, through malnutrition, hard labor, ill health, and high infant mortality, as well as a result of partners and parents being separated on different properties and by resale.[32] When the supply of new Africans was later cut to North America, plantation owners would explore slave breeding to increase profits, either by offering incentives or direct manipulation of female slave fertility.

What it meant to be a family in the early modern world was therefore to belong to a small but deeply unstable social unit. Nuclear families were uncommon, the precariousness of life notable. Memoirs, funerary monuments, and descriptions of indigenous mourning rituals reveal the heartfelt grief shown for loved ones. When he came to write his memoirs, the physician Felix Platter's sorrow for the death of his seventeenth-year-old sister Ursula, which had occurred some sixty years earlier, was still palpable.[33] Social history approaches and the history of mentalities have opened up new ways of understanding early modern family life and how families spoke of expectations of illness and death. When Josselin's infant son Ralph died in 1648, Josselin appeared to note the child's passing with stoicism: "it was the youngest, and our affections not so wonted unto it: the lord, ever the lord learne mee wisedome and to knowe his mind in this chastisement."[34] Yet his meticulous attention to the record of his son's funeral is suggestive of an alternative mode of affective expression.[35] Scholars have carefully studied such early modern emotional forms, effectively dispelling the notion that familial affectivity was lessened by high rates of infant mortality.

FAMILY AS AN AGENT OF HEALTH CARE

Perhaps even more important for the health of early modern families than medical tracts and therapies were everyday nutritional and hygiene behaviors. These have received far less attention in early modern scholarship, partly because they were often held in oral traditions and have been perceived as difficult to evaluate and historicize. Such views are now being challenged by scholars who argue that recipe books are indicative of the understanding and use of learned, lay, and practical bodily and natural knowledge in the home. Familial care was a vital part of the early modern health system that operated regardless of social position. The humanist author Juan-Luis Vivès was insistent that elite women should not leave the care of their families to servants in his 1524 *De institutione feminae Christianae*. Lady Margaret Hoby's diary indicates the range of medical tasks for family, neighbors, and tenants that elite women might perform. Physicians Charles Estienne and Jean Liébault's much reprinted and progressively expanded *L'Agriculture, et Maison Rustique* argued that economy demanded that country housewives be familiar with a range of natural remedies to aid the household in illness, while leaving more complex remedies to urban physicians.

Families were expected both to diagnose and treat themselves in a range of medical situations, and authors prepared texts to support them in these therapeutic activities. Published household literature in England increased over the late sixteenth century, instructing women on a combination of medicine, cookery, and household science. By 1600, female authorship emerged, such as Elizabeth Grey, Countess of Kent's 1653 *A Choice Manuall or Rare and Select Secrets of Physick & Chyrurgery*. Here, diet was conceptualized as a key component of preventative as well as curative medicine. This printed literature reflected the existence of a commonplace of the early modern English home that is now becoming well documented: the manuscript recipe book. Women held collections of regimens, herbals, and recipe collections that were practical working books serving families in their homes. Their additions and annotations are now considered important indicators of revisions and evolutions of this domestic expertise.

Similarly, early modern cleanliness has received little scholarly attention as a contribution to health and well-being of families and children. Yet theories of hygiene that understood the skin as permeable to disease made fabric and clothing critically important as protective barriers.[36] Like the oils and waxes applied to newborns, swaddling bandages offered protection for delicate infant skin. Although swaddling clothes have been generally overlooked in modern research, they were much more noteworthy to contemporary commentators. Ralph Josselin recorded the removal of his daughter Rebekah from swaddling bands at seven weeks in his diary of family life. Linens were included among the birth accessories compiled by expectant parents. By the eighteenth century, swaddling strips would be used as evidence of maternal care and preparation by women accused of infanticide, indicating their normative presence as appropriate newborn care in early modern societies.

Likewise, there is little scholarly discussion of the contrasting hygienic habits in Jewish and Christian cultures. Jewish sources noted how Christians did not frequently bathe. While the Jewish humanist scholar Leone Modena recalled horsing around with a friend near a commonplace ritual bath as a five-year-old, the ceremonial first immersion into bathwater of six-year-old Louis XIII was recorded by his physician as a significant event.[37] As early modern Christian culture shifted for its cleansing away from the bathhouse to the application of fresh linen on the body, it points to the importance (but as yet poorly documented) role of domestic labor in hygienic practices. Contemporary art, particularly from the Dutch Republic, provides potentially important insights into the cultural perceptions of domestic hygiene work such as cleaning, laundering, and delousing of fellow family members. Women's household management practices included an everyday but nonetheless skillful range of activities designed to soothe the body, the mind, and the atmosphere of family life in the home.

Views of familial roles and relationships formed a vital part of medical and natural knowledge during this period. All the available sources indicate that women were expected to—and did indeed—provide the majority of health care within the home. The author of the 1600 household and husbandry manual *Le théâtre d'agriculture et mésnage des champs,* Olivier de Serres, suggested that his discussion of therapeutics was more appropriate to women than men because their natural temperament was charitable. He envisaged a range of sicknesses that did not warrant the attention of a member of the professional medical community. The work of gender scholars has revealed how early modern terminology used to describe women's roles within the family as mothers, nurses, and matrons has obscured their health care work.

Family was a significant resource for medical care. In Jewish communities that lacked access to hospital facilities, the principle of *bikur cholim* enjoined family, relatives, and friends to visit the sick as a key mechanism for assistance. In the case of the mentally ill, few facilities existed for long-term support, making family the primary instrument for decision making, treatment, and support as poor-relief and criminal records have shown. Investigations into demonic possession and sanctity highlight that families made the first steps toward natural or supernatural diagnoses of their loved ones and sought relief accordingly. Family could also be the cause of mental illness. The loss of a life partner was recognized as a cause of melancholy and ill health of the kind that the Jewish merchant Glikl of Hameln described after the death of her husband, while greensickness might be cured in some cases by marrying adolescent female sufferers, fulfilling their expected social and physical role as wives.[38] Mental disturbances could thus be caused by familial relationships as well as by the lack of them.

Families were influential in the selection of medical attendants and advice, as is evident by physicians' pique when women judged their abilities and advised friends and relatives about the suitability of university-trained practitioners. In his 1612 *Ignorant Practisers of Physicke,* John Cotta devoted a chapter to female counselors and recommenders of medicine in which the head of household was warned to be wary of his wife. Family members also elected to seek treatment beyond, or in addition to, the professionally trained medical personnel, seeking intercession from saints, through pilgrimage, offerings, and prayers, as well as a myriad of alternative health practitioners. Anne of Brittany's inventories reveal that she sent amulets, icons, coins, and lizard tongues, as well as physicians, to safeguard the health of her children and their nurses.[39] Through their decisions about what medical help they required and which practitioners were most suitable to provide it, families—and especially, it seems, women—made important judgments about early modern science and health care.

FAMILY AS A SOURCE FOR NATURAL KNOWLEDGE, MEDICAL PRACTICE, AND THEORY

Childbirth and newborn health were areas of medical care in which women's experiences as mothers were particularly valued. Although physicians generally insisted that their theoretical training and focus on disease causation gave them superiority in matters of medicine, when it came to the treatment of women and children, they typically declined intervention in favor of midwives and mothers. In the southern German cities, from the fifteenth century, midwives were overseen in practice by boards of women who were selected by experience and class to create the patrician-based *Ehrbare Frauen* and later in the sixteenth century, the middle-class *Geschworene Weiber*.[40] This was a pattern familiar to many areas without a local university medical faculty such as London, where licensing was ecclesiastical rather than medical at this period. In the Puritan colonies of North America, religious ideologies rendered childbirth a strictly female matter.[41] At the same time in Paris, however, midwifery was becoming an expertise learned through supervised training rather than life experience. A 1556 royal edict concerning criminal acts such as infanticide and abortion also stipulated tightening the conditions under which midwives worked. Statutes from 1560 required theoretical training by a surgeon to accompany the conventional apprenticeship. Once the skills and knowledge of midwifery were made distinct from female bodily experiences, it was possible for men to argue their expertise in the field. By the seventeenth century, the male *accoucheur* had developed as an alternative birthing assistant competing for elite French clientele.[42] By contrast, in the nascent colonies of New England and New France, which lacked guild restrictions and were poorly served by university-trained practitioners and medical institutions, the role of midwives expanded to a more general health care role.[43]

The family experiences of practitioners were themselves important in creating their understanding of domestic life and dynamics. Physicians drew on their memories of childhood and their own family histories in their texts in important ways. Pictorius recalled his wife finding threadworms in the anus of his own children in his *Frawenzimmer*. He and Mercuriale devoted seven and ten chapters respectively to the topic of worms alone, indicating something of the contemporary concern for this particular childhood scourge. Modena, for one, described in his autobiography *Hayyei Yehudah* how he had been plagued by worms as a child. Personal experience of family life was not just a source of understanding but might also, it seems, act as a source of authority for particular medical opinions. In medical writing, subject matters were also slowly shifting from those favored by the ancients to those topics that were relevant to early modern life as medical authors saw and experienced it. A subject introduced at this period was that of treatment for burns, included in Omnibus Ferrarius's 1577 *De arte medica infantium*. Burn injuries and deaths were frequent within the early modern home, and girls were particularly susceptible to them because of their greater restriction to the domestic environment.

The concept of family could also act as a source of scientific understanding. Cultural and intellectual historians have recently begun to examine how family ideologies came to govern scientific perception. The emerging agrarian science of husbandry promoted a vision of the patriarchal father presiding over the domestic unit. The early modern study of bee colonies was typically constructed according to the organizational model of the patriarchal statecraft, mistaking the queen for a king bee. When Charles Butler identified in his 1609 *The Feminine Monarchie* that the queen bee was in fact female, he simply recast their social structure as a perfect model of industrious feminine domesticity. Within contemporary understanding of husbandry, bees were in other ways problematic. They were not properly domestic for they did not require human assistance for their subsistence, reproduction, or care. Thus, early modern texts offered methods to retain bees to one's household, including tanging (banging household pots and pans to freeze the flight of bees) and telling the bees (informing bees of deaths or marriages within the domestic unit, to prevent their flight in search of the missing family members).[44] The recommendations of such husbandry and agrarian texts were underpinned by contemporary notions of family roles and relationships.

In more concrete ways, the family could also serve as a site for the production and transfer of natural knowledge. The analysis of manuscript recipe books helps us to understand the household as a knowledge community whose conventions of shared authorship and proof through experimental practice contrasted with the university scientific traditions of individually authored and more abstract scholarship. Rather than a discrete form of expertise, these texts demonstrate that the domestic sphere produced knowledge integrating information from family, friends, professional practitioners, and the commercial sector, requiring its own instruments and equipment. The women who developed kitchen medicine were active producers of a contemporary natural knowledge that combined abstract and practical features.[45]

Scholars are discovering new ways to consider the impact of domestic ideologies and household spaces in natural knowledge creation. Within the bachelor communities of the university, scholars recast their role as parental figures by taking on boarders. However, others scholars' research was produced and communicated through the household, beyond the university communities and before the advent of exclusive scientific societies. Indeed, the historiography of Protestant science has carefully studied the impact of Martin Luther's casual remark about the work of Copernicus made at the dinner table that later appeared in his *Tischreden*.[46] Scholars such as John Dee, Mary Sidney Herbert, and Lady Grace Mildmay constructed laboratories and experiments in their homes. Family members were enlisted in the enterprise of science in their roles as wives, sons, and daughters, as both helpers and objects of study. John Dee's record of his wife Jane's menstrual cycle as a site for scientific study mirrored the interests of the physician Thomas Platter in attending the delivery of his first child. Jane also worked as a participant in the laboratory team based in her household.[47] Establishing authority of the domestic scientific household was problematic, though. Suggesting the powerful ideology of feminine domestic authority, John Aubrey opined in his biographical study that the wife of the mathematician William Oughtred "would not allow him to burne candle after supper, by which meanes many a good notion is lost, and many a problem unsolved."[48]

Additionally, the family served as a mechanism for the transmission of natural and medical knowledge in important ways. Many unregulated healers insisted that they had received training from their mothers and female relatives, as did Isabel de Montoya when she was called before the Inquisition of New Mexico in the 1660s.[49] Familial heritage as a pathway to medical professions was common across Jewish, Islamic, and Christian groups in Europe. Careers were established through marriage and inheritance of scientific equipment, laboratories, and even investigations. Social and prosopographical studies have examined sources such as wills, inventories, marriage patterns, and letters to understand family inheritance of natural knowledge. The statutes of some medical guilds allowed widows to maintain a husband's clientele and pass it onto their children, creating the possibility of familial dynasties managing medical knowledge. In England, the secret of the forceps was passed from father to son within the Huguenot refugee family of the Chamberlens. Scientific positions could be expected to pass from father to son in the university world too. Much to the amusement of his students, Thomas Clayton, who succeeded his father in the Regius Professorship of Medicine at Pembroke College Oxford in 1647, could not endure the sight of a bloodied body.[50]

Family background could both privilege and exclude groups from forms of natural and medical knowledge. In Spain, Muslim converts to Catholicism could not attend universities, and their medical traditions and health care provisions were thus segregated. Jewish converts to Catholicism were permitted to attend, however, and they were active in medical study and practice. Universities offered such students opportunities for social mobility and acted as centers for their own cultural knowledge. As physicians across early modern Europe, they wrote of a distinctive Jewish medical acumen and in defense of Jewish practitioners more broadly. Juan Huarte de San Juan, for example, rejected aspersions on Jewish capabilities for science in his 1575 work, *Examen de ingenios para los sciencias*, maintaining that Jews had a particular physical suitability and mental aptitude for medicine borne of their cultural and biological inheritance of servitude and affliction.[51]

CONCLUSIONS

Medical and natural knowledge were underpinned by assumptions about family as a model for the natural world, for scientific teamwork, for medical care, for authority to develop ideas, and for transmission of them. As a source of knowledge, family experiences, identities, and spaces were vital. In return, evidence produced by lay and university-trained knowledge communities provides us with insights into the expectations of life for children and family. They offer views about which family members could provide health care or assistance with natural knowledge work, the illnesses and experiments in which they could participate, and those matters that were considered beyond the domestic sphere. Family members, especially women, were embedded in medical and natural knowledge communities as theorists and practitioners who could determine the kind and quality of professional interactions within the household. Significantly, personal experiences of childhood and family life were a critical touchstone for how the natural world and bodily health were understood. Some were inspired to create knowledge because of their family lives; others grounded their particular focus in their identities as husbands, fathers, sons, sisters, wives, and mothers; and for yet others these roles provided a justification of their authority to speak in this domain. Family and childhood experiences were at once the product of early modern health and science, as well as among the most potent forces shaping these rich and varied knowledge traditions.

CHAPTER TEN

World Contexts

JAMES CASEY

One of the marks of a civilized people, thought the apostle of the American Indians Bartolomé de las Casas around 1550, was an ordered family structure, and in particular the "good and reasonable customs, in conformity with the natural law," observed in connection with marriage. By this standard, he argued, the Aztecs were a civilized, not a barbarian, people. Meanwhile, "the no small care and attention they devoted to the formation and proper rearing of their offspring" was further testimony to "the prudent rule and good order of this most rational people."[1]

Attempting to understand the other was one of the great challenges facing Europeans in the so-called Age of Discovery. This chapter seeks to explore the diversity of the childhood experience, and in particular how Europeans attempted to relate what they found to their own assumptions about family life. Most of the observers were Christian missionaries, and that has its own significance. "Nothing has impressed me more nor seemed more worthy of praise and recall," wrote the Jesuit Josè de Acosta in 1590, "than the care and good order with which the youth were brought up under the Mexica." For was not education "the whole future promise of a commonwealth"?[2] It was a characteristic note that found many an echo in the Europe of the Renaissance and of the twin religious upheavals of the Protestant Reformation and the Catholic Counter-Reformation. For Martin Luther, the family had come to stand as the very pillar and emblem of a godly life; for the Jesuits, the family and the school came to assume a moral significance that they had never quite enjoyed before.

The impact of these developments within Europe must be borne in mind as one looks at the attitudes to ways of doing things beyond Christendom.

And it was not just attitudes that were at stake. The considerable migration of peoples that followed in the wake of the voyages of exploration led in two different directions: one was the attempt to create in the New World a reproduction—more refined, more godly, but still a reproduction—of the family life of the European; the other was the involuntary emergence of a new kind of hybrid civilization, that of the mestizo, blending the values of the Indian and the European. Finally, one must consider the effects of the colonial experience itself: the consequences for society of the rearing of its elites from an impressionable age among companions of a race deemed inferior. What was borrowed and what was lost in the coming together of the populations of the world?

NEW WORLDS, YOUNG PEOPLE

One of the striking features of the premodern world is the youthfulness of its people. From the evidence of censuses, it is likely that a good third of the population in any part of Europe would not yet have reached their fifteenth or sixteenth birthday. By contrast, barely one person in twenty was over sixty years of age, and with orphanage and remarriage of widowers, up to a fifth of households sheltered the offspring of more than one couple. The household might be small in scale, but it was complex. The wealthier the family, the more servants they would have, and these were sometimes illegitimate children or poor relatives. Indeed, in seventeenth-century Poland, orphans would be assigned by the authorities to the serf family nearest in blood. Outside Europe, in Asia and America, the polygamy of the rich—always, of course, a minority—led to yet more complex arrangements. Celibacy was generally frowned on outside Christendom, and marriage tended to be universal and entered into when the girl, especially, was in her teens. But high mortality at all ages, combined with a feeling that a married couple should generally cook and sleep and live separately (though they might work together and share land), generally ensured that the experience of growing up in most civilizations was centered on some kind of nuclear family household. The exceptions we shall note in due course.

For most of the population most of the time there was little privacy. The seventeenth-century missionary Bernabé Cobo in his extensive travels through the Andes was appalled at the poverty of housing (though the situation in his native Spain at the time can hardly have been much better). The native houses resembled huts—"all simple, one storey constructions with a single room, which is at the same time entrance hall, living room, bedroom, pantry, wine cellar, kitchen and even stable." And elsewhere he remarked: "Everyone from a single household, both parents and children, normally sleeps inside one *chusi* (the woollen blanket which was doubled up as ground sheet and cover)."[3] Interesting here is the viewpoint of a European, whose own society at this time was just beginning the amplification and diversification of its dwelling places.

But the real focus of most of the world's family systems was less the house than the patrimony and the kinship group. In all preindustrial societies, the wider family conferred status and protection and access to property, either through marriage or through inheritance from the older generation. In this respect Europeans would find themselves at ease in many parts of the world. But reverence for the ancestors was carried by some cultures to extremes that merited comment. "A universal custom among all the Indian nations," noted the Jesuit Bernabé Cobo, "was to pay more attention to the dwelling that they were to have after death than to the one they had during their lifetime."[4] And he went on to describe the awesome commemoration of the dead among the Inca, involving the immolation of infants. More admiration was evoked in his fellow Jesuit, Saint Francis Xavier, by the customs of the Japanese, in particular their sense of inherited honor. "On no account would a poverty-stricken gentleman marry with someone outside the gentry, even if he were given great sums to do so," he wrote in 1549, "because they consider that they would lose their honor."[5] Audible here is the sigh of a Spanish gentleman at the greedy individualism of Renaissance Europe.

Much of the description of the tribal peoples by Europeans of the time seems to reflect what later ethnography would classify as matrilineal and sometimes matriarchal societies. Among the tribal Indians, though children were generally reared in small family groups, their basic loyalty was to their mother's clan, and above all to a kind of blood brother, the companion whom they had chosen out of the rambling network of their maternal cousins. The famous Jesuit missionary to the Iroquois, Joseph François Lafitau, pointed in his seminal treatise of 1724 to a crucial factor differentiating the experience of most Europeans from that of the natives of North America. "The husband and wife do not leave their family and lodge to set up a family and residence apart," he tells us. Instead, each counted as being of the wife's lodge and family, not the husband's.[6] Living in long houses that might shelter up to a dozen matrilineal families, comprising some fifty or sixty individuals, the Iroquois likely experienced childhood, growing up, and solidarity with others very differently than the Europeans who came to live among them. Among the Pántagoras, noted another missionary, women were married off by their nearest male kinsman, while remaining under the authority of the latter rather than of their spouse. If there was a dispute between man and wife, the latter would go back to her brother's people, taking her children with her, "and the fathers show no emotion nor try to stop them." This explained, he thought, why "the women are so free and even impudent ... getting up to mischief, which even though they know about it their husbands cannot punish."⁷ Hence perhaps the great indiscipline of Indian youngsters, also noted by observers, and the fact that Indian women lost no status—indeed, rather gained prestige—by having children by European men out of wedlock, as Las Casas remarked.

An accompanying feature of most Indian societies outside the empires of the Aztec and Inca was that, according to Columbus, "the women appear to work more than the men," as the Portuguese settlers were to find among the Tupinamba of Brazil, where the women did the agricultural work and the men confined themselves to hunting. These were, after all, still largely hunter-gatherer cultures, albeit semisedentary, lacking much property to pass on in the way of inheritance. "As far as I could see," noted Columbus, "whatever a man had was shared among all the rest."

The advance of arable farming, fixed settlement, and trade had led to the growing importance of the father among the Aztecs and Incas, controlling—though not completely—the transmission of land from one generation to the next. But patriarchy was loosely structured where the need for protection still fostered the solidarity of the clan. On the frontiers of urban civilization, huddling together in a dangerous environment still made sense. The conquistadors experienced the same need and had to adjust their household forms accordingly. Thus the chronicler of the conquest of the Aztecs, Bernal Díaz del Castillo obtained permission to arm his household in Guatemala against his fellow Spaniards (1551), while in 1602 we find the president of the Guadalajara high court accused of giving shelter to "nine sons, sons-in-law or grandsons, not to mention cousins of cousins and a host of Spanish friends and dependants of all these people."⁸

In these frontier territories general disorder could be linked to a weakly integrated family structure. Ireland in 1595 struck the poet and colonizer Edmund Spenser as being of this sort. Irish youngsters, "being (as they all be) brought up idly without awe of parents, without precepts of masters, without fear of offence, not being directed nor employed in any course of life which may carry them to virtue," sought to imitate the lawless daring portrayed for them in story and song.⁹ Given that land was held by the kin group and not by the individual, the rules of succession tended to favor the most able relative—a brother, perhaps, rather than the eldest son. Private armies and cattle raids flourished. One of the aims of the civilizing process that the English administration was keen to introduce into Ireland was domesticity: to settle the seminomadic pastoral clans on surveyed, individually owned plots of land (carefully reduced in size by about a third, it has to be added, with the argument that settled farmers would farm more intensively than pastoralists would). Something similar was being tried by the Spaniards through the resettlement program (the *reducciones*).

Violence was a feature of preindustrial society. Attempts to contain it included cathartic rituals in which youth had a prominent role. As part of the ritual year by which the community governed its affairs, those in authority would be reminded for a day or a week of the transitory nature of power. Thus, at carnival every year in Europe, the common people could freely usurp the clothes and bearing of their superiors, and every January, in memory of Herod's slaughter of the Jewish infants at the time of Christ's birth, a junior chorister would be solemnly invested by the bishop or sometimes the dean of the chapter with the regalia of earthly power, processing from the church in what often turned out to be a riotous encounter with the youth of the town. Prelates were found who defended these celebrations as morally uplifting, an exercise in humility, in face of the attacks mounted against them in the age of the Reformation. The youth were seen, then, almost by definition as the irresponsible members of society, entrusted with that supreme gift of making fun of a topsy-turvy world. There are echoes of this attitude in other world cultures as well. The adolescent in the Arab world, if he came from a poorer, weakly structured family, tended to join the street gangs that were always to be feared in urban riots. Though they called themselves *al-chuttâr* (the sharp-witted), they tended to be classed by the authorities simply as *al-ahdâth* (youngsters).[10] There was an understanding, then, of the distinctive nature of childhood as an antechamber to the adult world—a time, if not of innocence, at least of an imperfect discernment of right and wrong. This was to change, as the Europeans of the Age of Discovery began to look on childhood less as a stage in the cycle of life and more as a preparation for adulthood.

ATTITUDES TOWARD CHILDREN

After something close to half a millennium of propaganda and conflict, the Christian church in the West had by 1500 managed, with more or less success, to impose its idea of the family on a turbulent lay population. Marriage was to be a sacrament, not primarily for the procreation of children but, like the Holy Family in Nazareth, a moral support along the path of salvation.

Marriage was supposed to be freely entered into by the man and the woman. While respecting the strategic considerations of family interest and parental wishes, it was not be subject to these. For marriage was an unbreakable, life-time bond between one man and one woman. And it was expected to serve the good of the wider community, hence the formal prohibition of marrying anyone related within four degrees of kinship (i.e., the descendants of the same great-great-grandfather on either the mother's or the father's side). The aim of these prohibitions, theologians explained from the time of Saint Augustine onward, was to spread *caritas* ("good fellowship") throughout the society at large, avoiding the narrowing of solidarity to the kinship group. It was a remarkable system that through much dispute, agony, and conflict helped ultimately to fashion the individualism of European life.

That pioneering observer of Ming China, the Jesuit Matteo Ricci (1552–1610), ascribed much of the misery he found—slavery, poverty, prostitution, infertility—to an unnaturally early age at marriage: fifteen for men, he thought, instead of the twenty that he regarded as normal in his native Italy. Polygamy was a scourge, as was the selling of children whom parents could not support.[11] Better, thought Ricci, to follow the example of the Europeans, who married late and sometimes not at all, devoting their energies to spreading the word of God among all mankind (a nice justification of imperial outreach).

It was a familiar Christian attitude. The great apostle of the Indians of New Spain, Fray Toribio de Benavente (called "Motolinia," or "The Poor One," by the Indians because of his humility) noted in his treatise of 1541 that differing approaches to family life were one of the main impediments to the conversion of the natives. Some of the chiefs had up to 200 wives, he observed, leading to a serious imbalance of the sexes among the rest of the population. They would argue with the friars that the Spaniards also kept many women in their house-holds, "and if we said that they served as maids, they retorted, 'so do ours' ... since they kept them all busy weaving blankets."[12] Women, in fact, constituted a significant criterion of status and wealth for their husbands. In this vein, they played a crucial role as gifts in the Aztec and Inca empires, distributed to successful warriors before the Spaniards came, and after their arrival on the scene, as a means of attaching the conquistadors to alliance with local tribes.

However latitudinarian missionary practice might have been on the subject of marriage—and some acknowledgment that Indian matrimony had its own logic was forthcoming from Acosta, for example—the ultimate objective was to instill in the Indians the values of European civilization. The resettlements undertaken in Mexico and Peru were designed in part to create an environment in which a European family structure—monogamous, nuclear, and intimate—could flourish. Thus in 1567 the magistrate Juan de Matienzo set out the ideal grid pattern of the new towns where the Indians were to be resettled in Peru. They would have streets that led directly to the central plaza, surrounding which would stand the parish church, the office of the town council, the hospital, and the homes of the local governor and priest. Indian houses were to have two or three separate rooms, so that parents might sleep away from their offspring, and to have beds to prevent them from sleeping rough on the floor, and the front door was to open directly onto the street to facilitate supervision of who was living with whom.[13]

Not long before, the Franciscan Motolinía found much to praise in the poverty and simplicity of the Mexican Indian: "They are, of all the world's peoples," he thought, "those least concerned with acquiring and leaving an estate to their children." And he found the youngsters living "good and healthy lives, growing up well-built, tough, strong and cheerful," in spite of the harsh conditions.[14] Observers agreed that the Indians married very young: barely fifteen years of age in the case of Iroquois girls, twenty-one for their men folk. Breast-feeding among the Mexican Indians observed by Las Casas, as among the Iroquois studied by Lafitau, lasted for up to four years, inhibiting sexual relationships. All of this led to a fairly low fertility rate. Indian women, wrote Lafitau, "although of a strong and robust constitution, have not the fecundity seen elsewhere," not least among the French and English colonists at this time. In Ming China, in spite of early and universal marriage, fathers could expect to leave five or six offspring, spread perhaps over several marriages given the high rate of mortality and remarriage. In India one notes a fairly similar pattern: brides of sixteen, marriages interrupted by early death after fifteen years or so, and an issue of seven or eight children.[15]

European interest in Asian family structure was limited to the preoccupations of Christian missionaries. By contrast, Europeans had a more direct interest in the Americas, whose apparently empty lands beckoned settlers. Thousands of Europeans made the voyage to the New World, taking with them the principles of family life that had marked their own upbringings. This migration was more evident in the case of England than of Spain. Over the seventeenth century, some 530,000 English men and women settled in North America, a considerable proportion of a population of perhaps 4,000,000. Spain, by contrast, with 6,000,000 people, saw 250,000 leave for the New World during the sixteenth century. It was a serious enough hemorrhage for a country already bled white by the exodus of 7,000 or more of its young men every year to the battlefields of Europe.[16] Settling in a new world, with an apparent scarcity of native inhabitants and an abundance of land, the New

Englanders were able to set up for themselves at a relatively young age. Girls would marry around twenty years of age on average, the men folk somewhat later at twenty-seven (because there were more men than women in the early colonies). These figures are a good five years below the levels found back in the mother country. And these youthful households were prolific in offspring: eight or nine on average, ensuring a rapid growth of population.[17] Nor were their close neighbors, the French settlers in Canada, far behind, with twenty-two recorded as the average age at first marriage for girls and twenty-seven for men.

Spanish America had a rather distinct profile, given the shortage of women (at most, a third of the emigrants from Spain in the peak years of the later sixteenth century were female), and given the tendency of the conquistadors to produce offspring by native concubines. Illegitimate children accounted for nearly forty percent of births in the bigger cities of Latin America, considerably more than the rate of up to ten percent found at this time in Spanish towns like Granada or Seville, which in its turn was also perhaps twice the equivalent urban rate elsewhere in Europe. Discussion of illegitimacy is delicate, for we are not always sure what we are measuring. Foundlings may have been victims of poverty rather than shame, and it is not always clear that they should be counted with infants openly recorded as having no identifiable father. Clearly much of the urban population of colonial Latin America was made up of the unrecognized offspring of mixed racial encounters. In the countryside, by contrast, the Indians maintained more of a traditional family structure, albeit modified by official rules on monogamy. Studies are thin on the ground, but what we do have would suggest that an Indian boy and girl would live together for a time before getting married. The situation was not unlike that in peasant Europe at the time, and even though the hand of the church may have reshaped popular culture in this respect more speedily in Europe, it is notable that official illegitimacy rates do not appear to be much higher in the rural areas of the New World.

Bastard offspring were more an advantage than a problem in tribal societies where defense against enemies was always a major concern. But as urbanization spread, they came to be less welcome, given the primacy of the household and the need to limit dispersal of its patrimony. This coincided interestingly with movements for religious reform at the close of the Middle Ages, which adopted a harsher attitude toward sin, punishing the bastard in his own person for the lapse of his parents. In Shakespeare's *King Lear*, Edmund muses that since he is treated as an illegitimate son, he may as well act the character of a bastard: treacherous and unreliable—the very qualities that the Spaniards attributed to those of mixed race in the Indies. In *Telemachus* (1694), the tale of a young man's voyage of discovery of the world and himself, Fénelon portrayed one island people, offspring of veterans of the siege of Troy. He believed that "their illegitimate birth, the loose living of their mothers, the lack of discipline in their upbringing, gave them a certain wild and barbarous appearance." It was a common enough view of inhabitants generally of the overseas colonies: marginal men, who did not quite fit into European society, further contaminated by the doubtful customs of the native peoples.

The separation of sexual roles that we noted as a feature of the tribal Indians may explain why children were left so long at the breast, and how these early years of childhood were such a glorious age of indiscipline. John Demos, who has studied the fascination yet repulsion of the wilderness for the settler families of New England around 1700, notes that "Indian people … were notorious among Europeans for indulging—indeed, 'spoiling'—their young." One French commentator on the Iroquois commented at this time: "We may justly reproach them with the way in which they bring up their children; they do not so much as know what it is to correct them." Lafitau wrote in 1724 of the extensive freedom of Indian children, their turbulent play, their slow integration into the chores of housekeeping: "no one would dare to strike and punish them."[18]

There was great indulgence of newborns almost everywhere, indeed, even in more settled patriarchal societies. Montaigne contrasted the playful indulgence of infants in sixteenth-century France with the tension that developed as the youngsters came of an age to inherit. Outside Europe, where mothers were often in their teens, they would find in the birth of a son, perpetuator of the lineage, the affirmation of status and dignity. Given the age difference between man and wife that one finds in imperial China as among the Arab peoples, often amounting to fifteen or twenty years, the emotional tie drew the mother closer to her son than to her husband. Given the high mortality of young brides in childbirth in colonial Brazil, the significant tie seems to have been that between the black wet nurse and her master's son. Gilberto Freyre noted in this respect the age gap that frequently existed between the planters and the teenage mothers of their infant progeny. It was a system that bred great formality in intrafamily relationships. At an early age the young Brazilian boy became a man.

THE RELAY OF THE GENERATIONS

"I am young, it is true," declared the Cid in Corneille's famous play of 1636 as he prepared to duel with the master swordsman who had insulted his father, "but courage in the well-born does not count in years." Shortly before, Montaigne had written: "I reckon that our souls are as formed at twenty as they will ever be ... If they have not shown what they are capable of by that age, they never will in years to come."[19] Certainly the high mortality of the age meant that the relay of the generations often took place faster than would be the case today. But if children had to be ready everywhere to assume the burdens of adulthood before their time, there were contrasting views on whether this was to be welcomed or not. In Martorell's great chivalric tale *Tirant lo Blanc* (1490) the hermit count insists on sending all boys of eleven into battle, despite the pleas of his wife that their own son is too young.

Childhood was everywhere recognized, then, as a distinctive stage in the stepped pyramid of the ages of man—a relentless process of waxing and waning governed by the law of nature and minutely divided by each perceptible change in the physical and mental capacity of the person. But the process was perhaps more formal and ritualized, less geared to the individual's own development than to the needs of the wider community, than would be the case today. Europeans marked several turning points in the development of the young. In the great thirteenth-century Castilian law code, the *Siete Partidas,* those aged under ten and a half years could not be accused of any crime, nor could they be disinherited for any fault, "because it is not likely that one so young could wrong a father with malice aforethought." In criminal law, the concept of diminished responsibility and an accompanying leniency in punishment were accorded to those under the age of fourteen, or even in some cases the age of twenty-five. Certainly from accounts of how the system worked in Seville, we learn that those younger than sixteen were never condemned to death, but to flogging or the galleys. The church hesitated a little over exactly when a child had the full use of reason needed to commit a deadly sin. The diocese of Valencia in 1565 ordered that children become "accustomed" to annual confession of their sins from the age of "seven or eight," with an obligation to do so for those aged between twelve and fourteen, when "one begins to have a perfect use of reason." In other world cultures a similar transition to full responsibility for one's actions becomes evident around puberty. Thus, around the age of fourteen, as the Jesuit Cobo tells us, the young Inca would adopt a new name for himself, a chosen name that he as an individual would bear for the rest of his life—the affirmation, as it were, of his own personal identity.[20]

The rigorous training to which the youth of the great Indian empires—and especially the Aztecs—were exposed after their infant years impressed Europeans. Las Casas copied out the *huehuetlatolli,* the sayings of the elders, which the young Aztecs would learn as a preparation for adult responsibility.

And Acosta noted how the strenuous physical and mental training kept these adolescents from the "twin evils of youth, idleness and willfulness."[21] Some Europeans were impressed with the equality of opportunity afforded the young to engage in service to the community. Rather than the European system, which favored those of gentle birth, several civilizations appeared to confer status and power on the most able. Thus Busbecq, envoy of the Holy Roman Emperor to the Ottoman sultan, observed in his famous *Letters from Turkey* (1556–1564) that there "each man is rewarded according to his deserts, and offices are filled by men capable of performing them." Thus the sons of shepherds could be regularly found in the highest positions in government. In general, he concluded, "they do not consider that good qualities can be conferred by birth or handed down by inheritance, but regard them partly as the gift of heaven and partly as the product of good training and constant toil and zeal."[22] Acosta noted the same in China. There power lay in the hands of the literate class, those who could after much mental effort master the 120,000 characters of the Chinese script, thereby demonstrating their outstanding ability and fitness to rule. This mandarin elite was characterized by tension between the generations, noted by Acosta. Since the state examinations would determine rank and honor, the masters in school by day and the parents by night at home "make them study so much that their eyes turn red, and they whip them very often with canes."[23]

DISCIPLINE IMPOSED

In fact, two related cultural developments were to make European childhood significantly different from that of other world cultures. The first of these was the unfolding of Renaissance humanist thought, which sought to transform the school (known, of course, to virtually all societies, from Aztecs to Muslims to Chinese mandarins) from an apprenticeship for the priesthood to a nursery of citizens, with the focus shifting from the handing on of traditions to the questioning of received wisdom. The revival of the Greek and Roman classics, as well as of the Hebrew scriptures, opened European eyes to the lessons of comparative history, which they were to apply to the understanding of the languages and institutions of the New World. The second related development was the Reformation, reflecting a remarkable rise in literacy, among the urbanized populations especially, and a remarkable "flattering of the lay vocation." Godliness moved from the sacred space of the church to the intimacy of workshop and home.

Nor was this development confined to Protestants. The Jesuits, founded in 1540, became the very embodiment of this new reforming spirit, which emphasized that godliness was accessible to all, even those working within the world. People wondered, commented the early historian of the order, Pedro de Ribadeneira, why the Jesuits concentrated on grammar schools rather than the more prestigious role of university teachers. The key, he argued, was to be found in the nature of the Protestant heresies then sweeping Europe. Heresy was the placing of self above authority; it was a reflection of the breakdown of good order—not in the first instance a matter of belief but of behavior. The Jesuits judged, therefore, that "to come to grips with this fire and stop the house collapsing around us, it was necessary to reform lives and improve behavior." Nothing seemed more calculated to create a godly society than to accustom children from an early age to the practice of virtue, "imbibing good customs with their mother's milk and growing up with them," as second nature.[24] Cervantes in his *Coloquio de los Perros* (1610) summed up why the Jesuit schools were so successful—teaching by enthusiasm and example rather than by the rod—and how they were turning out graduates "who have more than most the qualities of prudence required to run the affairs of this world."

This was the model that the missionaries took with them to the New World. It implied optimism about the receptivity that native peoples would accord it, and at the same time an authoritarian approach to those who sought to escape the ferule. The Franciscan friar Jerónimo de Mendieta, toward the end of the sixteenth century, wrote of the great hopes to be placed in the Mexican peoples, if only they could be separated from the wiles and corruption of Europeans and indoctrinated in the way of salvation. Anticipating the famous Jesuit reservations in Paraguay shortly afterward, he affirmed his belief that "placed in subjection and obedience, there is no people or nation in the world more disposed to accept what they are told; by contrast, once you give in to their love of freedom and self-will, there are no wild beasts of the jungle more fierce than they."[25]

Motolinía, as we saw, described the pain caused by the abolition of polygamy. He also noted the conflict between generations to which Christianization had led, with the young, having been to the mission schools, taking more easily to the new ways than their parents did. For many boys, the sport of baiting the old and out-of-date seems to have had a charm of its own, as in the tragic tale of the assassination of an Aztec priest by a gang of schoolboys in the center of town in the full light of day. Somewhere between a hagiography and an adventure story was the case recounted also by Motolinía of young Cristóbal, son and heir of one of the Tlaxcalan tribal chiefs. After becoming a Christian he set about destroying any idols he could find in his father's house and breaking open the vats of "wine" (perhaps pulque), urging that drunkenness was the besetting sin of his people. The outraged parent turned on his son, clubbed him to death, and, when the boy's mother intervened, had her put to death as well. Interestingly, the father had initially tried to hide Cristóbal from the authorities, since he was next in line of succession to the chiefdom, dispatching his three younger sons to the mission school instead. Girls as well as boys were mobilized for this work of evangelization, Motolinía tells us, visiting friends and relatives, sometimes in the company of older women, but always spreading the Christian message. What would we have done, comments the great Franciscan missionary, without these child interpreters?[26]

The household became a focus of spiritual development, particularly among the Puritans, many of whom left England and the Old World in the early seventeenth century in order to create a new Jerusalem, a city of God, in the New World. Seeking to reform the established Anglican Church, whose emphasis on ritual seemed remote from the inner conversion to which they aspired, the Puritans sought to reconcile the doctrine of John Calvin, which held that the individual was predestined by God for no merit or fault of his own either to eternal salvation or damnation, with the enforcement of godly conduct on the population at large, starting with the members of their own households: children, servants, and dependants. The strict surveillance of self for clues to God's anger or favor, evidenced, for example, in Cotton Mather's late seventeenth-century diary with its daily annotation of at least one good action effected, gives the measure of self-awareness of the New England colonists and helps explain the proliferation of memoirs and diaries among this people. As Edmund Morgan explains, the Puritan faith shifted spiritual development from the church to the home, dispensing with intermediaries with God and focusing on the reading of scripture as the key to the development of the young mind. "Every morning immediately upon rising and every evening before retiring, a good Puritan father led his household in prayer, in scriptural reading and in singing of psalms."[27]

Religion was also beginning to play a part in the shaping of the Catholic family. Pedro de Luxán portrayed in 1550 what must have been a fairly typical upper middle-class household in Seville, where the father would gather wife and children and (it appears) servants round the fireplace after dinner. There he would get one of his sons to read aloud from a book that had caught his eye in the family library a little earlier. Even so, Catholic devotion was not exclusively family orientated. Of course, no two forms of transition were necessarily the same. In North America, the Puritans tried to introduce a family system that basically reproduced that of Europe, with their aim of building the city of God in the heathen wilderness. Indeed, the frontier setting provided a laboratory in a sense for more extreme versions of some features of the Old World. The gentry of Virginia reared their children in households where there were lots of servants or slaves, disciplining both sets of dependants more or less equally with the whip. The youngsters grew up with a cheerful acceptance of the hierarchy and traditions of their youth. By contrast, in New England the strict Puritan inhabitants were more concerned with making the child aware of the sinfulness of his behavior rather than with punishing him physically. Education in these colonies tended to take the form of an attempt to break the will by building up a sense of shame and internalized guilt from a very early age. These Puritan children would later recall in their adult journals the self-pride and rebelliousness of their youth, and the onset of a sense of sin, almost as a second birth. And from this awakening came a striving to do God's will not only in their own lives but in the world around them.[28]

The family helped shape the societies of the New World, not only in the patterns of education and discipline laid down for the younger generation, but perhaps equally in the patterns of interaction with the native peoples The traditional picture of a European elite imposing its values on other cultures regarded as inferior is increasingly being modified by more recent research into patterns of acculturation and assimilation. One of the pioneer revisionists was Gilberto Freyre, a sociologist who began in the 1930s a series of studies on the culture of his native Brazil, pointing out how much it owed to the native peoples and the black slaves. Given the scattered nature of European settlement, there was significant social and cultural exchange between masters and slaves. Given also the system of arranged marriages, which meant that girls of twelve or fourteen would be married off to planters of thirty or forty, the emotional center of the big house was likely to be the black wet nurses and nannies, who might well have to look after the master's children when his wife died early in childbirth. The songs, the folk tales, and the cuisine would all reflect a blending of Native American, Portuguese, and African strains. Thus, the fairy tale of European provenance began to acquire a jungle setting, a scenario where wild beasts were denser on the ground. Malign spirits of African origin tended to take over the role of the witch, more familiar to Europeans, in tales warning children to stay indoors after dark and to wash their faces before going to bed. Less benignly, the mixing of slave children in play with those of the master bred an early arrogance in the behavior and manners of the young European, as he forced his black playmate to take all the knocks—acting out the role of a steed whipped along by its rider, and so forth. In the earlier days of the colony, the Native Americans had played alongside their European counterparts, blending the games of Europe—the flying of the kite—with those more familiar to the

Indian—the bird trap, for example, or (of so much significance for Brazil's future triumphs) the rubber ball.[29]

The emergence of a hybrid culture was signaled in Spanish America by the famous report of Juan and Ulloa in 1749, which pointed to divisions between Spaniards freshly arrived in the colony and creoles (those of Spanish ancestry but born in America). Creoles were lazy, wasteful, and incompetent; they had taken on—so it was alleged—the coloring of the local society, and indeed were indistinguishable from it. Whether they also had some Indian blood in their veins seemed of less account.[30]

Nor did the circumstances of the Spanish conquest facilitate a stable family system. One of the great voices of the Indian people was that of Huaman Poma, the down-at-heel claimant to a provincial chiefdom, who as a result of his wanderings through the Andes came up with the material for an indictment of the colonial system (1615). The mixing of the two races, Spaniards and Indians, he claimed, led inevitably to sexual and economic exploitation. The Indians, overburdened, were leaving their villages and drifting to the towns, victims of alcoholism and prostitution. Priests were as guilty as anyone else of taking advantage of the poor Indian. The visible result was the decline of the pure Indian population, the rise of the mestizo or half-breed, rejected by both Spaniards and Indians as shifty and unreliable. The world was "turned upside down," as Huaman Poma put it.[31]

CONCLUSIONS

In his enormously influential study of other cultures (1772), the abbé Raynal suggested that a benchmark for civilization was the freedom of the individual. We are too fond of comparing the king to the father of a family, he thought, whereas a look at China should convince us of the deadening influence of patriarchy. "What is the effect on us of paternal despotism? a show of respect on the outside and within a secret, impotent hatred of our fathers. What has been and what is the effect in every land of civil despotism? vileness of conduct and the extinction of virtue."[32]

If Asian despotism could be linked to authoritarian upbringing in the home, the freedom of the Native American might be thought to stem from his rather different childhood. The great apostle of the Indies, Motolinía, could write of the virtue of the native peoples, freed from the preoccupation of gathering together property. And this became part of the legend on which the writers of the Enlightenment would draw for their picture of the so-called noble savage. But the preoccupations of the Europeans in the Age of Discovery was rather

that of imposing order—a freedom from the fear and chaos that still characterized the Old World of the fifteenth through seventeenth centuries.

It was that ordered society that the physician and educationalist Juan Huarte
de San Juan sought to build in his famous essay, *The Examination of Talents
for the Sciences* (1575). In the dedication to the king, Philip II, he set out the
baleful consequences for religion, law, and health of allowing the young to
take up professions for which they were not suited. The bulk of the text is
concerned with the formation of youth. There are those, it notes, who believe
in the inherited virtue of nobility. But surely nobility is like the figure zero,
worthless in itself but a magnifying factor when allied with talent. Yet it is not
sufficient to emphasize the virtues of education without taking into account the
content and method of what is being taught. Education must not become mere
instruction, a point that earlier pedagogues like Luis Vives had also stressed.
The educators of Renaissance Europe were keen to break with what one may
call the mandarin tradition of authority and received knowledge characteristic
of many of the world's cultures. All knowledge, affirms Huarte de San Juan
(several years before Montaigne), is relative and provisional. Religion, he has-
tened to add (though it did not save him from the Inquisition, which quickly
banned his book), is founded on faith and authority rather than human reason.
You can teach the young, lecture to them, and instruct them. But education is
something different: the awakening of the critical faculty, which depends very
much on the aptitude of the pupil.

Huarte de San Juan is a traditionalist in some ways. But his emphasis on
studying the natural world owes much to a Renaissance culture, which sought
to understand the world on its own terms. Above all, his focus on the shifting
basis of knowledge—one reason why the book was placed on the index of
the Inquisition—betrays an awareness of the diversity of cultures. In a world
of childhood seen as the guarantee of continuity, Europe pointed in another
direction: childhood as discovery.

NOTES

Introduction

1. Brunner 1970; Frigo 1985: 8–27; Luke 1989: 52; Niccoli 1995: 90–94; Zarri 1996.
2. Ajmar-Wollheim and Dennis 2006: 10–31.
3. Burguière 1996: 97–118.
4. Frigo 1985: 116–122; Luke 1989: 87.
5. Pollock 1987; Chavasse 2008: 69–84.
6. Bellavitis and Chabot 2006: 77.
7. Sarti 2009: 376–394.
8. Herlihy 1978: 120. See also Heywood 2001: 21.
9. Po-Chia-Hsia 1989: 113–144; Cunningham 1995: 60; Heywood 2001: 164.
10. Strauss 1976: 74–84; Sommerville 1992: 166.
11. Burns 1999; Coates 2001: 141–162; Premo 2005; Tank de Estrada 2007.
12. Crawford 2004; Lett 2004; Bastress-Dukehart 2008.
13. Broomhall 2008.
14. Milanich 2002; Premo 2005.
15. Mirrer 1992; Bremmer and Bosch 1995; Hufton 1995, ch. 6; Cavallo and Warner 1999; Froide 2005; Lanza 2007.
16. Gager 1996; Romano 1996; Vassberg 1998; Corbier 1999.
17. Berry and Foyster 2007.
18. Cavallo 2008.
19. Milanich 2002.
20. Eisenach 2004, ch. 5; Cowan 2007; Byars 2008.
21. Weinstein 2004.
22. Contadini 2006; Sarti 2009: 375.
23. Hajnal 1983; Laslett 1983.
24. Viazzo 2003; Sovič 2008.
25. Viazzo 2003: 123.

26. Sperling 2004, 2007; Poska 2005.
27. Villaseñor Black 2006.

Chapter 1

1. Romano 1996: 3–42.
2. Menchi 1997: 260, 264.
3. Garfagnini 1996: 22.
4. Niccoli 1995: 102.
5. Niccoli 1995: 101–103.
6. Armon 2008.
7. Dekker 2000: 23–30.
8. Villaseñor Black 2006.
9. Bailey 2007: 219–222.
10. Main 2001: 126–131.
11. Diefendorf 1996: 276–279, 282–283.
12. Foyster 2003: 317.
13. Cavallo 2006c: 76.
14. Niccoli 1995: 190.
15. Harris 2001: 254–256.
16. Riddy 2003: 215.
17. Van der Heijden and van den Heuvel 2007; Abreu-Ferreira 2000.
18. Abreu-Ferreira 2000; Poska 2005: 43–50.
19. Allegra 1997: 65–67.
20. D'Amelia 2001: 225, 240.
21. Dekker 2000: 26, 34–35.
22. D'Amelia 2001: 243.
23. Wunder 2001: 321.
24. D'Amelia 2001: 225–231.
25. Foyster 2003: 315.
26. D'Amelia 2001: 226–227, 238.
27. Harris 2001: 248–250.
28. Foyster 2003: 321.
29. Romano 1996: 86.
30. Klapisch-Zuber 2002: 489–490.
31. Cavallo 2006: 77–82.
32. Reher 1998.
33. Chaytor 1980; Ben-Amos 2000; Foyster 2003.
34. Chaytor 1980: 38–40.
35. Cavallo 2007: 112–126.
36. Cavallo 2007: 186–193; Lett 2003.
37. Romano 1996: 99–101.
38. Romano 1996: 153, 198–199; Brady 2008: 190–192.
39. Romano 1996: 105, see also 20, 42, 93, 136–138.
40. dos Guimaraes Sa 2007: 20.

41. Adams 2008: 108–110.
42. Niccoli 1995: 175.
43. Brady 2008: 192.
44. Vergara 2007.
45. Plane 2000: 101.
46. Adams 2008: 112–113.

Chapter 2

1. Stone 1979: 93–108.
2. Casey 1989: 156–157; Heal 1990: 153–168.
3. Kent 1978: 26–30; Romano 1987: 120–123; Peck 1990: 47–75; Heal and Holmes 1994: 166–175, 201–214; Zmora 2001: 8–21, 79–82.
4. Cooper 1976: 233–252; Grassby 1978; Casey 2007: 79–98.
5. Casey 2007: 87.
6. Harris 1990: 616–617, 624.
7. Casey 2007: 97–98.
8. Kettering 1988: 131–151; Larminie 1995: 124–141, 193; Casey 2007: 94–98; Daybell 2006: 26, 29.
9. Kettering 1988: 146–147; Heal and Holmes 1994: 282–289, 297–306; Whyman, 1999: 89–91; Casey 2007: 146–147; Ben-Amos 2008: 215–216.
10. Davis 2000: 37–42; Wrightson 2000: 70–75; Wiesner-Hanks 2006: 189–197; Ben-Amos 2008: 70–71.
11. Medick 1984: 317–339; Bennett 1992: 18–41; Cressy 1997; Wrightson 2000: 78.
12. Ogilvie 1997: 42–72; McIntosh 1998: 24–34; Wrightson 2000: 75–78; Ogilvie 2003: 21, 134–139, 266–268; Hindle 2004: 300–325.
13. Roper 1989; Wall 1995: 49–85; McIntosh 1998; Ferraro 2001; Lynch 2003: 144–155.
14. Wall 1995: 30–48; Gowing 1996; Ferraro 2001; Capp 2003: 185–266.
15. Wall 1995: 13, 49–57; Gowing 1996: 119–125; Ferraro 2001: 7; Capp 2003: 55–68, 185–266.
16. Wiesner-Hanks 2006: 185–215; Lynch 2003: 25–32.
17. Wiesner 1993: 92–106; Farr 2000: 145–152; Lynch 2003: 32–39; McIntosh 2005: 45–84.
18. Grassby 2001: 232–249; Ben-Amos 2008: 51–55, 77.
19. Ozment 1990: 47
20. Ozment 1990: 1–14, 21, 39.
21. Ozment 1990: 64–65, 75, 92.
22. Klapisch-Zuber 1985: 68–93; Brenner 1993: 72–73, 114–115, 128–140; Grassby 2001: 292–297; Murdoch 2006; Wiesner-Hanks 2006: 208.
23. Underdown 1993: 27–60. See also Archer 2000: 76–94; Ben-Amos 2008: 157–160.
24. Muldrew 1998; Casey 2007: 49, 256–257; Ben-Amos 2008: 359.
25. Kent 1978: 61–70; Klapisch-Zuber 1985: 81, 87–93; Whyman 1999: 63, 66–69.
26. Eckstein 1992; Davis 1994: 117–128; Farr 2000: 240–244.
27. Wall 1995: 14–17; Ferraro 2001; Capp 2003: 55–59; Foyster 2005: 170–171; Cavallo 2006a: 71–72; Hardwick 2006: 18–27; Ben-Amos 2008: 66–69.

28. Lis and Solly 1993: 1–30.
29. McIntosh 1988: 216; Terpstra 1995, 38–82; Black 2000: 9–10; Lynch 2003: 89–99.
30. Eisenbichler 1998; Terpstra 2000: 114–131; Black 2000: 9–29.
31. Farr 2000: 224–228, 230–240; Lynch 2003: 120–121.
32. Jütte 1994; Grell, Cunningham, and Arrizabalaga 1999; Lynch 2003: 103–135; Hindle 2004.
33. McIntosh 1988: 221; McCants 1997; Lynch 2003: 103–135, esp. 126, 128; Ben-Amos 2008: 113–139.
34. Jütte 1994: 143–177; Parker 1998: 15–17; Grell, Cunningham, and Arrizabalaga 1999.
35. Lynch 2003: 128–129; Cavallo 1995: 98–140; Ben-Amos 2008: 236–240.
36. Elliott 2006: 54–55; Horn 1994: 216–250.
37. Elliott 2006: 43–48; Horn 1994: 203–204.

Chapter 3

1. Sneyd 1847: 24–25.
2. Sneyd 1847: 43.
3. Wright and Halliwell 1841–1843: 196–199.
4. Fitzherbert 1532: fol. 50.
5. Hanawalt 1986: 157; Grosjean 1935: 17–19, 21–23.
6. Grosjean 1935: 275–276 (my translation); Hanawalt 1986: 158–159.
7. Vassberg 1983: 64; Cohn 1998: 109.
8. Vassberg 1983: 66–67; Freedman, 1999: 170–171.
9. Grosjean 1935: 293–294.
10. Vassberg 1983: 66, 70.
11. Vassberg 1983: 70–71; Kussmaul 1981: 3; Whittle 2005: 54, 65.
12. Herlihy and Klapisch-Zuber 1985: 112.
13. Fairchilds 2007: 150.
14. Ogilvie 2003: 155, 148; Loats 1997: 18–23.
15. Ozment 1989: 70–76.
16. Haas 1988: 178; King 2000: 135.
17. Davis 1986: 172.
18. Horowitz 1997: 89; Klapisch-Zuber 1985: 165–177; Goldberg 1992: 194–202; Ben-Amos 1994: 134, 150–151; Houlbrooke 1984: 154.
19. Gavitt 1990: 246, 245.
20. Gavitt 1990: 250, 251.
21. Terpstra 2005: 19–20; Safley 1997: 234–235.
22. Sharpe 1991: 253–256; Chojnacka and Wiesner-Hanks 2002: 22–30.
23. Tognetti 2005: 214–215.
24. Origo 1959: 192.
25. Kaplan 2005: 134; Jordan 2005: 175–179.
26. Davis 1971: 226–227.
27. Orme 2001: 313–315.

28. Jordan 2005: 171.
29. Jordan 2005: 155, 161, 165–167, 169, 171, 174.
30. Phillips 2003: 110; St. Clare Byrne 1981: vol. 3, 12–13; vol. 4, 150–152, 161–166.
31. Moody 1998; Davis 1971: 132 (my translation).
32. Wiedner 1960: 367–369.
33. Wiedner 1960: 377.
34. Burns 1998: 6.
35. Vergara 2007: 82–90.
36. Romero 2007: 40–41.
37. Griffiths 2008: 284–289; Jordan and Walsh 2007: 13, 76–85.

Chapter 4

1. I would like to thank the editors, Sandra Cavallo and Silvia Evangelisti, for their invaluable support and for providing useful bibliographic references. I am grateful to Patricia Fortini Brown for drawing my attention to the Valmarana family portrait. Hughes 1986: 7–38.
2. Goldthwaite 1993; Sarti 1999; Roche 2000; Franits 1993.
3. Frigo 1985.
4. Frigo 1985; Ajmar 2004: 149–176.
5. Matthews Grieco 2000: 290; Sheingorn 2004: 273–301.
6. Richardson 2003: 433–447; Bec 1967; Branca 1986; Macfarlane 1970.
7. Sarti 1999: 86–147; Roche 2000: 81–105 and 166–192; Main 2001: 203–237; Goldthwaite 1993: 212–255.
8. Richardson 2003: 445–446.
9. Brewer and Porter 1993; Roche 2000: 166–192; Main 2001: 203–237; St. George 1998: 15–113; Goldthwaite 1993: 212–255.
10. Richardson 2003: 447.
11. Sarti 1999: 96–147.
12. St. George 1998: 15–113; Main 2001: 203–237.
13. Alcock 2003: 449–468.
14. Alcock 2003: 449–468; Johnson 1993; Demos 2000: 36–51; St. George 1998: 15–113.
15. Demos 2000: 47–48.
16. Sarti 1999: 96–96; Roche 2000: 91, 123–30; Demos 2000: 36–51.
17. Lombardi 2001: 179–241.
18. Morrall 2002: 263–273.
19. Franits 1993: 142; Morrall 2002: 263–273.
20. Sarti 1999: 123–125; Roche 2000: 189–192; Ajmar-Wollheim 2006: 206–221.
21. Calvert 1992: 7.
22. Calvert 1992: 7.
23. Calvert 1992: 21.
24. Calvert 1992: 21.
25. Guillemeau 1612: 15.
26. Guillemeau 1612: 21.

27. Guillemeau 1612: 22.
28. *Childhood* 1988: 36, fig. 36.
29. Guillemeau 1612: 22.
30. Guillemeau 1612: 16–17.
31. Trusler 1999: 67; Cleland 1607: 20.
32. Calvert 1992: 33–37.
33. Calvert 1992: 33–37.
34. Trusler 1999: 109.
35. Langmuir 2006: 134.
36. Cavallo 2006b: 174–187; Musacchio 2005: 139–156.
37. Calvert 1992: 38.
38. Macfarlane 1970: 90.
39. Trusler 1999: 56.
40. Brown 2006: 140.
41. Trusler 1999: 54–61.
42. Gray 1996: 221; Trusler 1999: 61.
43. Dominici 1860: 144.
44. Franits 1993: 135.
45. Musacchio 1999.
46. Franits 1993: 132.
47. Certaldo 1912: 90–91.
48. Trusler 1999: 118.
49. Trusler 1999: 120.
50. Dolce 1545: 10^v–11^r. Dolce's dialogue is a rough Italian adaptation of Juan Luis Vives's *Institutio feminae Christianae*.
51. Dolce 1545: 14^v.
52. Orme 1995: 53 and footnote 31.
53. Orme 1995: 54.
54. Orme 1995: 54.
55. Orme 1995: 51.
56. Orme 1995: 56.
57. Ajmar 2004: 208–216; Ajmar-Wollheim 2006: 152–163; Mottola Molfino 1986: 277–293; Smith 1998: 375–391.
58. Giovanni di Dio da Venezia 1471: 53^v–54^r.
59. Dolce 1545: f. 14^v.

Chapter 5

1. From the *Zibaldone* of Giovanni Rucellai, cited Garin 1968: 26.
2. Garin 1968: 71–107, 142–169.
3. Margolin 1995: 286.
4. Luke 1989: 83–95.
5. Garin 1968: 201–216.
6. O'Malley 1993.
7. Coudert 2005: 403–406; Grendler 1991: 99.

8. Coudert 2005: 407.

9. Rapley 1990.

10. Strasser 2004.

11. Tarabotti 2007: 283.

12. Klapisch-Zuber 1984; Alexandre-Bidon and Lett 1997; Grendler 1991: 111–112.

13. King 1991: 226–231.

14. Ferrari 2000; Boitel-Souriac 2008.

15. Lopez 2007: 73–77.

16. Brizzi 1995; Braunstein 1992: 119; Colesanti 2006: 59; Bellavitis 2008: 143–161.

17. Cavallo 2007.

18. Michalove 1999; dos Guimarães Sá 2007: 28.

19. Michaud-Fréjaville 1982; Hanawalt 1993: 129–153; Bernardi 1993.

20. Gavitt 1990: 248–249, 299–300; Tropé 1996.

21. Chartier, Compère, and Julia 1976; Orme 2006: 334–335.

22. Grendler 1991: 49–79.

23. Luke 1989: 115.

24. Watt 2002: 445.

25. Kagan 1975.

26. Balestracci 2004: 120–124; Platter 1982.

27. Gonzalbo Aizpuru 1990: 32–36; Alaperrine-Bouyer 2002.

28. Vergara 2007.

29. Gourdeau 1994: 53.

30. Monaghan 2005: 57–59.

31. Monaghan 2005: 21.

32. Monaghan 2005: 22.

33. Monaghan 2005: 38.

34. Monaghan 2005: 31.

35. Monaghan 2005: 41.

36. Monaghan 2005: 43.

37. Houston 1988.

Chapter 6

1. Sears 1986: chs. 1–3 and all plates.

2. Dal and Skarup 1980: 59.

3. Sears 1986. For consistent representations of children at play or schooling, see, for example, plates 15, 19, 43, 45, 49, 56, 65–66, 68, 70, 84, 94. For planetary and humoral influences, see pp. 12–15 and 110–111, plates 45–51, 55.

4. Seymour, 1975: 292.

5. Sears 1986: pp. 64–65, 89, 98, 152.

6. Sears 1986: pp. 110–111, plates 45–51.

7. Phillips 1999: 1–24; Goldberg 2006: 413–414.

8. Dawes and Magilton 1980: 63, and see also 27.

9. Herlihy and Klapisch-Zuber 1985: 272, table 9.3; Wrigley, Davies, Oeppen, and Schofield, 1997: 217–223, figures 6.3, 6.6.

10. Gavitt 1990: 189; Gil'adi 1992: 26.
11. Fildes 1988: 44–46, 73.
12. Klapisch-Zuber 1985: 133–137.
13. Gavitt 1990: 188.
14. Gavitt 1990: 188–189, 206–209.
15. Crawford and Gowing 2000: 89.
16. Emmison 1964: 28–29.
17. Borthwick Institute, York, (hereafter BI), Cause Papers G. 1521.
18. Emmison 1964: 29; Klapisch-Zuber 1985: 137–138, 140.
19. Gavitt 1990: 164.
20. Centre for Kentish Studies, Maidstone, DRb/Pa 24 f. 12d.
21. Gavitt 1990: 196, 210, 212–219, table 11.
22. Allan 1937; figures from decade 1563–1572.
23. Orme 1995: 51; Klapisch-Zuber 1985: 149.
24. Seymour 1975: 291; Gavitt 1990: 191.
25. Gil'adi 1992: 23, 52–53.
26. Seymour 1975: 300.
27. Orme 2001: 242.
28. Ben-Amos 1994: 55–56.
29. Orme 2001: 245–246.
30. Vincent 2003: 57, 59–60.
31. Alexandre-Bidon and Lett 1997: chs. 6–7; Hanawalt 1993: 111, 113.
32. Crouzet-Pavan 1997: 177–179; Rossiaud 1988: 12–14.
33. Eisenbichler 1998: 191–197; Crouzet-Pavan 1997: 218–219.
34. Gavitt 1990: 189; Allan, 1937: figures from decade 1563–1572.
35. Willis and Merson 1968: xlii–lviii, 61–84.
36. Slack 1975: 67.
37. Ben-Amos 1994: 40–45.
38. Horn 2007: 144.
39. Slack 1975: 30.
40. Orme 1995: 51–54.
41. Hanawalt 1993: 112.
42. Clark 1985: 336.
43. Gil'adi 1992: 116.
44. Crouzet-Pavan 1997: 178–179.
45. BI, York, Cause Papers G. 61.
46. Norfolk and Norwich Record Office (hereinafter NNRO) Wills, Hyrnyng f. 85r.
47. Clark 1985: 341.
48. Hajnal 1982: 449–494.
49. Laslett 1983: 82; Herlihy and Klapisch-Zuber 1985: figure 7.2; 206, 221.
50. Maddern 2008: 55.
51. Laslett 1983: 82; Herlihy and Klapisch-Zuber 1985: figure 7.2, p. 206; Harris 2002: 56–57.
52. Furnivall 1897: 9–11, 12.
53. Laslett 1983: 86–87; Furnivall 1897: 25.
54. BI, York, Cause Papers Roll 89.

55. Swanson 1989: 31, 42.
56. Oliva 1998: 45–46.
57. York Minster Archives Visitations Book 1472–1550 L2 (3) c f. 51d; NNRO DCN 1/6/59, 1/6/61.
58. Quotes from Horn 2007: 978, 1056; see also Horn 2007: 934, 937, 973.
59. Quote from Greer 2000: 36. See also Clendinnen 1991: 189–192, 98–99.
60. Archer 1990: 479–481, Bremner 1970: 6–8 and 23–4.
61. Bremner 1970: 23.
62. Archer 1990: 490–491.
63. Bremner 1970: 38.
64. Bremner 1970: 73–4.
65. Minz 2004: 16–22; Bremner 1970: 74–75.
66. Herlihy and Klapisch-Zuber 1985: 282–286; Gavitt 1990: 162–172, 189.
67. Froide 2005: 2–3.

Chapter 7

1. The author thanks Susan Deans-Smith, Martha Newman, Robert Olwell, Bianca Premo, Cynthia Talbot, and Karin Wulf for their comments and suggestions on this chapter. Hindle 2001: 17–38, and passim; Beik 1985; Hanley 1989 and 2006; Pierce 2003; Strasser 2004.
2. Bodin quoted in Opitz 2003: 19; James I (as father) quoted in Aughterson 1995: 145 and (as father) in Smith 1998: 14.
3. Hanley 1989: 12.
4. Frye 1993: 158 and 55 (spelling modernized).
5. Hanley 1989; Strasser 2004.
6. Brown 1996.
7. Kingdon 1995.
8. Hardwick 2009; Ingram 2001; Ferraro 2001.
9. Soman 1997; Rublack 1999: 163–196; Wiesner-Hanks 2000.
10. Socolow 2000; Premo 2008.
11. McCants 1997; Safley 2005; Birn 2007: 677–708; Gerber 2004.
12. Premo 2005: 22; Hanley 1989.
13. Hanley 1989; Premo 2005: 1–42; Brewer 2005.
14. Premo 2005: 28–29; Hardwick 1992.
15. González and Premo 2007.
16. Premo 2005; Herndon and Murray 2009.
17. Hardwick 2009.
18. Hardwick unpublished manuscript; Gowing 1997; Soman 1990.
19. Hardwick 2006; Hardwick 2009.
20. Premo 2008.
21. Hardwick in published manuscript.
22. Levack 1995: 144–145.
23. Hardwick 2009.
24. Rublack 1999: 231–254; Hardwick 2009.

Chapter 8

1. Reinhard 1982; Po-Chia-Hsia 1989: 2–4.
2. Webb 2005 and 2007.
3. Arenal and Schlau 1989: 384–385.
4. Miller 2006: 325.
5. Swanson 1995: 124.
6. Banner 2005: 89.
7. Mattox 2006.
8. Palumbo Fossati 2004; Morse 2007.
9. Ajmar-Wollheim and Dennis, 2006; Cavallo and Evangelisti 2009.
10. Miller 2006: 325.
11. Morse 2007; Webb 2007.
12. Strauss 1978: 4; Gaimster and Gilchrist 2003.
13. Watt 1991: 217–253; Rublack 2005: 166–169.
14. Richetts 2005; Hamling 2007a, 2007b.
15. Cordier 1674: 200.
16. King 2008: 66.
17. King 2008: 71.
18. King 2008: 49.
19. Watt 2002; Spierling 2008.
20. Klapisch-Zuber 1985: 113–114; Battista 2002: 133–135.
21. King 2008: 67.
22. Po-Chia-Hsia 1989: 4, 113–116.
23. Watt 2001: 199–204.
24. Plebani 1996: 42–44.
25. Wiesner-Hanks 1996: 83–89; Leonard 2005: 64, 74.
26. Strohl 2001: 136–138.
27. Grendler 1989: 333–362; Po-Chia-Hsia 1989: 114; Houston 2002: 13–24, 37.
28. McCants 1997.
29. Kagan 1974: 19.
30. Kagan 1974: 11.
31. Arenal and Schlau 1989.
32. Wiesner-Hanks 2008: 143–163.
33. Rapley 1990; Diefendorf 2004; Lux-Sterritt 2005; Dinan 2006.
34. Atkinson 2001: 231–236.
35. Benavides 1630.
36. O'Malley and Bailey 2003: 315.
37. Tanck de Estrada 2007: 15–16.
38. Pinson 1997; Tanck de Estrada 2007: 18–19.
39. Atkinson 2001: 234.
40. Atkinson 2001: 236; see also Zemon-Davis 1995: 63–169 and Deslandres 2003: 139–141.
41. Sommerville 1992: 21–33; Romero 2007: 33–41.
42. Zemon-Davis 1975.
43. Niccoli 1995: 37; Taddei 200: 121–168.

44. Christian 1981: 215–222; Walsham 1994: 296–297.
45. Scaramella 1997: 9–20; Benvenuti Papi and Giannarelli 1991: 7–24.
46. Mascuch 2006: 114.
47. Walsham 1994: 293–294.
48. Walsham 1994: 296–298.

Chapter 9

 1. Ze'evi 2006: 37.
 2. Rosner 1977: 177.
 3. Ze'evi 2006: 37.
 4. Roth 2005: 200.
 5. Pollack 1971: 19.
 6. Rosner 1977: 44–45.
 7. Ballester 1996: 202.
 8. Ze'evi 2006: 37.
 9. Ballester 1996: 201.
10. Still 1965: 162–163.
11. Klapisch-Zuber 1985: 153–154; Nadeau 2001.
12. Otis 1986: 88.
13. Gavitt 1990: 189.
14. Klapisch-Zuber 1985: 154.
15. Bennassar 1967: 198.
16. Carmichael 1986: 41.
17. Klapisch-Zuber 1985: 38.
18. Davis 1978: 22; Davis 1991: 288, 290; Broomhall 2006: 122.
19. Demaitre 1977: 477.
20. Gavitt 1990: 217–218.
21. Cunningham 1977: 37–40.
22. Broomhall 2004: 167.
23. Klapisch-Zuber 1985: 146.
24. Salisbury 1996: 21–22.
25. Wear 2006: 221; Walter, Schofield, and Appleby 1991.
26. Eckert 1996.
27. Harding 1993.
28. Daniels 1992; Thornton 1997; Ubelaker 2000.
29. Salisbury 1996: 19.
30. Kiple 2002.
31. Galenson, 1996: 181–183.
32. Walvin 2001: 180–181.
33. Le Roy Ladurie 1997: 104.
34. Macfarlane 1976: 114.
35. Houlbrooke 1998: 235.
36. Vigarello 1988: 16.

37. Vigarello 1988: 16; Hallo, Ruderman, and Stanislawski 1984: 172.
38. Abrahams 1962; King 2004.
39. Le Roux de Lincy 1860: 135.
40. Wiesner 1993.
41. Wertz and Wertz 1989: 1–28; Rooks 1997: 19.
42. McTavish 2005.
43. Numbers 1987; Christianson 1997.
44. Tsing 1995: 120–121.
45. Leong and Pennell 2007; Leong 2008; Rankin 2008.
46. Barker 2005: 31–32.
47. Harkness 1997.
48. Gunther 1969: 37.
49. Megged 2006: 69.
50. Gunther 1968: 273–274.
51. Ruderman 1995: 273–307; García-Ballester 1996.

Chapter 10

1. Motolinía 1988: 153.
2. Acosta 1986: 431.
3. Cobo 1990: 196.
4. Cobo 1990: 246.
5. Parry 1968: 142–149.
6. Demos 1996: 143.
7. Pérez de Barradas 1968: 116–119.
8. Chevalier 1970: 161.
9. Englander 1990: 292–296.
10. Burguière 1986: II, 429–433.
11. Spence 1985: 219–220.
12. Motolinía 1988: 174.
13. Fraser 1990: 42–44.
14. Motolinía 1988: 115.
15. Burguière 1986: II, 243–388.
16. Elliott 2006: 28–56.
17. Demos 1970: 64–75.
18. Demos 1996: 143–146.
19. Montaigne 1965: I, 396.
20. Cobo 1990: 202.
21. Acosta 1986: 431.
22. Englander 1990: 303–304.
23. Acosta 1986: 396.
24. Ribadeneira 1946: 177–192.
25. Maravall 1982: 101–102.
26. Motolinía 1988: 276–289.

27. Morgan 1966: 136.
28. Greven 1977: 3–61.
29. Freyre 1974: 313–323.
30. Juan and Ulloa 1978: 218–224.
31. Huaman Poma 1986: vol. 3, 1022–1025.
32. Raynal 1981: 36–37.

BIBLIOGRAPHY

Abrahams, Beth-Zion, ed. and trans. 1962. *The life of Glückel of Hameln, 1646–1724, written by herself*. London: East and West Library.

Abreu-Ferreira, Darlene. 2000. "Fishmongers and shipowners: Women in maritime communities of early modern Portugal." *The Sixteenth Century Journal* 31(1): 7–23.

Acosta, José de 1986: *Historia Natural y Moral de las Indias* (1590). Madrid: Historia 16.

Adams, Tracy. 2008. "Fostering girls in early modern France." In *Emotions in the household 1200–1900*, ed. Susan Broomhall. Basingstoke, England: Palgrave.

Ajmar, Marta. 2004. Women as exemplars of domestic virtue in the literary and material culture of the Italian Renaissance. PhD diss., The Warburg Institute, University of London.

Ajmar-Wollheim, Marta, and Flora Dennis, eds. 2006. *At home in Renaissance Italy*. London: V&A Publications.

Alaperrine-Bouyer, Monique. 2002. "L'Education des Elites Indigènes au Début du XVIIe Siècle: la Politique de la Couronne et ses Effets." In *Famille et Education en Espagne et Amérique Latine*, ed. Jean-Louis Guereña. Tours, France: Université François Rabelais.

Alcock, Nathaniel Warren. 2003. "The medieval peasant at home." In *The medieval household in Christian Europe, c. 850–c. 1550*, ed. Cordelia Beattie, Anna Maslakoic, and Sarah Rees Jones. Turnhout, Belgium: Brepols Publishers.

Alexandre-Bidon, Danièle, and Didier Lett. 1997. *Les Enfants au Moyen Age*. Paris: Hachette.

Allan, George A. T., ed. 1937. *Christ's Hospital Admissions: Vol. I, 1554–1599*. London: Harrison.

Allegra, Luciano. 1997. "La Madre Ebrea nell'Italia Moderna: Alle Origini di uno Stereotipo." In *Storia della Maternità*, ed. Marina D'Amelia. Bari, Italy: Laterza.

Archer, Ian W. 2000. "Social networks in Restoration London: The evidence of Samuel Pepys's diary." In *Communities in early modern England*, ed. Alexandra

Shepard and Phil Withington. Manchester, England: Manchester University Press.

Archer, Richard. 1990. "New England mosaic: A demographic analysis for the seventeenth century." *The William and Mary Quarterly,* 3rd ser., 47: 477–502.

Arenal, Electa, and Stacey Schlau, eds. 1989. *Untold sisters: Hispanic nuns in their own words.* Albuquerque: University of New Mexico Press.

Armon, Chara. 2008. "Fatherhood and the language of delight in fifteenth-century Italian texts." In *Florence and Beyond. Culture, Society and Politics in Renaissance Italy,* ed. David. S. Peterson and Daniel E. Bornstein. Toronto: University of Toronto Press.

Atkinson, Clarissa W. 2001. "'Wonderful affection': Seventeenth-century missionaries to New France on children and childhood." In *The child in Christian thought,* ed. Marcia Bunge. Grand Rapids, Mich.: William B. Eerdmans.

Aughterson, Kate. 1995. *Renaissance women: A sourcebook: Constructions of femininity in England.* London: Routledge.

Bailey, Joanne. 2007. "Reassessing parenting in eighteenth-century England." In *The family in early modern England,* ed. Helen Berry and Elizabeth Foyster. Cambridge: Cambridge University Press.

Balestracci, Duccio. 2004. *Cilastro che Sapeva Leggere.* Ospedaletto (Pisa), Italy: Pacini.

Ballester, Rosa. 1996. "Ethical perspectives in the care of infants in sixteenth to eighteenth centuries." In *Medicine and medical ethics in medieval and early modern Spain: An intercultural approach,* ed. Samuel S. Kottek and Luis García-Ballester. Jerusalem: Magnes Press.

Banner, Lisa A. 2005. "Private rooms in the monastic architecture of Habsburg Spain." In *Defining the holy sacred space in medieval and early modern Europe,* ed. Andrew Spicer and Sarah Hamilton. Aldershot, England: Ashgate.

Barker, Peter. 2005. "The Lutheran contribution to the astronomical revolution: Science and religion in the sixteenth century." In *Religious values and the rise of science in Europe,* ed. John Brooke and Ekmeleddin Ihsanoglu. Istanbul: Research Centre for Islamic History, Art and Culture.

Bastress-Dukehart, Erica. 2008. "Sibling conflict within early modern German noble families." *Journal of Family History* 33(1): 61–80.

Battista, Giuseppina. 2002. *L'educazione dei figli nella regola di Giovanni Dominici (1355/6–1419).* Firenze, Italy: Pagnini e Martinelli Editori.

Beauvois, Daniel. 1981. "Enseignement et Pédagogie dans le Monde Slave." In *Histoire Mondiale de l'Education, de 1515 à 1815,* ed. Gaston Mialaret and Jean Vial. Paris: PUF.

Bec, Christian. 1967. *Les Marchands Ecrivains. Affaires et Humanisme à Florence, 1375–1434.* Paris: La Haye, Mouton.

Beik, William. 1985. *Absolutism and society in seventeenth-century France: State power and provincial aristocracy in Languedoc.* Cambridge: Cambridge University Press.

Bellavitis, Anna. 2008. *Famille, Genre, Transmission à Venise au XVIᵉ siècle.* Rome: Ecole Française de Rome.

Bellavitis, Anna, and Isabelle Chabot. 2006. "People and property in Florence and Venice." In *At home in Renaissance Italy,* ed. Marta Ajmar-Wollheim and Flora Dennis. London: V&A Publications.

Ben-Amos, Ilana Krausman. 1994. *Adolescence and youth in early modern England.* New Haven, Conn.: Yale University Press.

Ben-Amos, Ilana Krausman. 2000. "Reciprocal bonding. Parents and their offspring in early modern England." *Journal of Family History* 25(3): 291–312.

Ben-Amos, Ilana Krausman. 2008. *The culture of giving: Informal support and gift-exchange in early modern England.* Cambridge: Cambridge University Press.

Benavides, Alonso. 1630. *Memorial que Fray Iuan de Santander de la Orden de San Francisco, Comissario General de Indias, presenta a la Magestad Catolica de Rey Don Felipe Quarto nuestro Segnor.* Madrid: Emprenta Real. (For a modern English translation see: Benavides, Alonso. 1996. *A harvest of reluctant souls. The memorial of Fray Alonso de Benavides 1630.* Niwot: University Press of Colorado.)

Bennassar, Bartolomé. 1967. *Valladolid au siècle d'or: Une ville de Castille et sa compagne au XVIe siècle.* Paris: Mouton.

Bennett, Judith M. 1992. "Conviviality and charity in early modern England." *Past and Present* 134: 18–41.

Benvenuti Papi, Anna, and Elena Giannarelli, eds. 1991. *Bambini santi. Rappresentazioni dell'infanzia e modelli agiografici.* Turin, Italy: Rosemberg & Sellier.

Bernardi, Philippe. 1993. "Apprentissage et Transmission du Savoir dans les Métiers du Bâtiment à Aix-en-Provence à la Fin du Moyen Âge." *Education, Apprentissage, Initiation au Moyen-Âge. Les Cahiers du CRISIMA* 1: 69–79.

Berry, Helen, and Elizabeth Foyster, eds. 2007. *The family in early modern England.* Cambridge: Cambridge University Press.

Birn, Anne-Emanuelle. 2007. "Child health in Latin America: Historiographic perspectives and challenges." *Hist. cienc. saude-Manguinhos* 14(3): 677–708.

Black, Christopher F. 2000. "The development of confraternity studies over the past thirty years." In *The politics of ritual kinship: Confraternities and social order in early modern Italy,* ed. Nicholas Terpstra. Cambridge: Cambridge University Press.

Boitel-Souriac, Marie-Ange. 2008. "Quand Vertu Vient de l'Etude des Bonnes Lettres. L'Education Humaniste des Enfants de France de François 1er aux Derniers Valois." *Revue historique* 645: 33–59.

Borthwick Institute, York, Cause Papers.

Brady, Andrea. 2008. "'A share of sorrow': Death in the early modern English household." In *Emotions in the household 1200–1900,* ed. Susan Broomhall. Basingstoke, England: Palgrave.

Branca, Vittore. 1986. *Mercanti Scrittori. Ricordi nella Firenze tra Medioevo e Rinascimento.* Milan, Italy: Rusconi.

Braunstein, Philippe. 1992. *Un Banquier Mis à Nu.* Paris: Gallimard.

Bremmer, Jian, and Bosch, van den Lourens, eds. 1995. *Between poverty and the pyre: Moments in the history of widowhood.* London: Routledge.

Bremner, Robert H. 1970. *Children and youth in America. A documentary history.* Cambridge, Mass.: Harvard University Press.

Brenner, Robert. 1993. *Merchants and revolution: Commercial change, political conflict, and London's overseas traders, 1550–1653.* Cambridge: Cambridge University Press.

Brewer, Holly. 2005. *By birth or consent: Children, law, and the Anglo-American revolution in authority.* Chapel Hill: University of North Carolina Press.

Brewer, John, and Porter, Roy, eds. 1993. *Consumption and the world of goods*. London: Routledge.

Brizzi, Gian Paolo. 1995. "Le Marchand Italien à l'Ecole Entre Renaissance et Lumières." In *Cultures et Formation Négociantes*, ed. Franco Angiolini and Daniel Roche. Paris: EHESS.

Broomhall, Susan. 2004. *Women's medical work in early modern France*. Manchester, England: Manchester University Press.

Broomhall, Susan. 2006. "Understanding household limitation strategies among the sixteenth-century urban poor in France." *French History* 20(2): 121–137.

Broomhall, Susan, ed. 2008. *Emotions in the household 1200–1900*. Basingstoke, England: Palgrave.

Brown, Kathleen. 1996. *Good wives and nasty wenches and anxious patriarchs: Gender, race, and power in colonial Virginia*. Chapel Hill: University of North Carolina Press.

Brown, Patricia Fortini. 2006. "Children and education." In *At home in Renaissance Italy*, ed. Marta Ajmar-Wollheim and Flora Dennis. London: V&A Publications.

Brunner, Otto. 1970. "La 'Casa come Complesso' e l'Antica 'Economica' Europea." In *Per una Nuova Storia Costituzionale e Sociale*, ed. Otto Brunner. Milano, Italy: Vita e Pensiero.

Bunge, Marcia J, ed. 2001. *The child in Christian thought*. Grand Rapids, Mich.: William B. Eerdmans.

Burguière, André, ed. 1986: *Histoire de la Famille*. 3 vols. Paris: Armand Colin.

Burguière, André, ed. 1996: *A History of the Family: the Impact of Modernity*, vol. 2. Cambridge: Polity Press.

Burns, Kathryn. 1998. "Gender and the politics of Mestizaje: The Convent of Santa Clara in Cuzco, Peru." *The Hispanic American Historical Review* 78: 5–44.

Burns, Kathryn. 1999. *Colonial habits: Convents and the spiritual economy of Cuzco, Peru*. Durham, N.C.: Duke University Press.

Byars, Jane. 2008. "The long and varied relationship of Andrea Mora and Anzola Davide: Concubinage, marriage and the authorities in the early modern Veneto." *Journal of Social History* 41(3): 667–690.

Calvert, Karin. 1992. *Children in the house: The material culture of childhood, 1600–1900*. Boston: Northeastern University Press.

Capp, Bernard. 2003. *When gossips meet: Women, family, and neighbourhood in early modern England*. Oxford: Oxford University Press.

Carmichael, Ann G. 1986. *Plague and the poor in Renaissance Florence*. Cambridge: Cambridge University Press.

Casas, Bartolomé de las. 1974. *Los Indios de México y Nueva Espana: Antología* (c. 1550), ed. Edmundo O'Gorman. Mexico: Editorial Porrúa.

Casey, James. 1989. *The history of the family*. Oxford: Basil Blackwell.

Casey, James. 2007. *Family and community in early modern Spain: The citizens of Granada, 1570–1739*. Cambridge: Cambridge University Press.

Cavallo, Sandra. 1995. *Charity and power in early modern Italy: Benefactors and their motives in Turin, 1541–1789*. Cambridge: Cambridge University Press.

Cavallo, Sandra. 2006a. "The artisan's casa." In *At home in Renaissance Italy*, ed. Marta Ajmar-Wollheim and Flora Dennis. London: V&A Publications.

Cavallo, Sandra. 2006b. "Health, beauty and hygiene." In *At home in Renaissance Italy,* ed. Marta Ajmar-Wollheim and Flora Dennis. London: V&A Publications.

Cavallo, Sandra. 2006c. "L'Importanza della 'Famiglia Orizzontale' nella Storia della Famiglia Italiana." In *Generazioni. Legami di Parentela tra Passato e Presente,* ed. Daniela Lombardi and Ida Fazio. Rome: Viella.

Cavallo, Sandra. 2007. *Artisans of the body in early modern Italy. Identities, families, masculinities.* Manchester, England: Manchester University.

Cavallo, Sandra. 2008. "Bachelorhood and masculinity in Renaissance and early modern Italy." *European History Quarterly* 38(3): 375–397.

Cavallo, Sandra, and Evangelisti, Silvia, eds. 2009. *Domestic institutional interiors in early modern Europe.* Aldershot, England: Ashgate.

Cavallo, Sandra, and Warner, Lyndan, eds. 1999. *Widowhood in medieval and early modern Europe.* New York: Longman.

Centre for Kentish Studies, Maidstone, CRb/Pa 24.

Certaldo, Paolo di Pace da. 1912. *Il Libro di Buoni Costumi: Documento di Vita Trecentesca Fiorentina,* ed. Salomone Morpurgo. Florence, Italy: Accademia della Crusca.

Chartier, Roger, Compère, Marie-Madeleine, and Julia, Dominique. 1976. *L'Education en France du XVIe au XVIIIe Siècle.* Paris: SEDES.

Chavasse, Ruth. 2008. "Humanist education and emotional expectations of teenagers in late fifteenth-century Italy." In *Emotions in the household 1200–1900,* ed. Susan Broomhall. Basingstoke, England: Palgrave.

Chaytor, Miranda. 1980. "Household and kinship: Ryton in the late sixteenth and early seventeenth centuries." *History Workshop Journal* 10: 24–60.

Chevalier, François. 1970. *Land and society in colonial Mexico.* Berkeley: University of California Press.

Childhood: A loan exhibition of works of art. 1988. London: Sotheby's.

Christian, William Jr. 1981. *Apparitions in late medieval and renaissance Spain.* Princeton, N.J.: Yale University Press.

Christianson, Eric H. 1997. "Medicine in New England." In *Sickness and health in America: Readings in the history of medicine and public health,* ed. Judith Walzer Leavitt Walzer and Ronald L. Numbers. Madison: University of Wisconsin Press.

Chojnacka, Monica, and Wiesner-Hanks, Merry E. 2002. *Ages of woman, ages of man: Sources in European social history, 1400–1750.* Harlow, England: Pearson Education.

Clark, Elaine. 1985. "The custody of children in English manor courts." *Law and History Review* 3(2): 333–348.

Cleland, James. 1607. Ηρω-παιδεια, *or the institution of a young noble man.* Oxford: J. Barnes.

Clendinnen, Inga. 1991. *Aztecs.* Cambridge: Cambridge University Press.

Coates, Timothy J. 2001. *Convicts and orphans. Forced and state-sponsored colonizers in the Portuguese empire, 1550–1755.* Stanford, Calif.: Stanford University Press.

Cobo, Bernabé 1990. *Inca religion and customs* (1653), ed. Roland Hamilton. Austin: University of Texas Press.

Cohn, Jr., Samuel K. 1998. "Women and work in Renaissance Italy." In *Gender and Society in Renaissance Italy,* ed. Judith C. Brown and Robert C. Davis. London: Longman.

Colesanti, Gemma. 2006. *Caterina Llull I Cabastida: Una mercantessa catalana nella Sicilia del '400*. Universitat Girona. Available at: http://www.tesisenxarxa.net/TESIS_UdG/AVAILABLE/TDX-0203106.

Contadini, Anna. 2006. "Middle-Eastern objects." In *At home in Renaissance Italy*, ed. Marta Ajmar-Wollheim and Flora Dennis. London: V&A Publications.

Cooper, J. P. 1976. "Patterns of inheritance and settlement by great landowners from the fifteenth to the eighteenth centuries." In *Family and Inheritance: Rural Society in Western Europe 1200–1800*, ed. Jack Goody, Joan Thirsk, and E. P. Thompson. Cambridge: Cambridge University Press.

Corbier, Mireille, ed. 1999. *Adoption et Fosterage*. Paris: Éditions de Boccard.

Cordier, Jean. 1674. *La famiglia santa*. Macerata, Italy: Giacomo Filippo Pannelli.

Coudert, Allison P. 2005. "Educating girls in early modern Europe and America." In *Childhood in the Middle Ages and the Renaissance*, ed. Albrecht Classen. Berlin: De Gruyter.

Cowan, Alexander. 2007. *Marriage, manners and mobility in early modern Venice*. Aldershot, England: Ashgate.

Crawford, Patricia. 2004. "Sibling relationships." In *Blood, bodies and families in early modern England*, ed. Patricia Crawford. Harlow, England: Pearson.

Crawford, Patricia, and Gowing, Laura. eds. 2000. *Women's worlds in seventeenth-century England: A sourcebook*. London: Routledge.

Cressy, David. 1997. *Birth, marriage and death: Ritual, religion, and the life-cycle in Tudor and Stuart England*. Oxford: Oxford University Press.

Crouzet-Pavan, Elisabeth. 1997. "A flower of evil: Young men in medieval Italy." In *A history of young people; Vol. 1, Ancient and medieval rites of passage*, ed. Giovanni Levi and Jean-Claude Schmitt. Cambridge, Mass.: The Belknap Press of Harvard University Press.

Cunningham, Carole. 1977. "Christ's Hospital: Infant and child mortality in the sixteenth century." *Local Population Studies* 18: 37–40.

Cunningham, Hugh. 1995. *Children and childhood in Western society since 1500*. London: Longman.

Dal, Erik, and Skarup, Poul. 1980. *The ages of man and the months of the year: Poetry, prose and pictures outlining the Douze mois figures motif mainly found in shepherds' calendars and in Livres d'Heures (14th to 17th century)*. Copenhagen: Munksgaard.

D'Amelia, Marina. 2001. "Becoming a mother in the seventeenth century: The experience of a Roman noblewoman." In *Time, space, and women's lives in early modern Europe*, ed. Thomas Kuehn, Silvana Sidel Menchi, and Anne Jacobson Schutte. Kirksville, Mo.: Truman State University.

Daniels, John D. 1992. "The Indian population of North America in 1492." *William and Mary Quarterly* 49: 298–320.

Davis, Barbara B. 1991. "Poverty and poor relief in sixteenth-century Toulouse." *Historical Reflections* 17(3): 267–296.

Davis, Norman, ed. 1971. *Paston letters and papers of the fifteenth century*, part 1. Oxford: Clarendon Press.

Davis, Robert C. 1994. *The war of the fists: Popular culture and public violence in late Renaissance Venice*. New York: Oxford University Press.

Dawes, Jean, and Magilton, M. R. 1980. *The cemetery of St Helen-on-the-Walls, Aldwark*. York, England: Council for British Archaeology.

Daybell, James. 2006. *Women letter writers in Tudor England.* Oxford: Oxford University Press.

Dekker, Rudolf. 2000. *Childhood, memory and autobiography in Holland from the Golden Age to Romanticism.* Basingstoke, England: Macmillan.

Demaitre, Luke. 1977. "The idea of childhood and childcare in medical writings of the Middle Ages." *Journal of Psychohistory* 4: 461–490.

Delgado Criado, Buenaventura, ed. 1993. *Historia de la Educación en España y América. La Educación en la España Moderna (siglos XVI–XVIII).* Madrid: Fundación Santa Maria.

Demos, John. 2000. *A little commonwealth: Family life in Plymouth colony.* Oxford: Oxford University Press.

Demos, John. 1994. *The unredeemed captive: A family story from Early America.* New York: Alfred A. Knopf.

Deslandres, Dominique. 2003. "'In the shadow of the cloister': Representations of female holiness in New France." In *Colonial Saints: Discovering the Holy in the Americas,* ed. Allan Greer and Jody Bilinkoff. New York: Routledge.

Diefendorf, Barbara. 1996. "Give us back our children: Patriarchal authority and parental consent to religious vocations in early Counter-Reformation France." *Journal of Modern History* 68(2): 1–43.

Diefendorf, Barbara B. 2004. *From penitence to charity: Pious women and the Catholic Reformation in Paris.* Oxford: Oxford University Press.

Dinan, Susan. 2006. *Women and poor relief in seventeenth-century France: The early history of the Daughters of Charity.* Aldershot, England: Ashgate.

Dolce, Lodovico. 1545. *Dialogo della institutioe delle donne. Secondo li tre stati, che cadono nella vita umana.* Venice, Italy: G. Giolito de Ferrari.

Dominici, Giovanni. 1860. *Regola del Governo di Cura Famigliare,* ed. Donato Salvi. Florence, Italy: A. Garinei.

Earle, Tom F., and Lowe, Kate J., eds. 2005. *Black Africans in Renaissance Europe.* Cambridge: Cambridge University Press.

Eckert, Edward A. 1996. *The structure of plagues and pestilence in early modern Europe: Central Europe, 1560–1640.* Basle, Switzerland: Karger.

Eckstein, Nicholas A. 1995. *The district of the Green Dragon: Neighbourhood life and social change in Renaissance Florence.* Florence, Italy: Leo S. Olschki.

Eisenach, Emlyn. 2004. *Husbands, wives and concubines. Marriage, family, and social order in sixteenth-century Verona,* Kirksville, Mo.: Truman State University Press.

Eisenbichler, Konrad. 1998. *The boys of the Archangel Raphel: A youth confraternity in Florence, 1411–1785.* Toronto: University of Toronto Press.

Elliott, J. H. 2006. *Empires of the Atlantic world: Britain and Spain in America 1492–1830.* New Haven, Conn.: Yale University Press.

Emmison, F. G. 1964. *Tudor food and pastimes.* London: Ernest Benn Limited.

Englander, David, Diana Norman, Rosemary O'Day, and W. R. Owens, eds. 1990. *Culture and belief in Europe 1450–1600: An anthology of sources.* Oxford: Blackwell.

Fairchilds, Cissie. 2007. *Women in early modern Europe, 1500–1700.* Harlow, England: Pearson Education.

Farr, James R. 2000. *Artisans in Europe 1300–1914.* Cambridge: Cambridge University Press.

Fénelon, François de. 1968. *Les Aventures de Télémaque* (1694), ed. Jeanne Lydie Goré. Paris: Garnier Flammarion.

Ferrari, Monica. 2000. *"Per Non Manchar in Tutto del Debito Mio." L'Educazione dei Bambini Sforza nel Quattrocento*. Milan, Italy: Franco Angeli.

Ferraro, Joanne M. 2001. *Marriage wars in late Renaissance Venice*. Oxford: Oxford University Press.

Fildes, Valerie. 1988. *Wet nursing: A history from antiquity to the present*. Oxford: Basil Blackwell.

Fitzherbert, John. 1532. *Here Begynneth a Newe Tracte or Treatyse Moost Profytable for All Husbandmen*. London: Rycharde Pynson.

Flandrois, Isabelle. 1992. *L'Institution du Prince au Début du XVIIe Siècle*. Paris: PUF.

Foyster, Elizabeth. 2003. "Parenting was for life, not just for childhood: The role of parents in the married lives of their children in early modern England." *History* 86: 313–327.

Foyster, Elizabeth. 2005. *Marital violence: An English family history, 1660–1857*. Cambridge: Cambridge University Press.

Franits, Wayne E. 1993. *Paragons of virtue: Women and domesticity in seventeenth-century Dutch art*. Cambridge: Cambridge University Press.

Fraser, Valerie. 1990. *The architecture of conquest: Building in the Viceroyalty of Peru 1535–1635*. Cambridge: Cambridge University Press.

Freedman, Paul. 1999. *Images of the medieval peasant*. Stanford, Calif.: Stanford University Press.

Freyre, Gilberto. 1974. *Maîtres et Esclaves: La Formation de la Société Brésilienne* (1933). French edition, Paris: Gallimard.

Frigo, Daniela. 1985. *Il Padre di Famiglia. Governo della Casa e Governo Civile nella Tradizione dell'Economica tra Cinque e Seicento*. Rome: Bulzoni.

Froide, Amy M. 2005. *Never married: Single women in early modern England*. Oxford: Oxford University Press.

Frye, Susan. 1993. *Elizabeth I: The competition for representation*. New York: Oxford University Press.

Furnivall, Frederick J., ed. 1897. *Child-marriages, divorces, and tatifications, &c in the diocese of Chester, A.D. 1561–6*. Early English Text Society, Original Series 108. London: Trübner & Co.

Gager, Kristin E. 1996. *Blood ties and fictive ties: Adoption and family life in early modern France*. Princeton N.J.: Princeton University Press.

Gaimster, David, and Gilchrist, Roberta, eds. 2003. *The archaeology of Reformation 1480–1580*. Leeds, England: Maney.

Galenson, David W. 1996. "The settlement and growth of the colonies: Population, labor, and economic development." In *The Cambridge economic history of the United States I: The colonial era*, ed. Stanley L. Engerman and Robert E. Gallman. Cambridge: Cambridge University Press.

García-Ballester, Luis. 1996. "Minorities and medicine in sixteenth-century Spain: Judaizers, 'moriscos' and the Inquisition." In *Medicine and Medical Ethics in Medieval and Early Modern Spain: An Intercultural Approach*, ed. Samuel S. Kottek and Luis García-Ballester. Jerusalem: Magnes Press.

Garfagnini, Manuela Doni. 1996. "Autorità Maschili e Ruoli Femminili. Le Fonti Classiche degli 'Economici." In *Donna, Disciplina, Creanza Cristiana dal XV al XVII Secolo: Studi e Testi a Stampa,* ed. Gabriella Zarri. Roma, Italy: Edizioni di Storia e Letteratura.

Garin, Eugenio. 1968. *L'Education de l'Homme Moderne, 1400–1600.* Paris: Fayard.

Gavitt, Philip. 1990. *Charity and children in Renaissance Florence: The Ospedale degli Innocenti, 1410–1536.* Ann Arbor: University of Michigan Press.

Gerber, Matthew. 2004. The end of bastardy: Illegitimacy in France from the Reformation to the French Revolution. PhD. diss, University of California at Berkeley.

Gil'adi, Avner, 1992. *Children of Islam: Concepts of childhood in medieval Muslim society.* Basingstoke, England: MacMillan.

Giovanni di Dio da Venezia. 1471. *Decor Puellarum.* Venice, Italy: Nicolaus Jenson.

Goldberg, P.J.P. 1992. *Women, work, and life cycle in a medieval economy: Women in York and Yorkshire* c. *1300–1520.* Oxford: Clarendon Press.

Goldberg, P.J.P. 2006. "Life and death: The ages of man." In *A Social History of England 1200–1500,* ed. Rosemary Horrox and W. Mark Ormrod. Cambridge: Cambridge University Press.

Goldthwaite, Richard A. 1993. *Wealth and the demand for art in Italy 1300–1600.* Baltimore, Md.: Johns Hopkins University Press.

Gonzalbo Aizpuru, Pilar. 1990. *Historia de la Educacion en la Epoca Colonial. El Mundo Indigena.* Mexico City: El Colegio de Mexico.

González, Ordina E., and Premo, Bianca, eds. 2007. *Raising an empire: Children in early modern Iberia and colonial Latin America.* Albuquerque: University of New Mexico Press.

Gourdeau, Claire. 1994. *Les Délices de nos Coeurs. Marie de l'Incarnation et ses Pensionnaires Amérindiennes, 1639–1672.* Silléry, France: Septentrion.

Gowing, Laura. 1996. *Domestic dangers: Women, words, and sex in early modern London.* Oxford: Oxford University Press.

Gowing, Laura. 1997. "Secret births and infanticide in seventeenth-century England." *Past and Present* 156(1): 87–115.

Grassby, Richard. 1978. "Social mobility and business enterprise in seventeenth-century England." In *Puritans and revolutionaries: Essays in seventeenth-century history presented to Christopher Hill,* ed. Donald Pennington and Keith. Oxford: Clarendon Press.

Grassby, Richard. 2001. *Kinship and capitalism: Marriage, family, and business in the English-speaking world, 1580–1740.* Cambridge: Cambridge University Press.

Gray, Todd, ed. 1996. *Devon household accounts: 1627–59.* Exeter, England: Devon and Cornwall Record Society.

Greer, Allan, ed. 2000. *The Jesuit relations. Natives and missionaries in seventeenth-century North America.* Boston: Bedford/St. Martins.

Grell, Ole Peter, Cunningham, Andrew, and Arrizabalaga, Jon, eds. 1999. *Health care and poor relief in Counter-Reformation Europe.* London: Routledge.

Grendler, Paul F. 1989. *Schooling in Renaissance Italy: Literacy and learning 1300–1600.* Baltimore, Md.: The Johns Hopkins University Press.

Grendler, Paul F. 1991. *La Scuola nel Rinascimento Italiano.* Bari, Italy: Laterza.

Greven, Philip. 1977. *The Protestant temperament: Patterns of child-rearing, religious experience and the self in early America.* New York: Alfred A. Knopf.

Griffiths, Paul. 2008. *Lost Londons: Change, crime, and control in the capital city, 1550–1660.* Cambridge: Cambridge University Press.

Grosjean, Paul S. J. 1935. *Henrici VI Angliae Regis Miracula Postuma: Ex Codice Musei Britannici Regio 13. c. viii.* Brussels: Société des Bollandistes.

Guillemeau, Jacques. 1612. *The nursing of children.* London: A. Hatfield.

dos Guimaraes Sa, Isabel. 2007. "Up and out. Children in Portugal and the empire (1500–1800)." In *Raising an empire: Children in early modern Iberia and colonial Latin America,* ed. Ordina E. González and Bianca Premo. Albuquerque: University of New Mexico Press.

Gunther, R. T. 1968. *Early science in Oxford.* Vol. 11. Winchester, England: Warren.

Gunther, R. T. 1969. *Early science in Cambridge.* Winchester, England: Warren.

Haas, Louis. 1988. *The Renaissance man and his children: Childbirth and early childhood in Florence 1300–1600.* Houndmills, England: Macmillan Press.

Hajnal, J. 1982 "Two kinds of preindustrial household formation system." *Population and Development Review* 8: 449–494.

Hajnal, J. 1983. "Two kinds of pre-industrial household formation system." In *Family forms in historic Europe,* ed. Richard Wall, Jean Robin, and Peter Laslett. Cambridge: Cambridge University Press.

Hallo, William W., David B. Ruderman, and Michael Stanislawski, eds. 1984. *Heritage: civilisation and the Jews.* New York: Praeger.

Hamling, Tara. 2007a. "The appreciation of religious images in plasterwork." In *Art re-formed: Reassessing the impact of the Reformation on the visual arts,* ed. Tara Hamling and Richard L. Williams. Newcastle, England: Cambridge Scholars Publishing.

Hamling, Tara. 2007b. "To see or not to see? The presence of religious imagery in the Protestant household." *Art History* 30(2): 170–197.

Hanawalt, Barbara A. 1986. *The ties that bound: Peasant families in medieval England.* New York: Oxford University Press.

Hanawalt, Barbara A. 1993. *Growing up in medieval London. The experience of childhood in history.* Oxford: Oxford University.

Hanley, Sarah. 1989. "Engendering the state: Family formation and state building in early modern France." *French Historical Studies* 16(1): 4–27.

Hanley, Sarah. 2006. "The family, the state, and the law in seventeenth- and eighteenth-century France: The political ideology of male right versus an early theory of natural rights" *Journal of Modern History* 78 (June): 289–332.

Harding, Vanessa. 1993. "Burial of the plague dead in early modern London." Working paper given at the symposium Epidemic Disease in London: From the Black Death to Cholera, Institute of Historical Research, March 19, 1992. Available at: http://www.history.ac.uk/cmh/epipre.html.

Hardwick, Julie. 1992. "Widows and widowhood in early modern France." *Journal of Social History* 26(1): 133–148.

Hardwick, Julie. 2006. "Early modern perspectives on the long history of domestic violence: The case of seventeenth-century France." *Journal of Modern History* 78 (1): 1–36.

Hardwick, Julie. 2009. *Family business: Litigation and the political economies of daily life in early modern France.* Oxford: Oxford University Press.

Hardwick, Julie. Unpublished manuscript. *Sex and the (seventeenth-century) city: The social world of young workers in early modern France.*

Harkness, Deborah E. 1997. "Managing an experimental household: The Dees of Mortlake and the practice of natural philosophy." *Isis* 88: 247–262.

Harris, Barbara J. 1990. "Property, power, and personal relations: Elite mothers and sons in Yorkist and early Tudor England." *Signs* 15(3): 606–632.

Harris, Barbara J. 2001. "Space, time and power of aristocratic wives in Yorkist and early Tudor England (1450–1550)." In *Time, space, and women's lives in early modern Europe,* ed. Thomas Kuehn, Silvana Sidel Menchi, and Anne Jacobson Schutte. Kirksville, Mo.: Truman State University.

Harris, Barbara J. 2002. *English aristocratic women, 1450–1550: Marriage and family, property and careers.* Oxford: Oxford University Press.

Heal, Felicity. 1990. *Hospitality in early modern England,* Oxford: Clarendon Press.

Heal, Felicity, and Holmes, Clive. 1994. *The gentry in England and Wales, 1500–1700,* Basingstoke, England: Macmillan.

Herndon, Ruth Wallis, and Murray, John E., eds. 2009. *Children bound to labor: The pauper apprenticeship system in early America.* Ithaca, N.Y.: Cornell University Press.

Herlihy, David. 1978. "Medieval children." In *Essays in medieval civilization,* ed. Bede K. Lackner and Kenneth R. Philp. Austin: University of Texas Press.

Herlihy, David, and Klapisch-Zuber, Christine. 1985. *Tuscans and their families: A study of the Florentine catasto of 1427.* New Haven, Conn.: Yale University Press.

Heywood, Colin. 2001. *A history of childhood. Children and childhood in the West from medieval to modern times.* Cambridge: Polity.

Hindle, Steve. 2001. *The state and social change in early modern England.* London: Palgrave.

Hindle, Steve. 2004. *On the parish? The micro-politics of poor relief in rural England c. 1550–1750.* Oxford: Oxford University Press.

Horn, James. 1994. *Adapting to a New World: English society in the seventeenth-century Chesapeake.* Chapel Hill: University of North Carolina Press.

Horn, James, ed. 2007. *Captain John Smith: Writings with other narratives of … the first English settlement of America.* New York: The Library of America.

Horowitz, Elliott. 1997. "The worlds of Jewish youth in Europe, 1300–1800." In *A history of young people in the West. Volume one: Ancient and medieval rites of passage,* ed. G. Levi and Jean-Claude Schmitt, trans. Camille Naish. Cambridge, Mass.: Belknap Press.

Houlbrooke, Ralph A. 1984. *The English family 1450–1700.* London: Longman.

Houlbrooke, Ralph A. 1998. *Death, religion and the family in England, 1480–1750.* Oxford: Clarendon Press.

Houston, Ralph A. 1988. *Literacy in early modern Europe. Culture and education 1500–1800.* London: Longman.

Huaman Poma, Felipe. 1986. *Nueva Crónica y Buen Gobierno* (1615), ed. J. V. Murra, R. Adorno, and J. L. Urioste, 3 vols. Madrid: Siglo XXI.

Huarte de San Juan, Juan. 1990. *Examen de Ingenios para las Ciencias* (1575), ed. Felisa Fresco Otero. Madrid: Espasa-Calpe.

Hufton, Olwen. 1996. *The prospect before her: A history of women in Western Europe 1500–1800*. London: Random House.

Hughes, Diane Owen. 1986. "Representing the family: Portraits and purposes in early modern Italy." *Journal of Interdisciplinary History* 17(1): 7–38.

Ingram, Martin. 1987. *Church courts, sex, and marriage in England, 1570–1640*. New York: Cambridge University Press.

Ingram, Martin. 2001. "Child sexual abuse in early modern England." In *Negotiating power in early modern Society: Order, hierarchy, and subordination in Britain and Ireland*, ed. Michael J. Braddick and John Walker. New York: Cambridge University Press.

Juan, Jorge, and de Ulloa, Antonio. 1978. *Discourse and political reflections on the kingdoms of Peru* (1749), ed. John J. TePaske and Besse E. Clement. Norman: University of Oklahoma Press.

Johnson, Matthew H. 1993. *Housing culture: Traditional architecture in an English landscape*. London: UCL Press.

Jordan, Annemarie. 2005. "Images of empire: Slaves in the Lisbon household and court of Catherine of Austria." In *Black Africans in Renaissance Europe*, ed. Tom F. Earle and Kate J. Lowe. Cambridge: Cambridge University Press.

Jordan, Don, and Walsh, Michael. 2007. *White cargo: The forgotten history of Britain's white slaves in America*. Edinburgh: Mainstream Publishing.

Jütte, Robert. 1994. *Poverty and deviance in early modern England*. Cambridge: Cambridge University Press.

Kagan, Richard L. 1974. *Students and society in early modern Spain*. Baltimore, Md.: The Johns Hopkins University Press.

Kagan, Richard L. 1975. "Universities in Castile, 1500–1810." In *The university in society* (vol. 2), ed. Lawrence Stone. Princeton, N.J.: Princeton University.

Kaplan, Paul H. D. 2005. "Isabella d'Este and black African women." In *Black Africans in Renaissance Europe*, ed. Tom F. Earle and Kate J. Lowe. Cambridge: Cambridge University Press.

Kent, Dale. 1978. *The rise of the medici: Faction in Florence 1426–1434*. Oxford: Oxford University Press.

Kettering, Sharon. 1988. "Gift-giving and patronage in early modern France." *French History* 2(2): 131–151.

King, Helen. 2004. *The disease of virgins: Green sickness, chlorosis, and the problems of puberty*. London: Routledge.

King, Margaret L. 1991. *Le Donne nel Rinascimento*. Bari, Italy: Laterza.

King, Margaret L. 2008. "The school of infancy: The emergence of mother as teacher in early modern times." In *The Renaissance in the streets, schools, and studies. Essays in honour of Paul F. Grendler*, ed. Konrad Eisenbishler and Nicholas Terpstra. Toronto: Centre for Reformation and Renaissance Studies.

King, Ross. 2000. *Brunelleschi's dome*. London: Chatto & Windus.

Kingdon, Robert. 1995. *Adultery and divorce in Calvin's Geneva*. Cambridge, Mass.: Harvard University Press.

Kiple, Kenneth F. 2002. *The Caribbean slave: A biological history*. Cambridge: Cambridge University Press.

Klapisch-Zuber, Christiane. 1984. "Le Chiavi Fiorentine di Barbablù: l'Apprendimento della Lettura a Firenze nel XV secolo." *Quaderni Storici* 57(3): 765–792.

Klapisch-Zuber, Christiane. 1985. *Women, family, and ritual in Renaissance Italy,* trans. Lydia Cochrane. Chicago: University of Chicago Press.

Klapisch-Zuber, Christiane. 2002. "La Vie Domestique et Ses Conflits Chez un Maçon Bolonais du XVe Siècle." In *Le petit Peuple dans l'Occident Médiéval. Terminologies, Perceptions, Réalités,* ed. Pierre Boglioni, Robert Delort, and Claude Gauvard. Paris: Publications de la Sorbonne.

Kuehn, Thomas, Menchi, Silvana Sidel, and Schutte, Anne Jacobson, eds. 2001. *Time, space, and women's lives in early modern Europe.* Kirksville, Mo.: Truman State University.

Kussmaul, Ann. 1981. *Servants in husbandry in early modern England.* Cambridge: Cambridge University Press.

Langmuir, Erika. 2006. *Imagining childhood.* New Haven, Conn.: Yale University Press.

Lanza, Janine. 2007. *From wives to widows in early modern Paris: Gender, economy and law* Aldershot, England: Ashgate.

Larminie, Vivienne. 1995. *Wealth, kinship and culture: The seventeenth-century Newdigates of Arbury and their world.* Woodbridge, England: Boydell Press.

Laslett, Peter. 1983. "Family and household as work group and kin group: Areas of traditional Europe compared." In *Family forms in historic Europe,* ed. Richard Wall, Jean Robin, and Peter Laslett. Cambridge: Cambridge University Press.

Laslett, Peter. [1983] 2005. *The world we have lost—further explored.* London: Routledge.

Leonard, Amy. 2005. *Nails in the wall. Catholic nuns in Reformation Germany.* Chicago: University of Chicago Press.

Leong, Elaine. 2008. "Making medicines in the early modern Household." *Bulletin of the History of Medicine* 82: 145–168.

Leong, Elaine, and Pennell, Sara. 2007. "Recipe collections and the currency of medical knowledge in the early modern 'medical marketplace.'" In *Medicine and the market in England and its colonies, c. 1450–c. 1850,* ed. Mark S. R. Jenner, and Patrick Wallis. Houndmills, England: Palgrave Macmillan.

Le Roux de Lincy. A.J.V. 1860. *Vie de la reine Anne de Bretagne*, vol. 1. Paris: L. Curmer.

Le Roy Ladurie, Emmanuel. 1997. *The beggar and the professor: A sixteenth-century family saga,* trans Arthur Goldhammer. Chicago: University of Chicago Press.

Lett, Didier. 2003. "Vieux Frères et Oncles Jeunes. Ecart de Génération et Ecart d'Age dans les Familles de la Fin du Moyen Age." In *Lorsque l'Enfant Grandit,* ed. Jean-Pierre Bardet, Jean-Noel Luc, Isabelle Robin-Romero, and Catherine Rollet. Paris: Presse de l'Université Paris Sorbonne.

Lett, Didier. 2004. *Histoire des Frères et des Soeurs.* Paris: Editions De La Martinière.

Levack, Brian P. 1995. *The witch-hunt in early modern Europe.* London: Longman.

Lis, Catharina, and Soly, Hugo. 1993. "Neighbourhood social change in west European cities: Sixteenth to nineteenth centuries." *International Review of Social History* 38: 1–30.

Loats, Carol L. 1997. "Gender, guilds, and work identity: Perspectives from sixteenth-century Paris." *French Historical Studies* 20(1): 15–30.

Lombardi, Daniela. 2001. *Matrimoni di antico regime.* Bologna, Italy: Il Mulino.

Lopez, Denis. 2007. "L'éducation du prince au XVIIe siècle: regards sur l'enfance." In *Regards sur l'enfance au XVIIe siècle,* ed. Anne Defrance, Denis Lopez, and François-Joseph Ruggiu. Tubingen, Germany: Biblio.

Luke, Carmen. 1989. *Pedagogy, printing and Protestantism: The discourse on childhood.* New York: Albany State University.

Lux-Sterritt, Laurence. 2005. *Redefining female religious life: French Ursulines and English ladies in seventeenth-century France.* Aldershot, England: Ashgate.

Luxán, Pedro de. 1943. *Coloquios Matrimoniales* (1550). Madrid: Ediciones Atlas.

Lynch, Catherine, A. 2003. *Individuals, families, and communities in Europe, 1200–1800: The urban foundations of Western society.* Cambridge: Cambridge University Press.

Macfarlane, Alan. 1970. *The family life of Ralph Josselin: A seventeenth-century clergyman.* London: Cambridge University Press.

Maddern, Philippa. 2008. "'In myn own house': the troubled connections between servant marriages, late-medieval English household communities, and early modern historiography." In *Women, identities and communities in early modern Europe,* ed. Susan Broomhall and Stephanie Tarbin. Aldershot, England: Ashgate.

Main, Gloria L. 2001. *Peoples of a spacious land: Families and cultures in colonial New England.* Cambridge, Mass.: Harvard University Press.

Maravall, José Antonio. 1982: *Utopía y Reformismo en la Espana de los Austrias.* Madrid: Siglo XXI.

Margolin, Jean-Claude. 1995. *Erasme, Précepteur de l'Europe.* Paris: Julliard.

Marten, James, ed. 2007. *Children in Colonial America.* New York: New York University Press.

Martorell, Joanot. 1969. *Tirant lo Blanc* (1490), 2 vols., ed. Martí de Riquer. Barcelona: Seix Barral.

Mascuch, Michael. 2006. "The godly child's 'power and evidence' in the word: Orality and literacy in the ministry of Sarah Wright." In *Childhood and Children's Books in Early Modern Europe, 1550–1800,* ed. Andrea Immel and Michael Witmore. New York: Routledge.

Matthews Grieco, Sara. 2000. "Persuasive pictures: Didactic prints and the construction of the social identity of women in sixteenth-century Italy." In *Women in Italian Renaissance Culture and Society,* ed. Letizia Panizza. Oxford: Legenda.

Mattox, Philip E. 2006. "Domestic sacral space in the Florentine Renaissance palace." *Renaissance Studies* 20(5): 658–673.

McCants, Anne E. C. 1997. *Civic charity in a Golden Age: Orphan care in early modern Amsterdam.* Urbana: University of Illinois Press.

McIntosh, Majorie K. 1988. "Local responses to the poor in late medieval and Tudor England." *Continuity and Change* 3(2): 209–245.

McIntosh, Majorie K. 1998. *Controlling misbehaviour in England, 1370–1600.* Cambridge: Cambridge University Press.

McIntosh, Majorie K. 2005. *Working women in English society 1300–1620.* Cambridge: Cambridge University Press.

McTavish, Lianne. 2005. *Childbirth and the display of authority in early modern France.* Aldershot, England: Ashgate.

Medick, Hans. 1984. "Village spinning bees: Sexual culture and free time among rural youth in early modern Germany." In *Interest and emotion: Essays on the study of family and kinship,* ed. Hans Medick and David W. Sabean. Cambridge: Cambridge University Press.

Megged, Amos. 2006. "The inquisitorial perspectives of an unmarried mulatta woman in mid-seventeenth-century Mexico." In *Voices from the Bench: The Narratives of Lesser Folk in Medieval Trials,* ed. Michael Goodich. Houndmills, England: Palgrave Macmillan.

Menchi, Silvana Sidel, Thomas Kuehn, and Anne Jacobson Schutte, eds. 1997. *Tempi e spazi di vita femminile tra medioevo ed età moderna.* Bologna, Italy: Il Mulino.

Michalove, Sharon D. 1999. "Equal in opportunity? The education of aristocratic women, 1450–1540." In *Women's Education in Early Modern Europe. A History,* ed. Barbara J. Whitehead. New York: Garland.

Michaud-Fréjaville, Françoise. 1982. "Bons et Loyaux Services. Les Contrats d'Apprentissage en Orléanais (1380–1480)." In *Les Entrées dans la Vie. Initiations et Apprentissages.* Nancy, France: Presses Universitaires.

Milanich, Nara 2002. "Historical perspectives on illegitimacy and illegitimates in Latin America." In *Minor omissions. Children in Latin American history and society,* ed. Tobias Hecht. Madison: The University of Wisconsin Press.

Miller, Elizabeth. 2006. "Prints." In *At home in Renaissance Italy,* ed. Marta Ajmar-Wollheim and Flora Dennis. London: V&A Publications.

Minz, Steven. 2004. *Huck's raft. A history of American childhood.* Cambridge, Mass.: The Belknap Press.

Mirrer, Louise, ed. 1992. *Upon my husband's death: Widows in the literature and histories of medieval Europe.* Ann Arbor: University of Michigan Press.

Monaghan, E. Jennifer. 2005. *Learning to read and write in colonial America.* Amherst: University of Massachusetts.

Montaigne, Michel de. 1965. *Les Essais* (1588), 3 vols. Paris: Flammarion.

Moody, Joanna, ed. 1998. *The private life of an Elizabethan lady: The diary of Lady Margaret Hoby, 1599–1605.* Stroud, England: Sutton Publishing.

Morgan , Edmund S. 1966. *The Puritan family: Religion and domestic relations in seventeenth-century New England.* New York: Harper and Row.

Morrall, Andrew. 2002. "Protestant pots: Morality and social ritual in the early modern Home." *Journal of Design History* 15(4): 263–273.

Morse, Margaret M. 2007. "Creating sacred space: The religious visual culture of the Renaissance Venetian *casa.*" *Renaissance Studies* 21(2): 151–184.

Motolinía (Fray Toribio de Benavente). 1988. *Historia de los Indios de la Nueva España* (1541), ed. Giuseppe Bellini. Madrid: Alianza.

Mottola Molfino, Alessandra. 1986. "Nobili, Sagge e Virtuose Donne. Libri di Modelli per Merletti e Organizzazione del Lavoro Femminile tra Cinquecento e Seicento." In *La Famiglia e la Vita Quotidiana in Europa dal '400 al '600. Fonti e Problemi,* ed. Renato Grispo. Rome: Ministero per il beni culturali e ambientali.

Muldrew, Craig. 1998. *The economy of obligations: The culture of credit and social relations in early modern England.* Basingstoke, England: MacMillan.

Murdoch, Steve. 2006. *Network north: Scottish kin, commercial and covert associations in northern Europe, 1603–1746*. Boston: Brill.

Musacchio, Jacqueline M. 1999. *The art and ritual of childbirth in Renaissance Italy*. London: Yale University Press.

Musacchio, Jacqueline M. 2005. "Lambs, coral, teeth, and the intimate intersection of religion and magic in Renaissance Italy." In *Images, relics, and devotional practices in late medieval and Renaissance Italy*, ed. Scott Montgomery and Sally Cornelison. Tempe, Ariz.: Medieval and Renaissance Texts and Studies.

Nadeau, Carolyn A. 2001. "Blood mother/milk mother: Breastfeeding, the family, and the state in Antonio De Guevara's *Relox de Príncipes* (Dial of Princes)." *Hispanic Review* 69(2): 153–174.

Niccoli, Ottavia. 1995. *Il Seme della Violenza. Putti, Fanciulli e Mammoli in Italia tra Cinque e Seicento*. Roma, Italy: Laterza.

Norfolk and Norwich Record Office, Wills, Hyrnyng.

Norfolk and Norwich Record Office Dean and Chapter Records DCN 1/6.

Numbers, Ronald L., ed. 1987. *Medicine in the New World: New Spain, New France, and New England*. Knoxville: University of Tennessee Press.

Ogilvie, Sheilagh. 1997. *State corporatism and proto-Industry; the Württemberg Black Forest, 1580–1797*. Cambridge: Cambridge University Press.

Ogilvie, Sheilagh. 2003. *A bitter living: Women, markets, and social capital in early modern Germany*. Oxford: Oxford University Press.

Oliva, M. 1998. *The convent and the community in late medieval England: Female monasteries in the diocese of Norwich, 1350–1540*. Woodbridge, England: The Boydell Press.

O'Malley, John W. 1993. *The first Jesuits*. Cambridge, Mass.: Harvard University.

O'Malley, John S. J., and Bailey, Gauvin A., eds. 2003. *The Jesuits and the arts 1540–1773*. Philadelphia, PA: Saint Joseph's University Press.

Opitz, Claudia. 2003. "Female sovereignty and the subordination of women in the works of Martin Luther, Jean Calvin, and Jean Bodin." In *Political and historical encyclopedia of women*, ed. Christine Faure. London: Routledge.

Origo, Iris. 1959. *The merchant of Prato, Francesco di Marco Datini*. London: Reprint Society.

Orme, Nicholas. 1995. "The culture of children in medieval England." *Past and Present* 148: 48–88.

Orme, Nicholas. 2001. *Medieval children*. New Haven, Conn.: Yale University Press.

Orme, Nicholas. 2006. *Medieval schools, from Roman Britain to Renaissance England*. New Haven, Conn.: Yale University.

Otis, Leah L. 1986. "Municipal wet nurses in fifteenth-century Montpellier." In *Women and Work in Preindustrial Europe*, ed. Barbara A. Hanawalt. Bloomington: Indiana University Press.

Ozment, Steven. 1989. *Magdalena and Balthasar: An intimate portrait of life in sixteenth-century Europe revealed in the letters of a Nuremberg husband and wife*. New Haven, Conn.: Yale University Press.

Ozment, Steven. 1990. *Three Behaim boys: Growing up in early modern Germany*. New Haven, Conn.: Yale University Press.

Palumbo Fossati, Isabella. 1984. "L'interno della casa dell'artigiano e dell'arte nella Venezia del Cinquecento." *Studi veneziani* 8: 109–53.

Parker, Charles, H. 1998. *The reformation of community: Social welfare and Calvinist charity in Holland, 1572–1620.* Cambridge: Cambridge University Press.

Parry, J. H. 1968. *The European reconnaissance: Selected documents.* London: Macmillan.

Peck, Linda L. 1990. *Court patronage and corruption in early Stuart England.* London: Routledge.

Pérez de Barradas, José. 1968: *Los Mestizos de América.* Madrid: Espasa-Calpe.

Phillips, Kim M . 1999. "Maidenhood as the perfect age of woman's life." In *Young medieval women,* ed. Katherine J. Lewis, Noel James Menuge, and Kim M. Phillips. New York: St. Martin's Press.

Phillips, Kim M. 2003. *Medieval maidens: Young women and gender in England, 1270–1540.* Manchester, England: Manchester University Press.

Pierce, Leslie. 2003. *Morality tales: Law and gender in the Ottoman court of Aintab.* Berkeley: University of California Press.

Pinson, Jean-Pierre. 1997. "Le Plain-chant en Nouvelle France aux XVIIe et XVIIIe siècles: Vers une première syntèse." In *Plain-chant et liturgie en France au XVII siècle,* ed. Jean Duron. Paris: Éditions du Centre De Musique Baroque de Versailles, Éditions Klincksieck.

Plane, Anne Marie. 2000. *Colonial intimacies. Indian marriages in early New England.* Ithaca, N.Y.: Cornell University Press.

Platter, Thomas. 1982. *Ma vie.* Lausanne, Switzerland: L'âge d'homme.

Plebani, Tiziana. 1996. "Nascita e caratteristiche del pubblico di lettrici tra medioevo e prima età moderna." In *Donna, Disciplina, Creanza Cristiana dal XV al XVII Secolo: Studi e Testi a Stampa,* ed. Gabriella Zarri. Roma, Italy: Edizioni di Storia e Letteratura.

Po-Chia-Hsia, Ronald. 1989. *Social discipline in the Reformation: Central Europe, 1550–1750.* London: Routledge.

Pollack, Herman. 1971. *Jewish folkways in Germanic lands (1648–1806): Studies in aspects of daily life.* Cambridge, Mass.: The MIT Press.

Pollock, Linda. 1987. *A lasting relationship: Parents and children over three centuries.* London: Fourth Estate.

Poska, Alison. 2005. *Women and authority in early modern Spain. The peasants of Galicia.* Oxford: Oxford University Press.

Premo, Bianca. 2005. *Children of the father king: Youth, authority, and legal minority in colonial Lima.* Chapel Hill: University of North Carolina Press.

Premo, Bianca. 2008. "How Latin America's history of childhood came of age." *Journal of the History of Childhood and Youth* 1(1): 63–76.

Rankin. Alisha. 2008. "Duchess, heal thyself: Elisabeth of Rochlitz and the patient's perspective in early modern Germany." *Bulletin of the History of Medicine* 82: 109–44.

Rapley, Elizabeth. 1990. *The Dévotés. Women and church in seventeenth-century France.* Montreal: McGill-Queen's University.

Raynal, Guillaume T. 1981. *Histoire Philosophique et Politique des Deux Indes* (1772), ed. Yves Benot. Paris: Maspéro.

Reher, David S. 1998. "Family ties in western Europe: Persistent contrasts." *Population and Development Review* 24: 203–234.

Reinhard, Wolfgang. 1982. "Confessionalizzazione forzata? Prolegomeni ad una teoria dell'etá confessionale." *Annali dell'Istituto Storico Italo-Germanico in Trento* 8: 13–37.

Ribadeneira, Pedro de. 1967. *Vida de Ignacio de Loyola* (1592). Madrid: Espasa-Calpe.

Richardson, Catherine. 2003. "Household objects and domestic ties." In *The medieval household in Christian Europe, c. 850–c. 1550,* ed. Cordelia Beattie, Anna Maslakoic, and Sarah Rees Jones. Turnhout, Belgium: Brepols Publishers.

Ricketts, Annabel, et al. 2005. "Designing for Protestant worship: The private chapels of the Cecil family." In *Defining the holy sacred space in medieval and early modern Europe,* ed. Andrew Spicer and Sarah Hamilton. Aldershot: Ashgate.

Riddy, Felicity. 2003. "Looking closely: Authority and intimacy in the late medieval urban home." In *Gendering the master narrative. Women and power in the Middle Ages,* ed. Mary C. Erler and Maryanne Kowaleski. Ithaca, N.Y.: Cornell University Press.

Roche, Daniel. 2000. *A history of everyday things: The birth of consumption in France, 1600–1800.* Cambridge: Cambridge University Press.

Romano, Dennis. 1987. *Patricians and Popolani: The social foundations of the Venetian state.* Baltimore, Md.: Johns Hopkins University Press.

Romano, Dennis. 1996. *Housecraft and statecraft. Domestic service in Renaissance Venice, 1400–1600.* Baltimore, Md.: Johns Hopkins University Press.

Romero, R. Todd. 2007. "Colonizing childhood: Religion, gender, and Indian children in southern New England, 1620–1720." In *Children in colonial America,* ed. James Marten. New York: New York University Press.

Rooks, Judith. 1997. *Midwifery and childbirth in America.* Philadelphia: Temple University Press.

Roper, Lyndal. 1989. *The holy household: Women and morals in Reformation Augsburg.* Oxford: Oxford University Press.

Rosner, Fred. 1977. *Medicine in the Bible and the Talmud: Selections from classical Jewish Sources.* New York: Yeshiva University Press.

Rossiaud, Jacques. 1988. *Medieval prostitution.* Oxford: Basil Blackwell.

Roth, Norman. 2005. *Daily life of the Jews in the Middle Ages.* Westport, Conn.: Greenwood Press.

Rublack, Ulinka. 1999. *The crimes of women in early modern Germany.* Oxford: Oxford University Press.

Rublack, Ulinka. 2005. *Reformation Europe.* Cambridge: Cambridge University Press.

Ruderman, David B. 1995. *Jewish thought and scientific discovery in early modern Europe.* New Haven, Conn.: Yale University Press.

Safley, Thomas Max. 1997. *Charity and economy in the orphanages of early modern Augsburg.* Atlantic Highlands, N.J.: Humanities Press.

Safley, Thomas. 2005. *Children of the laboring poor: Expectation and experience among the orphans of early modern Augsburg.* Leiden, The Netherlands: Brill.

Salisbury, Neal. 1996. "The history of Native Americans from before the arrival of Europeans and Africans until the American Civil War." In *The Cambridge Eco-*

nomic History of the United States I: The Colonial Era, ed. Stanley L. Engerman and Robert E. Gallman. Cambridge: Cambridge University Press.

Sarti, Raffaella. 2002. *Europe at home. Family and material culture 1500–1800.* New Haven, Conn.: Yale University Press.

Sarti, Raffaella. 2009. "Cultura materiale e Consumi in Europa e nel Mediterraneo." In *Storia d'Europa e del Mediterraneo,* gen. ed. Alessandro Barbero, sezione 5. *Età Moderna,* vol. 10, *Ambiente, Popolazione, Società,* ed. by Roberto Bizzocchi. Rome: Salerno Editrice.

Scaramella, Pierroberto. 1997. *I Santolilli. Culti dell'infanzia e santità infantile a Napoli alla fine del XVII secolo.* Rome: Edizioni di Storia e Letteratura.

Schorn-Schutte, Luise. 1999. "Il Matrimonio come Professione: la Moglie del Pastore Evangelico." In *Time, space, and women's lives in early modern Europe,* ed. Thomas Kuehn, Silvana Sidel Menchi, and Anne Jacobson Schutte. Kirksville, Mo.: Truman State University.

Sears, Elizabeth. 1986. *The ages of man: Medieval interpretations of the life cycle.* Princeton, N.J.: Princeton University Press.

Seymour, M. C. ed., 1975. *On the properties of things: John Trevisa's translation of Bartholomaeus Anglicus De Proprietatibus Rerum,* vol. 1. Oxford: Clarendon Press.

Shahar, Shulamith. 1990. *Childhood in the Middle Ages.* London: Routledge.

Sharpe, Pamela. 1991. "Poor children as apprentices in Colyton, 1598–1830." *Continuity and Change* 6(2): 253–270.

Sheingorn, Pamela. 2004. "Appropriating the holy kinship: Gender and family History." In *Medieval families: Perspectives on marriage, household and children,* ed. Carol Neel. Toronto: University of Toronto Press.

Slack, P., ed. 1975. *Poverty in early-Stuart Salisbury.* Devizes, England: Wiltshire Record Society v. 31.

Smith, Alison. 1998. "Gender, ownership and domestic space: Inventories and family archives in Renaissance Verona." *Renaissance Studies* 12: 375–391.

Smith, David Lawrence. 1998. *A history of the modern British Isles, 1603–1707: The double crown.* London: Blackwell.

Sneyd, Charlotte Augusta, ed. 1847. *A relation, or rather a true account, of the island of England: With sundry particulars of the customs of these people and of the royal revenues under King Henry the Seventh, about the year 1500.* London: Camden Society, first series, 37. London: J. B. Nichols and Son.

Socolow, Susan. 2000. *The women of colonial Latin America.* Cambridge: Cambridge University Press.

Sofaer Derevenski, Joanna. 2000. *Children and material culture.* London: Routledge.

Soman, Alfred. 1990. "Le témoinage maquille: Encore un aspect de l'infra-justice a l'époque moderne." In *Les Archives du délit: Empreinte de société,* ed. Yves-Marie Bercé and Yves Castan. Toulouse, France: Editions Universitaires du Sud.

Soman, Alfred. 1997. "Anatomy of an infanticide trial: The case of Marie-Jeanne Bartonnet (1742)." In *Changing identities in early modern France,* ed. Michael Wolfe. Durham: University of North Carolina Press.

Sommerville, John C. 1992. *The discovery of childhood in Puritan England.* Athens: The University of Georgia Press.

Sovič, Silvia. 2008. "European family history: Moving beyond stereotypes of 'East' and 'West.'" *Cultural and Social History* 5(2): 141–163.

Spence, Jonathan D. 1985. *The memory palace of Matteo Ricci*. London: Faber and Faber.

Sperling, Jutta. 2004, "Marriage at the time of the Council of Trent (1560–70): Clandestine marriages, kinship prohibitions, and dowry exchange in European comparison." *Journal of Early Modern History* 8(1–2): 67–108.

Sperling, Jutta. 2007. "Dowry or inheritance? Kinship, property, And women's agency in Lisbon, Venice, and Florence (1572)." *Journal of Early Modern History* 11(3): 197–238.

Spicer, Andrew, and Hamilton, Sarah, eds. 2005. *Defining the holy sacred space in medieval and early modern Europe*. Aldershot, England: Ashgate.

Spierling, Karen E. 2008. "Father, son, and pious Christian. Concepts of masculinity in Reformation Geneva." In *Masculinity in the Reformation era*, ed. Scott H. Hendrix and Susan C. Karant-Nunn. Kirksville Mo.: Truman State University Press.

St. Clare Byrne, Muriel. 1981. *The Lisle letters*. 6 vols. Chicago: University of Chicago Press.

St. George, Robert Blair. 1998. *Conversing by signs: Poetics of implication in colonial New England culture*. Chapel Hill: University of North Carolina Press.

Still, George Frederic. 1965. *The history of paediatrics*. Oxford: Oxford University Press.

Stone, Lawrence. 1979. *The family, sex and marriage in England 1500–1800*, abridged ed. New York: Harper and Row.

Strasser, Ulrike. 2004. *State of virginity. Gender, religion and politics in an early modern Catholic state*. Ann Arbor: The University of Michigan Press.

Strauss, Gerald. 1976. "The state of pedagogical theory c. 1530: What Protestant reformers knew about education." In *Schooling and society: Studies in the history of education*, ed. Lawrence Stone. Baltimore, Md.: Johns Hopkins University Press.

Strauss, Gerald. 1978. *Luther's house of learning. Indoctrination of the young in the German Reformation*. Baltimore, Md.: The Johns Hopkins University Press.

Strohl, Jane E. 2001. "The child in Luther's theology: 'For what purpose do we older folks exist, other than to care for … the young?'" In *The child in Christian thought*, ed. Marcia Bunge. Grand Rapids, Mich.: William B. Eerdmans.

Swanson, R. N. 1989. *Church and society in late medieval England*. Oxford: Blackwell.

Swanson, Robert N. 1995. *Religion and devotion in Europe, c. 1215–c. 1515*. Cambridge: Cambridge University Press.

Taddei, Ilaria. 2001. *Fanciulli e giovani: crescere a Firenze nel Rinascimento*. Florence, Italy: Olschki.

Tanck de Estrada, Dorothy. 2007. "Indian children in early Mexico." In *Children in colonial America*, ed. James Marten. New York: New York University Press.

Tarabotti, Arcangela. 2007. *La Semplicità Ingannata*, ed. Simona Bertot. Padua, Italy: Il Poligrafo.

Terpstra, Nicholas. 1995. *Lay confraternities and civic religion in Renaissance Bologna*. Cambridge: Cambridge University Press.

Terpstra, Nicholas. 2000. "*In loco parentis:* Confraternities and abandoned children in Florence and Bologna." In *The politics of ritual kinship: Confraternities and social order in early modern Italy,* ed. Nicholas Terpstra. Cambridge: Cambridge University Press.

Terpstra, Nicholas. 2005. *Abandoned children of the Italian Renaissance: Orphan care in Florence and Bologna*. Baltimore, Md.: John Hopkins University Press.

Thornton, Russell. 1997. "Aboriginal North American population and rates of decline, ca. AD 1500–1900." *Current Anthropology* 38(2): 310–315.

Tognetti, Sergio. 2005. "The trade in black African slaves in fifteenth-century Florence." In *Black Africans in Renaissance Europe,* ed. Tom F. Earle and Kate J. Lowe. Cambridge: Cambridge University Press.

Trexler, Richard C. 1980. *Public life in Renaissance Florence*. New York: Academic Press.

Tropé, Hélène. 1996. "La Formation des Enfants Orphelins à Valence aux XVIe-XVIIe Siècles." In *La Formation de l'Enfant en Espagne aux XVIe et XVIIe Siècles,* ed. Augustin Redondo. Paris: Publications de la Sorbonne.

Trusler, Lucy. 1999. The material culture of childhood in Renaissance England. Master's thesis, V&A/RCA History of Design, Royal College of Art, London.

Tsing, Anna Lowenhaupt. 1995. "Empowering nature or: Some gleanings in bee culture." In *Naturalizing power: Essays in feminist cultural analysis,* ed. Sylvia Yanagisako and Carol Delaney. New York: Routledge.

Ubelaker, Douglas H. 2000. "Patterns of disease in early North American populations." In *A population history of North America,* ed. Michael R. Haines and Richard Hall Steckel. Cambridge: Cambridge University Press.

Underdown, David. 1993. *Fire from heaven: Life in an English town in the seventeenth century*. London: Fontana.

Van der Heijden, Manon, and van den Heuvel, Danielle. 2007. "Sailors' families and the urban institutional framework in early modern Holland." *The History of the Family* 12: 296–309.

Vassberg, David E. 1983. "Juveniles in the rural work force of sixteenth-century Castile." *Journal of Peasant Studies* 11(1): 62–75.

Vassberg, David E. 1998. "Orphans and adoption in early modern Castilian villages." *The History of the Family* 3(4): 441–458.

Vergara, Teresa C. 2007. "Growing up Indian: Migration, labor, and life in Lima (1570–1640)." In *Raising an empire: Children in early modern Iberia and colonial Latin America,* ed. Ordina E. González and Bianca Premo. Albuquerque: University of New Mexico Press.

Viazzo, Pier Paolo. 2003. "What's so special about the Mediterranean? Thirty years of research on household and family in Italy." *Continuity and Change* 18(1): 111–137.

Vigarello, Georges. 1988. *Concepts of cleanliness: Changing attitudes in France since the Middle Ages,* trans Jean Birrell. Cambridge: Cambridge University Press.

Villaseñor Black, Charlene. 2006. *Creating the cult of Saint Joseph. Art and gender in the Spanish empire*. Princeton, N.J.: Princeton University Press.

Vincent, Susan. 2003. *Dressing the elite: Clothes in early modern England*. Oxford: Berg.

Wall, Helena M. 1995. *Fierce communion: Family and community in early America*. Cambridge, Mass.: Harvard University Press.

Walsham, Alexandra. 1994. "'Out of the mouths of babes and sucklings': Prophecy, Puritanism, and childhood in Elizabethan Suffolk." *The Church and Childhood: Studies in Church History* 31: 285–299.

Walter, John, Schofield, Roger, and Appleby, Andrew B. 1991. *Famine, disease and the social order in early modern society*. Cambridge: Cambridge University Press.

Walvin, James. 2001. *Black ivory: Slavery in the British Empire*. 2nd ed. Oxford: Blackwell.

Watt, Jeffrey R. 2001. "L'impatto della riforma e della controriforma." In *Storia della famiglia in Europa dal cinquecento alla rivoluzione francese,* ed. Marzio Barbagli and David I. Kertzer. Rome: Laterza.

Watt, Jeffrey R. 2002. "Calvinism, childhood and education: The evidence from the Genevan consistory." *Sixteenth Century Journal,* 33(2): 439–456.

Watt, Tessa. 1991. *Cheap print and popular piety, 1550–1640*. Cambridge: Cambridge University Press.

Wear, Andrew. 2006. "Medicine in early modern Europe, 1500–1700." In *The Western medical tradition: 800 BC to AD 1800,* ed. Lawrence I. Conrad, Michael Neve, Vivian Nutton, Roy Porter, and Andrew Wear. Cambridge: Cambridge University Press.

Webb, Diana. 2005. "Domestic space and devotion in the Middle Age." In *Defining the holy sacred space in medieval and early modern Europe,* ed. Andrew Spicer and Sarah Hamilton. Aldershot, England: Ashgate.

Webb, Diana. 2007. *Privacy and solitude in the Middle Ages*. London: Continuum.

Weinstein, Roni. 2004. *Marriage rituals Italian style. A historical anthropological perspective on early modern Italian Jews*. Leiden, The Netherlands: Brill.

Wertz, Richard, and Wertz, Dorothy C. 1989. *Lying-in: A history of childbirth in America*. New Haven, Conn.: Yale University Press.

Whitehead, Barbara J., ed. 1999. *Women's education in early modern Europe. A history*. New York: Garland.

Whittle, Jane. 2005. "Housewives and servants in rural England, 1440–1650: evidence of women's work from probate documents." *Transactions of the Royal Historical Society* 15: 51–74.

Whyman, Susan E. 1999. *Sociability and power in late-Stuart England*. Oxford: Oxford University Press.

Wiedner, Donald L. 1960. "Forced labor in colonial Peru." *The Americas* 16: 357–383.

Wiesner-Hanks, Merry E. 1993. "The midwives of southern Germany and the private/pub lic dichotomy." In *The art of midwifery: Early modern midwives in Europe,* ed. Hilary Marland. London: Routledge.

Wiesner-Hanks, Merry E. 1996. *Convents confront the Reformation: Catholic and Protestant nuns in Germany*. Milwaukee: Marquette University Press.

Wiesner-Hanks, Merry. 2000. *Christianity and sexuality in the early modern world*. London: Routledge.

Wiesner-Hanks, Merry. 2006. *Early modern Europe, 1450–1789*. Cambridge: Cambridge University Press.

Wiesner-Hanks, Merry E. 2008. *Women and gender in early modern Europe*. Cambridge: Cambridge University Press.

Willis A. J., and Merson, A. L., eds. 1968. *A calendar of Southampton apprenticeship registers, 1609–1740*. Southampton, England: Southampton University Press.

Wright, Thomas, and Halliwell, James Orchard. 1841–1843. *Reliquiæ antiquæ: Scraps from ancient manuscripts, illustrating chiefly early English literature and the English language*, 2 vols. London: William Pickering.

Wrightson, Keith. 2000. *Earthly necessities: Economic lives in early modern Britain*. New Haven, Conn.: Yale University Press.

Wrigley, E. A., Davies, R. S., Oeppen, J. E., and Schofield, R. S., eds. 1997. *English population history from family reconstitution, 1580–1837, Cambridge studies in population, economy, and society in past time*. Cambridge: Cambridge University Press.

Wunder, Heide. 2001. "Construction of masculinity and male identity in personal testimonies: Hans von Schwenichen (1552–1616) in his Memorial." In *Time, space, and women's lives in early modern Europe*, ed. Thomas Kuehn, Silvana Sidel Menchi, and Anne Jacobson Schutte. Kirksville, Mo.: Truman State University.

York Minster Archives Visitations Book 1472–1550 L2(3) c.

Zarri, Gabriella, ed. 1996. *Donna, Disciplina, Creanza Cristiana dal XV al XVII Secolo: Studi e Testi a Stampa*. Roma, Italy: Edizioni di Storia e Letteratura.

Ze'evi, Dror. 2006. *Producing desire: Changing sexual discourse in the Ottoman Middle East, 1500–1900*. Berkeley: University of California Press.

Zemon-Davis, Natalie. 1975. *Society and culture in early modern France*. Stanford, Calif.: Stanford University Press.

Zemon-Davis, Natalie. 1986. "Women in the crafts in sixteenth-century Lyon." In *Women and Work in Preindustrial Europe*, ed. Barbara A. Hanawalt. Bloomington: Indiana University Press.

Zemon-Davis, Natalie. 2000. *The gift in sixteenth-century France*. Madison: University of Wisconsin Press.

Zmora, Hillay. 2001. *Monarchy, aristocracy and the state in Europe 1300–1800*. London: Routledge.

CONTRIBUTORS

Marta Ajmar-Wollheim is tutor in graduate studies (Renaissance) on the history of design postgraduate program at the Victoria and Albert Museum, London. She co-curated the exhibition *At Home in Renaissance Italy* (V&A, 2006) and co-edited the accompanying publication (London, 2006) and *Approaching the Italian Renaissance Interior* (2007). She is author of essays in material culture in various multi-authored volumes.

Cordelia Beattie is senior lecturer in history at the University of Edinburgh and author of *Medieval Single Women: The Politics of Social Classification in Late Medieval England* (2007) and editor, with Anna Maslakovic, of *The Medieval Household in Christian Europe, c. 850–1550: Managing Power, Wealth and the Body* (2003).

Anna Bellavitis is professor of early modern history at the University of Rouen (France) and author of *Identité, mariage, mobilité sociale. Citoyennes et citoyens à Venise au XVIe siècle* (2001); *Famille, genre, transmission à Venise au XVIe siècle* (2009) and co-editor of *Identités, appartenances, revendications identitaires (XVIe-XVIIIe siècle)* (2005); *Mobilité et transmission dans l'Europe moderne* (2009) and *Famiglie e poteri in Italia tra Medioevo ed epoca moderna* (2009).

Ilana Krausman Ben-Amos is associate professor in the Department of General History at Ben-Gurion University of the Negev, Israel, and author of *Adolescence and Youth in Early Modern England* (1994) and *The Culture of Giving: Informal Support and Gift-Exchange in Early Modern England* (2008).

Susan Broomhall is professor of history at the University of Western Australia and author of *Women and the Book Trade in Sixteenth-Century France* (2002); *Women's Medical Work in Early Modern France* (2004) and *Women and Religion in Sixteenth-Century France* (2006). She is editor of *Emotions in the Household, 1200–1900* (2008) and, with Stephanie Tarbin, of *Women, Identities and Communities in Early Modern France* (2008).

James Casey was reader in history at the University of East Anglia until his retirement in 2009. He has published extensively on the social history of early modern Spain. His several books include *The History of the Family* (1989) and *Family and Community in Early Modern Spain: The Citizens of Granada 1570–1739* (2007).

Sandra Cavallo is professor of early modern history at Royal Holloway, University of London and author or editor of *Charity and Power in Early Modern Italy: Benefactors and Their Motives in Turin 1541–1789* (1995); *Widowhood in Medieval and Early Modern Europe* (1998); *Artisans of the Body in Early Modern Italy: Identities, Families, Masculinities* (2007); *Spaces, Objects and Identities in Early Modern Italian Medicine* (2008); and *Domestic Institutional Interiors in Early Modern Europe* (2009).

Silvia Evangelisti is lecturer in European history at the University of East Anglia and author or editor of *Nuns: A History of Convent Life 1400–1750* (2007); *Unmarried Men and Women in Early Modern Italy and Europe* (2007); and *Domestic Institutional Interiors in Early Modern Europe* (2009).

Julie Hardwick is professor of history and director of the Institute for Historical Studies at the University of Texas at Austin. She is the author of *The Practice of Patriarchy: Gender and the Politics of Household Authority in Early Modern France* (1998) and *Family Business: Litigation and the Political Economies of Daily Life in Early Modern France* (2009).

Philippa Maddern is professor in medieval history at the University of Western Australia. She is the author of *Violence and Social Order: East Anglia 1422–1442* (1992) and has published many articles on families and households in late medieval England.

Stephanie Tarbin is lecturer in history at the University of Western Australia. She co-edited the collection *Women, Identities and Communities in Early Modern Europe* (2008) and is completing a monograph on moral regulation in Tudor London.

INDEX